Mental Health
Assessment and
Therapeutic
Intervention
with Older Adults

Senior Contributors

Dan G. Blazer, M.D., Ph.D.
Associate Professor of Psychiatry
Duke University Medical Center
Durham, North Carolina

Steven H. Herman, Ph.D.
Assistant Professor of Medical Psychology
Duke University Medical Center
Durham, North Carolina

Mary Ann Matteson, M.S.N.
Clinical Assistant Professor
University of North Carolina School of Nursing
Chapel Hill, North Carolina

Alice C. Myers, A.C.S.W.
Social Worker, Psychotherapist, and Consultant
Adult Counseling Services, Inc.
Durham, North Carolina

Alan D. Whanger, M.D.
Professor of Psychiatry
Duke University Medical Center
Durham, North Carolina

Mental Health Assessment and Therapeutic Intervention with Older Adults

Editors
Alan D. Whanger, M.D.
Professor of Psychiatry
Duke University Medical Center
Durham, North Carolina

Alice C. Myers, A.C.S.W.
Social Worker, Psychotherapist,
and Consultant
Adult Counseling Services, Inc.
Durham, North Carolina

AN ASPEN PUBLICATION®
Aspen Systems Corporation
Rockville, Maryland
Royal Tunbridge Wells
1984

Library of Congress Cataloging in Publication Data
Main entry under title:

Mental health assessment and therapeutic intervention
with older adults.

"An Aspen publication."
Includes bibliographies and index.
1. Geriatric psychiatry. I. Whanger, Alan D., 1930- .
[DNLM: 1. Geriatric Psychiatry. WT 150 M54934]
RC451.4.A5M444   1984   618.97′689   84-12433
ISBN: 0-89443-861-1

Publisher: John Marozsan
Associate Publisher: Jack W. Knowles, Jr.
Editorial Director: Margaret M. Quinlin
Executive Managing Editor: Margot G. Raphael
Managing Editor: M. Eileen Higgins
Editorial Services: Jane Coyle
Printing and Manufacturing: Debbie Collins

Copyright © 1984 by Aspen Systems Corporation

Library of Congress Catalog Card Number: 84-12433
ISBN: 0-89443-861-1

Printed in the United States of America

1   2   3   4   5

Table of Contents

Preface

Mental Health Assessment and Therapeutic Intervention with Older Adults was written for professional therapists and counselors who are also gerontologists. Nurses, social workers, psychologists, psychiatrists, physicians, pastoral counselors, family counselors, physical therapists, occupational therapists, recreational therapists, administrators, and other professionals who work with older adults will find this book helpful. The authors have considered three specific target groups. The first is composed of mental health professionals who have responsibility for providing services to older adults in mental health outpatient clinics, day treatment centers, and psychiatric hospitals. While the book is multidisciplinary in scope, it will be of particular interest to psychiatrists and other physicians who may not have much formal training or experience in working with older patients. The second group includes professional therapists and counselors, working in senior centers, day-care centers, retirement homes, nursing homes, hospitals, home health agencies, social service departments, district health departments, and other public or private agencies that provide services to older adults and their families. The third target group consists of students on their way to becoming therapists and gerontologists.

The philosophy shared by the authors is best characterized by the phrase *interdisciplinary team approach*. This approach benefits patients and team members. Older patients with mental health problems can best be evaluated by a team of professionals with varied knowledge and skills. Older patients need to be seen within their total environment so that their functioning in significant areas of their lives—social, physical, mental, economic, and daily activities—may be accurately assessed. The value to team members of this kind of approach accrues from their mutual support and collaboration. Each member realizes at times during the assessment and treatment process that the expertise of another team member is needed to provide some specific service or to help work through a difficult or complex situation.

The basic evaluation and treatment team represented by the authors includes a psychiatrist, a social worker, a nurse, and a psychologist. This basic composition was chosen because the most common mental health team includes representatives of two or more of these disciplines. Furthermore, the authors' combined experience, amounting to 60 years, has chiefly occurred in the context of such a basic team. In clinical practice the appropriate use of consultants, not represented on the basic team, is of great value. In combination, the consultants and the basic team become an extended team, which may include geriatricians, physical therapists, occupational therapists, and any other specialists or service providers in the community.

The authors are clinicians and researchers affiliated with the Duke University Center for the Study of Aging and Human Development. They have worked extensively with patients whose problems are related to aging. They have published books and journal articles on many aspects of the aging process and have provided classes and supervision for professionals working with older adults. These professionals included geropsychiatrists, nurses, physicians, psychologists, social workers, and pastoral counselors.

The purpose in preparing this volume was not to add to the growing number of textbooks on gerontology or of mental disorders of the aging. Information about mental disorders and different aspects of gerontology is provided only as an introduction to, and background for, the simulated and illustrative case material that is the special feature of this book. We have used the word *simulated* to refer to the cases because—although the case material is based on real-life people and situations—we have modified and disguised the information to protect the privacy of individual clients and patients. In some cases two or more histories may have been combined for illustrative purposes. Both terms, *patient* and *client*, are used, for a patient—someone who is ill—and a client—someone who is receiving a service—may be one and the same.

Part I provides information about the aging process and mental health needs and discusses the authors' philosophy of assessment and intervention. In Chapter 1 the common physical, emotional, intellectual, and social changes that occur in the aging population are discussed, enabling the reader to appreciate the older person's vulnerability to mental health problems. Aging adds another dimension to any mental health problem. The mental health needs of older adults and their opportunities for therapeutic intervention are also discussed in Chapter 1. Conventional therapy may be only one of the interventions to be considered. All available resources for each patient or client need to be explored. The most appropriate treatment or social care plan must be developed with consideration of resources available and each individual's ability and willingness to be actively involved.

In Chapter 2 the rationale for a multidimensional functional assessment is discussed. The separate elements of a functional assessment are described, and a simulated assessment interview is provided. The components of a basic clinical assessment are reviewed. The results of the combined functional and clinical assessment are summarized with implications for intervention. The value of team conferences and the philosophy of an interdisciplinary approach are emphasized.

Part II presents the special feature of this book—namely, the presentation of simulated cases to illustrate assessment and intervention techniques related to specific disorders. In each chapter, mental disorders are reviewed with attention given to the special problems of diagnosis and treatment. The second part of each chapter consists of simulated case histories demonstrating assessment and intervention. The cases are presented first as they would be provided to an intake treatment conference. Comments and questions by other team members are also presented. A treatment plan is described and its rationale given. When possible, the patient is followed over a period of time, with information presented regarding success or failure and/or adjustment of the intervention. The case presentations in each chapter in Part II differ from those in Chapter 2 in that the functional and clinical assessments are summarized briefly rather than being completely reproduced. No attempt has been made by the presenting clinician to explain or justify the content or varied format of the case studies. The authors are aware that in the real world of mental health clinics and counseling centers, the content of initial assessments varies for multiple reasons. The cooperativeness of the client, the time available for the assessment, reliable informants in addition to the client, and the experience of the clinician are some of the bases for varied content. The questions and comments by other clinicians during the case conference represent interdisciplinary team involvement and can be especially helpful to the evaluating clinician as he or she continues the assessment and intervention in subsequent sessions with the patient or client.

Part III describes two very different ways to think systematically about improving services. Epidemiologic survey data from community populations is of use in planning mental health services for the elderly. The final chapter describes the Living Textbook of Geriatric Care, an automated information system developed from a research base and applicable to research training and patient care. Unfortunately, funding cutbacks have forced the discontinuation of this informative system at our center for the time being, but it is a useful method and tool.

The therapists, counselors, and students for whom this book is written represent a wide spectrum of knowledge and experience. Therefore, they may find the material helpful in very different ways. For the student with little experience in geropsychiatry or the mental health field, the book will be an introduction to the real world of assessment and intervention with older persons. Students will be able to learn from experienced therapists important aspects of working with people who have a variety of disorders and are in varying situations. They will also have an opportunity to read about the rewards and frustrations experienced by these therapists. For professional therapists who are new to gerontology, the book will point out how they can apply their knowledge and experience to people in a new age group, alerting them to the ways that assessment and intervention are the same for all age groups and the ways they are different for older adults. For those who are both experienced therapists and gerontologists, the book should stimulate discussion and dialogue about various skills and styles of assessment and intervention. The authors hope that questions will be raised to motivate additional clinical research.

Alice C. Myers

Acknowledgments

We have all been fortunate to have been associated with the Duke University Center for the Study of Aging and Human Development and its affiliated programs, which have helped to provide a support setting for our programs, guidance for our research, examples for our treatments, stimulation for our growth, and teachers for our trainees. In particular we would like to recognize the leadership of Dr. Ewald W. Busse, Dr. Carl Eisdorfer, Dr. George Maddox, and Dr. Harvey Cohen, all of whom have ably directed the Center. Three others who have contributed much to the development and continuation of the various research and treatment programs are Dr. Adrian Verwoerdt, who started the Geropsychiatry Training Program at Duke Medical Center in 1966; Dr. Eric Pfeiffer, the first OARS Project Director; and Dr. Virginia Stone, a widely recognized leader in geriatric nursing. Two others who have contributed significantly and directly to the psychiatric aspect of the OARS Program are Dr. James Moore and Dr. William M. Taylor.

In writing a team-oriented book such as ours, it is difficult to say exactly where the list of primary authors should end. We want to specially acknowledge the following. Dr. David B. Larson, first a fellow in Geropsychiatry and later a staff geropsychiatrist, and his wife, Susan S. Larson, an activity therapist who has worked with her husband in family and marital therapy with the elderly, made a major contribution to Chapter 10, Personality, Marital, Family, Psychosexual and Sleep Disorders. Dr. George Maddox, who is also Professor of Medical Sociology, contributed in a substantial way to the writing of Chapter 11, Epidemiologic Survey Data. And Dr. Gerda S. Fillenbaum, a Senior Fellow in the Duke Center for the Study of Aging, shared the authorship of Chapter 12, The Living Textbook.

Our deep gratitude goes to the American Psychiatric Association and its Division of Public Affairs for permission to quote and adapt from the

Diagnostic and Statistical Manual of Mental Disorders, Third Edition (DSM-III). A substantial part of our book is disease- and problem-oriented, and we have attempted as far as possible to update and refine the definitions and descriptions of various disorders of older adults in terms of DSM-III. Older people are complex entities and their problems may be multiple and atypical; we hope that we have struck a reasonable and comprehensible balance between the standardized descriptions so vital to accurate diagnosis and proper statistical tabulation of mental disorders, and the problems as we experience them clinically among older persons.

As we have combined teaching with our own continuing education, we have become especially aware of the contributions our students make by raising questions and bringing new enthusiasm and insight to old problems. It would be impossible to name all of them, but we especially wish to acknowledge the contributions of Derek Hybels, Barry Phillips, Edna L. Ballard, and Margie Freeman, who were graduate students at the OARS Clinic while this publication was being developed. Our appreciation goes to Becky Heron for her advice and review of the simulated questionnaire in Appendix A.

We would like to thank those people at Aspen Systems Corporation with whom we have had the opportunity to work over the years and through the complexities of preparing a book for publication. We would especially like to acknowledge the major contribution and stimulation of R. Curtis Whitesel, Editorial Director, whose untimely death saddened us all.

Much of the behind-the-scenes work of manuscript preparation goes unheralded, but we wish to thank both families and colleagues for their major contributions to these efforts, especially Mrs. Ruth Wortman.

Most importantly, we acknowledge the contributions of our patients and their families. While they are deliberately made anonymous in this volume, they are well known to us as individuals in our clinical relationships. They have shared their life histories and current problems with us and entrusted us to work and grow with them. We hope that through our efforts in this book we keep faith with them by helping others to better understand the mental health problems of older adults and to work more effectively to improve the quality of life for many.

Alan D. Whanger

Part I

A Positive Approach to Geriatric Mental Health Care

Chapter 1

Understanding the Aging Process and the Mental Health Needs of Older Adults

Alice C. Myers

"One thing I can tell you," said the 80-year-old grandmother to her grandson on his fortieth birthday: "The second 40 years is not as long as the first 40." For many older adults, the speed with which the years go by in the last half of their lives is one of the first changes they notice. The words *change* and *loss* characterize old age. Many changes in the lives of older adults challenge even the best adjusted and most mature. Changes in general appearance, vision, hearing, physical health, social roles, income, intellectual functioning—all these changes and others have an impact on older people.

In recent years researchers and clinicians have published a growing number of articles and books in the field of gerontology and have done much to correct stereotypes and myths regarding aging.[1] Most older people are not depressed, neglected, and alone. The majority of older persons continue to function well and lead productive, meaningful lives. Nevertheless, in our enthusiasm to view old age in a more positive light and to root out "agism," we must not ignore the vulnerability of the elderly that is due to the many changes and losses that occur in their lives.

The normal or expected changes that occur in the lives of older persons may cause mild to moderate depression for some and adjustment disorders for others without previous emotional problems. Many older persons are able to adjust without much trouble to the losses and changes in their lives, but others need help. Help may come from friends, relatives, and community agencies. Older adults with more serious mental health problems require professional assessment and treatment.

The professional therapist needs to gain an understanding of the aging process, not only from professional authorities but also from personal authorities. The personal authorities are one's own clients and patients, as well as parents, grandparents, uncles, aunts, and friends. All have their own life stories to tell, and some elders have published those stories of what it was like to grow older.

Old age is now considered a developmental stage of life with its own problems, rewards, and compensations. Young professionals who work with older adults will eventually become older adults themselves and, in their own interest, will need to know something of aging and of the conditions of growing older. Chances of reaching the ranks of the 60-, 70-, and 80-year-olds are good. Those ranks now contain 25 million Americans. According to the 1980 census bureau report, the median age of the population is 30, that is, half of the population is 30 years of age or older. Of that group, 11.3 percent is over 65. The life expectancy of women is 76; of men, nearly 70.[2]

To understand the aging process, one needs to consider the biological, psychological, and social aspects of aging. Biological aging refers to changes that take place in the body over time and that end with death. For our discussion, it is helpful to think of aging in terms of primary and secondary aging.[3] Natural changes are rooted in heredity. They apparently occur independent of stress, trauma, or disease and result in deterioration and a decrease in functioning. This inevitable decline is known as primary aging. Additional disabilities and decline in functioning related to trauma, loss, and disease are known as secondary aging. Even in the area of primary aging, we are told that the three biological components—two are cellular and one is noncellular—age at different rates. Some cells, such as skin cells and white blood cells, are able to reproduce. Other cells, such as neurons of the central nervous system and the brain, cannot reproduce; thus they cannot be replaced once they are lost. The reader is referred to other authors for a more detailed discussion of the numerous theories of biological aging.[4] For our immediate purpose of gaining some understanding of the aging process, it is enough to know that natural biological changes take place in each person in different components of the body at varying rates of speed. In addition, trauma and disease may affect various body parts. One's heart may age earlier than one's brain. The reverse, of course, may also be true.

Age-related psychological changes include those in sensori- and psychomotor processes, perception, mental ability, drives, and emotions. Research indicates that although sensory acuity—vision, hearing, balance, taste, and smell—declines with age, the majority of older adults do not experience significant limits on their activities due to sensory loss before age 75.[5] Of course, individuals vary in this respect. Perceptual functions as well as psychomotor responses seem to decline. Some impairment of learning and some memory loss can be expected. Sexual and activity drives decline. Some emotions, such as loneliness, increase with age.[6] The degree to which social factors either minimize or aggravate age-related psychological changes varies markedly among individuals.

The social situation of older persons is continuously changing even as they are changing. As older persons learn and relearn how to function in their changing social milieu, their ability to adjust and satisfy their current needs depends both on their coping patterns and on the attitudes of the significant others in their environment. The life course, role changes, and changes in relationships and in the physical environment are all elements of the social situation for the older adult. Robert Atchley describes the life course as "an idealized and age related progression or sequence of roles and group memberships that individuals are expected to follow as they mature and move through life."[7]

The idea of there being a time for everything is not new. It has been with us for many centuries. "For everything there is a season, and a time for every matter under heaven; a time to be born, and a time to die; a time to plant, and a time to pluck up what is planted" (Ecclesiastes 3:1–2). Subcultures develop their own ideas about the life course. There seem to be some generally accepted standards that make up the master timetable for respective populations. The majority within a culture agrees with the schedule, as in contemporary American society: starting school, completing school, finding a job, marrying, having children, adjusting to the empty nest, finding a second career, and retiring. For the most part, social behavior conforms to expected patterns. Neugarten and Datan found that the majority within a culture stay reasonably on schedule and, when veering off or getting stalled, are motivated to resume the pattern and the normative pace.[8]

The number and quality of social roles assigned and accepted by individuals are influenced by many factors. However, a person's position on the life course is especially significant for the changing social roles of older persons. Retirement is expected in the general life course. For some, the loss of job roles also represents the loss of identity and a familiar, comfortable routine. For others, it means the loss of a challenging and rewarding daily experience. Successful retirement is a reality for many, but even a successful retirement means a different life style and the natural stress that comes even with positive change.

Widowhood is a common role change in the expected life course of women. For some, after an appropriate time of grieving, a new identity and relief from responsibility enables them to wear their new roles well. Others never seem able to adjust and continue to grieve over their loss of identity as married women as well as their loss of a spouse.

Older adults have a variety of life styles, as do other age groups. Some operate within the traditional and expected life course, others frequently depart. There are many changes from what was once considered normal. The dual career elderly, the single older person, and childless older couples are examples of those who have their own special life course issues. Success is not to be measured by fulfillment of the traditional life course. It is hoped that the older person will be first considered a unique individual.

Dependency is the most feared role change of independent adults. For many, to be physically or financially dependent means to give up their privacy and to always be grateful for whatever they receive. Dependency may affect one's self-image more than any other factor.

It is possible for many older persons to accept and adjust to the new and sometimes devastating changes that occur in their lives. Some view the changes as challenges and opportunities for further adult development. Others are not as fortunate, however, and do not cope well in late life.

Why is the aging process experienced differently? What clues can be found that will point to successful aging, and what clues will help us identify those who need help or are likely to need help?

Erikson's view is helpful. He has described human development in terms of the life cycle.[9] The phases of that cycle, accordingly, include: basic trust, autonomy, initiative, industry, identity, intimacy, generativity, and integrity. Each phase contains various opportunities and developmental goals. The degree to which people successfully complete each phase has important implications for their ability to meet the demands and gain the rewards of the next phase. For example, failure to develop a sense of basic trust makes the achievement of autonomy more difficult. The last phase, integrity, is the specific task of old age. It is the task of accepting the outcome of one's life and taking responsibility for it. Integration and integrity are more possible and probable for those who have completed the developmental tasks of the preceding phases.

For older adults the challenge is to continue to grow and adapt in the midst of changes and losses that are part of the aging experience. As already stated, many older persons accept this new challenge as they have earlier ones and consistently amaze everyone with their flexibility and resiliency. Others need help to find new ways to cope with changes themselves and in their world. Some of those needing help in later years have had difficulty negotiating the earlier developmental tasks.

Estimated percentages of older people in trouble and needing mental health services vary greatly. Most mental health authorities agree that 15 to 20 percent is a conservative estimate. A number of epidemiologic studies indicate that 5 to 10 percent of older persons in the community have significant psychiatric impairment, and that 10 to 40 percent have mild to moderate impairment.[10]

Among older adults who need help to cope with emotional problems and mental disorders, the types of problems or disorders and their severity vary widely. Many disorders are related to physical causes, but many more are related to life experiences and personality problems that have hampered the successful completion of earlier developmental phases.

Two broad groups are to be considered when mental health needs are discussed. The first group includes those individuals who have from good to excellent mental health most of the time. These older adults draw on a lifetime of learning and past experience to help them adjust to the social and physical changes of late life. For this group, life is sometimes difficult because of specific or accumulated stress. They will need some additional help. These needs may be met by their natural environment of family, friends, and community. Intervention and treatment by mental health professionals will be required by others. The case studies included in this book illustrate the variety and complexity of mental health difficulties for this group.

The second group consists of people most often recognized as having emotional problems or mental disorders. For these, life has always been a struggle. The aging process brings additional dimensions. Not all in this group are easily identified, however, some have indeed required assistance and intervention for all or most of their lives. Other emotionally fragile persons may function adequately and draw little attention to themselves until the additional stresses of late life are too much for them. The reader will also recognize representatives from the second group in the case studies.

Identification of the mental health needs of any individual is a complicated and continuous process. This is true both of the person experiencing new difficulties and of the person with long-standing emotional problems. A careful and thoughtful *initial* assessment provides the information necessary to proceed with *initial* interventions. Additional or alternate interventions are often indicated during the course of treatment as the therapist gains a better understanding of the patient and as the needs of the patient shift and change. The philosophy and method of assessment are presented in Chapter 2. As specific disorders are discussed, major attention is given to assessment. Treatment plans and interventions are considered after each assessment presentation. Comments are often made about the adaptation of specific interventions for older patients in the following chapters.

Therapeutic intervention has received increasing attention from clinicians in recent years. As early as 1959, however, Rechtschaffer reviewed the existing literature and presented a summary of modifications for the psychotherapeutic approach to elderly patients. These modifications included the following: the therapist must take a more active role; some educational techniques may be used; environmental manipulation may be desirable; resistance and transference should be handled gently; and therapy is more often tapered than terminated.[11] It is impossible to review each possible intervention in detail in this book. Readers are referred to the writings of our colleagues in the geropsychiatric field[12] and are encouraged to develop their own preferred intervention skills. Verwoerdt suggests that most psychotherapy with aged patients is supportive in nature. The goal is to support existing coping mechanisms and bring the patient back to a satisfactory condition.[13] The preferred intervention and mode of therapy depends both on the individual client's potential for growth and the knowledge and skills of the therapist. Whanger has contributed numerous publications regarding treatment within institutions, nutrition, and drug management.[14,15] Burnside and others have contributed greatly to our understanding of the values of group process and techniques with the elderly.[16]

The purpose of therapeutic intervention is to promote positive change and to prevent further deterioration. An intervention may be a simple environmental manipulation or an intricate combination of medication and insight-oriented therapy. Therapists who choose to work with older adults require the same essential preparation as other therapists. Additional supervised experience in geriatric settings is helpful as they learn to adapt interventions to older clients. The intervention possibilities increase in number in direct relation to the skill and creativity of the therapist. The choice of intervention for an individual may be limited by many factors, however, including personality characteristics, physical condition, motivation, economic considerations, available facilities, and personal and community resources.

Therapeutic intervention includes the appropriate utilization of services available to older adults. These services vary greatly from one community to another. Therapists working with the elderly must become familiar with services and service providers. Service providers must know about the range of mental health services in their community. Most cities and counties have community resource directories, which are a good place to start but cannot substitute for direct contact. Local councils on aging, departments of social services, health departments, home health agencies, and community mental health centers should be among the first service providers contacted to find out what is available for older adults in each community. Some counselors and therapists in private practice are prepared to work with older adults. Geriatric outpatient clinics and geriatric hospital wards are available in some places. It is hoped that a greater number of services and a larger number of professionals will offer a wider variety of therapeutic interventions in the future.

NOTES

1. Further Reading List.

2. U.S. Bureau of Census, *General Population Characteristics*, (Washington, D.C.: 1980).

3. E.W. Busse and D.G. Blazer, "The Theories and Processes of Aging," in *Handbook of Geriatric Psychiatry*, eds. E.W. Busse and D.G. Blazer (New York: Van Nostrand Reinhold, 1980), p. 4.

4. Ibid., pp. 4–16.

5. Robert C. Atchley, *The Social Forces in Later Life,* 2nd ed., (Belmont, California: Wadsworth Publishing, 1977), p. 63.

6. Ibid., p. 64

7. Ibid., p. 88

8. B.L. Neugarten and N. Datan, "Sociological Perspectives on the Life Cycle," in *Life Span Developmental Psychology: Personality and Socialization,* eds. P.D. Baltes and K.W. Shaie (New York: Academic Press, 1973).

9. Erik H. Erikson, *Identity* (New York: W.W. Norton, 1968).

10. Busse and Blazer, eds., *Handbook of Geriatric Psychiatry,* p. 253.

11. A. Rechtschaffen, "Psychotherapy with Geriatric Patients: A Review of the Literature," *Gerontology* 14: 1959, pp. 73–84.

12. Further Reading List.

13. A. Verwoerdt, *Clinical Geropsychiatry,* 2nd. ed. (Baltimore: Williams & Wilkins, 1981), p. 179.

14. A.D. Whanger and E.W. Busse, "Geriatrics," in *The Therapist's Handbook: Treatment Methods of Mental Disorders,* ed. B.B. Wolman (New York: Van Nostrand Reinhold, 1976), pp. 287–324.

15. A.D. Whanger, "Treatment within the Institution" and "Nutrition, Diet, and Exercise," in *Handbook of Geriatric Psychiatry,* eds. E.W. Busse and D.G. Blazer (New York: Van Nostrand Reinhold, 1980). pp. 453–497.

16. I.M. Burnside, ed., *Working with the Elderly: Group Process and Techniques* (North Scituate, Mass.: Duxbury Press, 1978).

FURTHER READING LIST

J.E. Birren and R.B. Sloane, eds., *Handbook of Mental Health and Aging* (Englewood Cliffs, N.J.: Prentice-Hall, 1980).

D.G. Blazer and I.C. Siegler, eds. *A Family Approach to Health Care of the Elderly* (Menlo Park, Calif.: Addison-Wesley, 1984).

E.W. Busse and E. Pfeiffer, eds., *Behavior and Adaptation in Late Life* (Boston: Little, Brown, 1969).

E.W. Busse and E. Pfeiffer, eds., *Mental Illness in Later Life* (Washington, D.C.: American Psychiatric Association, 1973).

R.N. Butler and M.I. Lewis, *Aging and Mental Health* (St. Louis: C.V. Mosby, 1973).

E. Palmore, ed., *Normal Aging* (Durham, N.C.: Duke University Press, 1970).

E. Palmore, ed., *Normal Aging II* (Durham, N.C.: Duke University Press, 1974).

B. Silverstone and H.K. Hyman, *You and Your Aging Parent* (New York: Pantheon Books, 1976).

Chapter 2

A Multidimensional and Interdisciplinary Approach to Assessment and Intervention

Alice C. Myers

A comprehensive and systematic assessment is the first goal of mental health professionals who work with older patients. Various factors influence the assessment process. They include the emotional and physical condition of the patient; the patient's desire to cooperate with, and/or ability to tolerate, the assessment process; the availability of concerned relatives or other reliable informants; and, of course, the skill and patience of the clinician(s). Even the most cooperative of patients and family members may be unable to provide an adequate early personal history; the patient may not remember, and younger family members may never have known. Other older patients may be reluctant to answer questions about personal history, hopes, fears, financial resources, and the like, because they resent what they regard as an intrusion. For most people a therapeutic relationship must be developed over a period of time before they are willing to share certain information. The clinician must also be alert to the possible pathology of other family members and to family dynamics in general. Considering the foregoing factors, it becomes even more clear that a systematic approach to assessment for older adults is essential.

Three separate components of initial assessment and intervention are demonstrated in this chapter by following one person through the assessment process. The multidimensional functional assessment, the clinical evaluation, and the interdisciplinary team conference are all discussed in the context of Mr. Johns. The name *Mr. Johns* is fictitious to ensure privacy to the patient; the material has been modified for the same purpose.

MULTIDIMENSIONAL FUNCTIONAL ASSESSMENT

Most mental health professionals agree that the older patient's current ability to function in the varied dimensions of his life needs to be assessed. Many clinicians choose to use an unstructured patient interview, combined with reports from reliable informants. Others choose a structured questionnaire, such as the Older Americans Resources and Services (OARS) instrument.[1] The OARS instrument, a multidimensional functional questionnaire, was developed at the Duke University Center for the Study of Aging and Human Development. It has continued since 1972 to be part of the initial evaluation for patients in the OARS Geriatric Evaluation and Treatment Clinic.[2] The OARS multidimensional functional assessment questionnaire (MFAQ) consists of two parts, each of which can be used independently: Part A is functional assessment and Part B, services assessment. Five dimensions are covered by the assessment questionnaire: social resources, economic resources, mental health, physical health, and activities of daily living. The purpose of the functional assessment is to obtain an overall impression of the subject's functional level in each of the five dimensions at the time of the assessment.

There are times when it is not appropriate to proceed with the MFAQ: when the patient is too anxious, paranoid, or physically weak or is unable to answer the questions for whatever reason. The preliminary questionnaire on page 2 of the MFAQ measures the patient's reliability. A total error score of 4 or more indicates that the patient may be unable to give factual answers. Other factors should be weighed, however. The subject's educational level, if third grade or lower, may account for some errors. Therefore, the interviewer should continue through question 14. If the patient appears to have little difficulty answering, continue. If not, ask the patient subjective questions—those in boxes. Direct the remaining questions to an informant. Questions 73 through 82 are always asked of an informant.

The simulated functional assessment interview with Mr. Johns is reproduced here in order to demonstrate its usefulness in a clinical setting. In the process of administering the MFAQ in a clinical setting, the interviewer may take note of statements and expressed feelings that will need to be explored later in a less structured clinical interview. Observations recorded to aid in continuing work with the patient are in parentheses; explanations to the reader are enclosed in brackets. On the completed questionnaire, printed in Appendix A, significant statements by the patient are set off by quotation marks to distinguish them readily from the interviewer's observations. The MFAQ is utilized for research as well as for immediate clinical purposes; therefore, care is taken to adhere closely to the questionnaire.[3]

A comparison of the interview with the completed questionnaire will reveal a few contrasts: namely, explanations and comments that are made in the interview, but are absent from the questionnaire, are for the purpose of relieving the patient's anxiety and establishing rapport. The patient was assured, for example, that the interviewer had not forgotten information provided earlier; the interviewer expressed interest in hearing more on certain points in the next interview.

Some clinicians who are unfamiliar with the MFAQ object to its length. It requires approximately 45 minutes to administer. Concern has also been expressed about the number of sensitive questions it includes. Most patients seem to respond well when assured of confidentiality, however. Most patients find comfort and security in the knowledge that the same questionnaire is given to every patient and that some questions may not apply to them. Interest, concern and respect expressed by the interviewer seem to evoke a good response in most patients.

Prior to the assessment interview with Mr. Johns, the interviewer had a brief telephone conversation with him and with his physician of several years. The patient was referred for recurring depression and for help in adjusting to disabilities resulting from a stroke.

Multidimensional Functional Assessment Interview

Clinician: Hello, Mr. Johns. I'm Mrs. Myers. We talked by phone the other day to arrange this appointment. I'm glad that you could come today.

Patient: Thank you. I'm glad I could come, too.

Clinician: Please come into my office. (Patient is using cane and is somewhat unsteady on his feet.) [It is helpful to explain clinic evaluation procedures and to give the patient an opportunity to ask questions, as demonstrated next.]

Clinician: Mr. Johns, we talked briefly on the phone about your recent physical problems and your current need for different living arrangements. I want to hear more about that. I also want to hear about your physical problems and any other problems that you might have. I mentioned to you by phone that our evaluation procedure is rather lengthy here at the clinic. I want to review that with you again, and see if you have any questions about it. As I mentioned on the phone, the people who come to our clinic have many different problems. However, we have the same procedures for evaluating their situations and their resources. (Patient is very attentive and keeps good eye contact.) The first part of our evaluation procedure is a questionnaire that we give to everyone. It has lots of questions, and some of the questions may seem relevant to you and some may not. I ask only that you bear with us and answer them to the best of your ability. Then, following the formal questionnaire, I will want to talk to you more about your recent problems, your present living arrangements, and your past social, medical, and family history. Also, you will have the opportunity to talk with other people on our staff when that seems appropriate. Now, I have done a lot of talking already. Do you have any questions about what I have said?

Patient: No, I just hope I can answer all the questions.

Clinician: Don't worry about that. Please tell me if you become tired.

Patient: I feel pretty good. My daughter tells me I am quite a talker. (Patient smiles.) [Use of questionnaire starts here. See Appendix A.]

Clinician: All right, what is the date of today?

Patient: The fifth of September, 1979.

Clinician: What day of the week is it?

Patient: Tuesday.

Clinician: What is the name of this place?

Patient: The Pickens Building, I believe. [The OARS Clinic is located in the Pickens Building.]

Clinician: What is your telephone number?

Patient: 963-9876.

Clinician: How old are you, Mr. Johns?

Patient: I was 64 last—no, I was 65 last June.

Clinician: When were you born?

Patient: The ninth of June, 1914.

Clinician: Who is the President of the United States now?

Patient: Carter is.

Clinician: Who was the President before him?

Patient: Mr. Ford, Mr. Gerald Ford.

Clinician: What was your mother's maiden name?

Patient: Lucille Thomas.

Clinician: Subtract 3 from 20, and keep subtracting 3 from each new number you get, all the way down.

Patient: Oh, that's easy, I'm good with numbers. Let's see, from 20, you said. That's 17, 14, 11, 8, 5, 2. (Patient is smiling and seems to enjoy attention from clinician.)

Clinician: Very good. Tell me, Mr. Johns, how far did you go in school?

Patient: I had a couple of years in college.

Clinician: I'm going to want to hear more about that later, but we will just proceed with these questions now. [I want to let the patient know that I want to know more about this, but need to keep to the structured questions for now.] I have a few questions to ask about your family and friends. Are you single, married, divorced, or separated?

Patient: My wife died about 10 years ago. (Client appears very sad.) [Clinician will note this on questionnaire and explore sadness further in clinical evaluation.]

Clinician: Who lives with you now?

Patient: No one. I live alone. That's part of the problem with my present physical difficulty. You see, since I had the stroke, I cannot do things as I would like to do for myself, and it makes it very difficult for me to live alone. (Patient seems distressed.)

Clinician: I understand that, Mr. Johns, and I hope together we can work out a living situation where you can be comfortable. Now, I have a few questions about your friends and your family. How many people do you know well enough to visit in their own homes? Five or more, 3 or 4, 1 or 2, or none?

Patient: Oh, I would say 3, I guess. [Clinician will want to pick up on this later to ask who those people are and what kind of a relationship he has with each of them.]

Clinician: About how many times did you talk to someone—friends, relatives, or others—on the telephone in the past week? Once a day or more, two to six times, once, not at all?

Patient: My daughter called me every day since I have been sick—while I was in the hospital and after I got out. [Clinician will want to ask in evaluation interview about social contacts prior to illness.]

Clinician: All right, thank you, Mr. Johns. How many times during the past week did you spend some time with someone who does not live with you? That is, you went to see them or they came to visit you, or you went out to do things together. Once a day or more, two to six times a day, once, not at all?

Patient: I didn't feel much like seeing anybody last week. Only my son came to see me last week.

Clinician: Mr. Johns, do you have someone you can trust and confide in?

Patient: Yes, I can talk to my brother. I have a brother that I can talk to. (Patient speaks of brother with affection.)

Clinician: Do you find yourself feeling lonely quite often, sometimes, or almost never?

Patient: Well, sometimes, I guess. Sometimes more often than others. But yes, sometimes.

Clinician: All right, do you see your relatives and friends as often as you want to, or are you somewhat unhappy about how little you see them?

Patient: Well, they are very busy. I understand they have their own lives. I don't know. [Clinician repeats question, hoping for a definite answer.]

Clinician: Do you see your relatives and friends as often as you want to, or are you somewhat unhappy about how little you see them?

Patient: Umm, often as I want, I guess. (Client seems very ambivalent about this statement.) [Clinician will explore this ambivalence in clinical evaluation interview.]

Clinician: Is there someone who would give you any help at all if you were sick or disabled—for example, a member of your family or a friend?

Patient: Well, I have a sister and a brother, and there's my son—they're all willing to help, but they're not able to help. They all work. My daughter does not live here. See, that's part of my problem. That's why I need to move somewhere or get some help some way. (Patient seems irritated.)

Clinician: I understand that your family would like to help but they are not able to help. I do remember that your need for a better living arrangement is one reason you are here today, but I do need to ask these questions so I will have a better understanding of your total situation. (Patient nods; irritation is not evident.) Now I'd like to ask you some questions about your work situation. I understand from talking with you on the phone that your work was disrupted because of your recent stroke. So would you say that you are presently employed full-time, employed part-time, retired, retired on disability, or would you choose another way to describe your present work situation?

Patient: I'm on sick leave now. I hope I can go back to work. I was just working part-time. I retired last year.

Clinician: What kind of work have you done most of your life?

Patient: Well, I have been a salesman for the best part of my working years. However, I have not been working as a salesman recently. I just took this part-time job in an office supply store. (Patient appears embarrassed about present employment.)

Clinician: Mr. Johns, did your wife ever work?

Patient: Yes, she was a secretary—a good one.

Clinician: Mr. Johns, I need to ask you a few questions about your income.

Patient: I don't have very much money. My insurance isn't good, and my time in the hospital and other family situations—I, uh, well all I have is my Social Security and another little pension I have from another job. Of course, I'm not getting any money from the part-time job now. (Patient is not hesitant to discuss finances, but appears sad again.)

Clinician: All right, Mr. Johns, do you mind telling me what your monthly income is from Social Security?

Patient: Two eighty.

Clinician: And I believe you said you had a retirement pension. What amount is that monthly?

Patient: Ninety-five.

Clinician: Thank you, Mr. Johns. Now is that the extent of your income at present? That is, do you have any money from savings or regular assistance from your family?

Patient: No.

Clinician: Do you have income from rental or interest from investment or insurance? Do you receive a VA or disability payment?

Patient: No, I wish I did.

Clinician: How many people altogether live on your income?

Patient: I am the only one.

Clinician: Mr. Johns, do you own your own home?

Patient: No.

Clinician: I believe you told me on the phone that you rent your own apartment, and you told me at that time how much you were paying, but I forgot. Do you mind telling me again how much that is per month?

Patient: No, I don't mind. I told you I pay a hundred and thirty-five dollars.

Clinician: Do you live in public housing or receive a rent subsidy?

Patient: No, I live in a regular apartment near here. Do you think I could live in a subsidized housing or get help with my rent?

Clinician: Mr. Johns, we will certainly look into that. There is a long waiting list for the public housing apartments for senior citizens, but you can certainly apply and get on that waiting list. However, we will need to think together about other alternatives before one of those apartments would become available. Now, just a few more questions about finances. Are your assets and financial resources sufficient to meet emergencies?

Patient: No, they are not. (Sadness)

Clinician: Are your expenses so heavy that you cannot meet the payments, or can you barely meet the payments, or are your payments no problem to you?

Patient: I can just barely meet the payments. And I don't think I can stay where I am, because I don't think I can care for myself well enough to be independent in the apartment.

Clinician: Mr. Johns, I know this next question may sound very much like the previous one, but I need to ask, is your financial situation such that you feel you need financial assistance or help beyond what you are already getting?

Patient: Yes, I do need some help.

Clinician: Do you pay for your own food, or do you get any regular help at all with cost of food or meals?

Patient: I pay for all my food myself, but I am not able to fix it like I could before all this happened to me.

Clinician: Mr. Johns, do you feel you need food stamps?

Patient: I don't know, I don't really want to go into that. I mean, I don't really want to apply for food stamps.

Clinician: OK. Now just a couple of questions about health or medical insurance. Are you covered by any kind of health or medical insurance?

Patient: I have Medicare and some other Blue Cross for hospitalization, for when I'm in the hospital only.

Clinician: Is that Medicare Plan A?

Patient: Yes.

Clinician: Mr. Johns, I have been asking a lot of questions about financial matters. Please tell me how well you think you are doing financially as compared to other people your age—better, about the same, or worse?

Patient: Well, I don't know. I don't know.

Clinician: How well does the amount of money you have take care of your needs—very well, fairly well, or poorly?

Patient: Well, that—I don't know how I'm going to manage. It has taken care of me, I mean I have had enough money to take care of me—to get along fairly well—but I don't know, I don't know now. (Stressful subject)

Clinician: Mr. Johns, I can see that it's difficult for you to talk about the financial situation because it is difficult for you to make ends meet. Now I have a few questions I want to ask you about how you feel about life. How often would you say that you worry about things—very often, fairly often, or hardly ever?

Patient: Well, I worry a lot now. I would say—yes, I would say very often.

Clinician: In general, Mr. Johns, do you find life exciting, pretty routine, or dull?

Patient: Pretty routine. Yes, although my life hasn't been routine, but of those choices I would say pretty routine—not exactly dull, but it's not exciting.

Clinician: Taking everything into consideration, how would you describe your satisfaction with life in general at the present time—good, fair, or poor?

Patient: Well, I've had, I've had some good times, I—it's been good. Right now it's not good, but it has been good. [Clinician repeats question in hopes of receiving specific answer.]

Clinician: How would you describe your satisfaction with life at the present time—good, fair, poor?

Patient: Just fair, I guess, just fair.

Clinician: Mr. Johns, I have another list of questions that I want you to answer yes or no as they apply to you now. There are no right or wrong answers—only what best applies to you. Occasionally a question may not seem to apply to you, but please answer either yes or no, whichever is more clearly correct.

Patient: All right, OK.

Clinician: Do you wake up fresh and rested most mornings?

Patient: Yes.

Clinician: Is your daily life full of things that keep you interested?

Patient: Uh, well, it has been, but right now, since I've been sick, I guess the answer is no.

Clinician: Does it seem that no one understands you?

Patient: No—no, I wouldn't say that—I wouldn't say that.

Clinician: Have you periods of days, weeks, or months when you couldn't take care of things because you couldn't get going?

Patient: Yes, since I've been sick this time, yes, there have been days like that.

Clinician: Is your sleep fitful and disturbed?

Patient: No, I've been sleeping pretty well.

Clinician: Are you happy most of the time, Mr. Johns?

Patient: Yes, yes, I guess you would say so.

Clinician: Are you being plotted against?

Patient: (Laughs) No, no, I don't think so.

Clinician: Do you certainly feel useless at times?

Patient: Yes, yes, I feel useless. Yes, I do. (Patient is sad.)

Clinician: During the past few years, have you been well most of the time?

Patient: Yes, until this past illness, yes.

Clinician: Do you feel weak all over much of the time?

Patient: Yes, since the stroke.

Clinician: Are you troubled by headaches?

Patient: No, no, I don't have headaches much.

Clinician: Have you had difficulty in keeping your balance in walking?

Patient: Yes, since the stroke.

Clinician: Are you troubled by your heart pounding and by shortness of breath?

Patient: Yes.

Clinician: Even when you are with people, do you feel lonely much of the time?

Patient: No. No, I wouldn't say so.

Clinician: Mr. Johns, how would you rate your mental or emotional health at the present time—excellent, good, fair, or poor?

Patient: Oh, good, I guess. (Patient is sad or uncertain of answer.)

Clinician: Is your mental or emotional health now better, about the same, or worse than it was five years ago?

Patient: Well, I don't know how to answer that. I don't believe I can answer that. No.

Clinician: Mr. Johns, let's talk about your health now. I know that you've given me some information again on the phone, and of course I will be requesting records from your physician, but there are a few specific questions I would like to ask you at this point. About how many times have you seen a doctor during the past six months other than as an inpatient in the hospital?

Patient: Well, let's see. Uh, I've been to see one twice, uh, no, once after I fell at work. He sent me to the hospital and then three times since I've been out of the hospital.

Clinician: All right. During the past six months how many days have you been so sick that you are unable to carry on your usual activities—such as going to work or working around the house?

Patient: About, uh, one, it's been almost a month now.

Clinician: How many days in the past six months were you in the hospital for physical health problems?

Patient: Oh, let's see, just two weeks and one day.

Clinician: How many days in the past six months were you in a nursing home or rehabilitation center for physical health problems?

Patient: There was some talk about that, but I did not go there from the hospital.

Clinician: Do you feel that you need medical care or treatment beyond what you are receiving at this time?

Patient: No. Dr. Smith is taking care of me. He's been my doctor for some time. I think he's fine, and he referred me here. That's mostly because, well, he said you all would help me find a place, but also he thinks that all this has kinda got me down.

Clinician: Yes, I'm glad Dr. Smith referred you to us. I want to talk more later about how your health problems and your living situation have gotten you down. Right now, I have a list of common medicines that people take. Would you tell me if you have taken any of the following in the past month.

Patient: Well, I can tell you I'm taking Lithium and, uh, meprobamate. That's all I'm taking right now.

Clinician: All right, Mr. Johns, would you mind if I just read this list over to see if you think that you've taken any of them in the past month, and not just what you're taking right now.

Patient: All right.

Clinician: Arthritis medication? Prescription pain killer? High blood pressure medicine? Pills to make you lose water or salt? Digitalis? Pills for the heart? Nitroglycerin tablets for chest pain? Blood pressure medicine? Drugs for poor circulation? Insulin injections for diabetes? Pills for diabetes? Prescription ulcer medicine? Seizure medication? Thyroid pills? Cortisone pills or injections? Antibiotics? Tranquilizers and nerve medicine? [Patient continues to shake head to give negative answer until tranquilizers are mentioned.]

Patient: Yes, uh, Librium.

Clinician: Prescription sleeping pills? Hormones?

Patient: No.

Clinician: What other prescription drugs have you taken in the past month?

Patient: I'm not sure what they gave me in the hospital.

Clinician: Fine, we will send for the medical records. Mr. Johns, again I have a long list of illnesses that I want to read for you, and I would like for you to tell me if you have any of the following illnesses at the present time and, if so, how much they interfere with your activities. Arthritis or rheumatism?

Patient: Yes. [Clinician will want more details later.]

Clinician: Glaucoma?

Patient: No.

Clinician: Asthma?

Patient: No.

Clinician: Emphysema?

Patient: No.

Clinician: Chronic bronchitis?

Patient: No.

Clinician: Tuberculosis?

Patient: No.

Clinician: High blood pressure?

Patient: No.

Clinician: Heart trouble?

Patient: Yes. [Clinician will ask for more history later.]

Clinician: Circulation trouble in arms and legs?

Patient: No.

Clinician: Diabetes?

Patient: No.

Clinician: Ulcers?

Patient: No.

Clinician: Other stomach or intestinal disorders?

Patient: No.

Clinician: Gall bladder problems?

Patient: No.

Clinician: Liver disease?

Patient: No.

Clinician: Kidney disease?

Patient: No.

Clinician: Other urinary tract disorders?

Patient: No.

Clinician: Cancer or leukemia?

Patient: No.

Clinician: Anemia?

Patient: No.

Clinician: Effects of the stroke?

Patient: Yes. Well at least I've been weak since whatever that was that happened to me when I went to the hospital.

Clinician: Parkinson's disease?

Patient: No.

Clinician: Epilepsy?

Patient: No.

Clinician: Cerebral palsy?

Patient: No.

Clinician: Multiple sclerosis?

Patient: No.

Clinician: Muscular dystrophy?

Patient: No.

Clinician: Effects of polio?

Patient: No.

Clinician: Thyroid or other glandular disorders?

Patient: No.

Clinician: Skin disorders such as pressure sores, leg ulcers, or severe burns?

Patient: No.

Clinician: Speech impediment or impairment?

Patient: No.

Clinician: Now you have indicated that you are troubled with arthritis. Would you say that interferes with your activities a little, a great deal, or not at all?

Patient: A little.

Clinician: And you also indicated that you do have heart trouble. Would you say that that interferes with your activities a little, a great deal, or not at all?

Patient: Not at all.

Clinician: And the effects of the stroke or whatever it was that affected you prior to the hospitalization—would you say that interferes with your activities not at all? A little? A great deal?

Patient: A little. (Clinician is surprised at this answer but decides at this point not to challenge the answer. The previous conversations on the phone and prior comments in this interview have led the clinician to think that the stroke has interfered with a great deal of his activities.)

Clinician: How is your eyesight—excellent, good, fair, poor?

Patient: Good, I would say it's good.

Clinician: Do you have any other physical problems or illnesses at the present time that seriously affect your health?

Patient: No. No, not that we have not discussed.

Clinician: Now I want to ask a few questions about supportive devices and prostheses. Do you use any of the following aids all or most of the time? Cane?

Patient: No.

Clinician: Walker?

Patient: Yes, I didn't bring it with me today, but I do use a walker. I had someone help me into the building.

Clinician: Wheelchair?

Patient: No.

Clinician: Leg brace?

Patient: No.

Clinician: Back brace?

Patient: No.

Clinician: Hearing aid?

Patient: No.

Clinician: Colostomy equipment?

Patient: No.

Clinician: Catheter?

Patient: No.

Clinician: Kidney dialysis machine?

Patient: No.

Clinician: Any other?

Patient: No.

Clinician: Do you need any aids that you currently do not have?

Patient: No.

Clinician: Do you have a problem with your health because of drinking, or has your physician advised you to cut down on drinking?

Patient: No, I've never liked to drink.

Clinician: How would you rate your overall health at the present time— excellent, good, fair, or poor?

Patient: Poor. I guess I'd have to say poor right now.

Clinician: Is your health better now, about the same, or worse than it was five years ago?

Patient: Worse.

Clinician: How much do your health problems stand in the way of your doing the things that you want to do—not at all, a little, or a great deal?

Patient: A great deal. (Again client seems very sad as he is discussing his physical problems now.)[Note that his answer to this question is different from that to a similar question asked in relation to specific illnesses.]

Clinician: Now I'd like to ask you about some of the activities of daily living, things that we all need to do as part of our daily lives. I'd like to know if you can do these activities without any help at all, or if you need some help to do them, or if you can't do them at all. Can you use the telephone without help, including looking up numbers and dialing; with some help; or are you completely unable to use the telephone?

Patient: Oh, I can. I can use the telephone. It's not easy for me to look up numbers now, because as I said, my eyesight is not as good lately, but I can. I can do that.

Clinician: Good. Can you get to places out of walking distance without help, with some help, or are you unable to travel unless emergency arrangements are made for a specialized vehicle like an ambulance?

Patient: Well, I got here today. A taxi brought me. But it's not easy. I'd rather have somebody with me, but I can get to places.

Clinician: Yes, that is difficult. I can see that that's difficult for you. Can you go shopping for groceries or clothes without help, or are you completely unable to go shopping?

Patient: Well, I need some help. I can't carry things, and I can't stay on my feet long at a time.

Clinician: All right. Can you prepare your own meals without help, with some help, or are you completely unable to prepare any meals?

Patient: Well, I haven't been cooking for myself since I've been out of the hospital. I've only been out a few days. I guess—no, I'm not sure if I could. My son's been bringing me some things, and I've been eating some cereal. I don't think I could cook a full meal for myself, but I always have. I don't think I could now.

Clinician: All right. I want to come back and talk some more about the grocery shopping and the meal preparation and getting places. Can you do your own housework without help, with some help, or are you completely unable to do any housework?

Patient: Well, I don't think I can do any housework now.

Clinician: All right. Can you take your own medicines without help, with some help, or are you completely unable to take your medicine?

Patient: Oh, I can take my medicine. I don't have any trouble with that. You mean, do I remember it, or—yes, I can do that.

Clinician: Mr. Johns, can you eat without help, with some help?

Patient: Well, if a—no, I can do that.

Clinician: Can you take care of your own appearance—for example, shaving and so forth—without help, or do you need some help?

Patient: No, I can do that all right. I can use an electric razor.

Clinician: Let's see, the next question is, can you walk without help, with some help from a person, or with the use of a walker? I believe you told me you have used a walker.

Patient: I use a walker sometimes.

Clinician: Can you get in and out of bed without any help or aids?

Patient: Oh, yes, I can do that.

Clinician: Can you take a bath or shower without help, or do you need some help getting in and out of the tub?

Patient: I can take a shower. I wouldn't—but I'm not very sure—I'd rather there be someone there.

Clinician: Do you have trouble getting to the bathroom on time?

Patient: No. No, I haven't had that problem.

Clinician: Mr. Johns, is there someone who helps you with the things we've been talking about—the shopping, the housework, the bathing and getting dressed, and getting around?

Patient: Well, there is right now, but he, he's only here for a short time.

Clinician: And who is that?

Patient: My son.

Clinician: And his name?

Patient: Mr. Will Johns.

Clinician: Mr. Johns, you have answered a lot of questions already and been very patient. I do want to talk with you further to get some information about your family and medical history, as well as a few more details about what happened to you just prior to hospitalization. First, though, I would like for you to rest a few minutes. Would you like a cup of coffee?

Patient: Yes, I think I would. All right, thank you.

Clinician: Will you just wait outside my office and I'll get you a cup. You rest a few minutes and we'll talk again.

Patient: OK.

[Due to frailty of patient, clinician decided to use first section of the questionnaire and then proceed with the clinical evaluation. Clinician takes a few minutes to review questions already answered by the client and prepares for additional hour with client. If an informant had accompanied the client, the informant would be interviewed at this point.]

A quick review of the assessment interview with Mr. Johns presents a picture of moderate impairment in all five dimensions and alerts the evaluating clinicians to areas for further exploration. His social relationships appear adequate, but help with his daily needs is available only now and then. His son, who has been bringing in meals and helping in other ways, is visiting only for a few more days. The patient mentions several relatives who are concerned about him, but quickly explains why they cannot help him more. He explains that sister, brother, and son work and that both his son and daughter live elsewhere. I wonder if he believes that his relatives could help more, if he is angry and feeling rejected, or if—by what he tells me—he wants me to know that he is cared for and valued by his family, even though they can do no more. He seems distressed when talking about living alone and his difficulty with managing. I want to learn about his friends, particularly those he knows well enough to visit, and how often he sees them and family members. He seems uncertain of whether or not he wants to see them more often. He is embarrassed about his present employment. His income is somewhat inadequate, and he has no reserves in property or investments. He appears despondent when talking of his economic resources. He does not report receiving any regular financial assistance from family members.

I would rate his mental health as moderately impaired. He worries frequently and lives routinely, and—by his own description—his satisfaction with life in general is fair. At times he feels useless. His condition could be related to the aftereffects of his stroke. However, he has been a widower for 10 years, and his part-time job prior to his stroke is a source of embarrassment. I will need to know more about his personal history, but I suspect that he is depressed as a result of his life review, complicated by his present vulnerable emotional and physical condition following the recent stroke.

Current physical problems include the effects of his stroke, heart trouble, and some arthritis. He made conflicting statements regarding how disabled he is because of the stroke. The medical records have been requested, but I will want to hear his view of his medical history, including the heart trouble.

He regularly requires assistance with shopping, meal preparation, housework, and walking. Family members are not available on a long-term basis. I will need to find out what alternative living arrangements he has considered and rejected, or is still considering.

After reviewing the current functional assessment of Mr. Johns and my observations, I am ready to proceed with a second interview—the clinical evaluation.

CLINICAL EVALUATION

Discussion of the clinical evaluation, the second component of the assessment process, follows the presentation of the functional assessment, because the clinical evaluation builds on the information and impressions gained from the structured assessment interview. In my work with Mr. Johns, I had the advantage of administering the MFAQ as well as proceeding with the clinical evaluation. When assisted by an assessment interviewer, the evaluating clinician is responsible for reviewing both the questionnaire information and comments from the assessment interview.

The MFAQ concentrates on the current functional capacity of the patient, whereas the clinical evaluation is a less structured interview. It does explore specific areas of the patient's life: (1) the presenting problems as perceived by the patient and informants; (2) mental status and psychiatric symptomatology; (3) personal, medical, and psychiatric history; (4) family and social relationships, past and present; and (5) coping and adaptive patterns.

The presenting problem is usually addressed in the first few minutes of the clinical evaluation. The patient expects to talk about the problems that brought him to the clinic. Because his perception of the problem may be different from that of a family member, the family physician, or some other referring source, his version is important. For example, a daughter may be concerned about her mother's ability to care for herself, while her mother is frightened at the prospect of nursing home care. Their problems are related, but their perspectives are different.

The perceptions of current problems by patients and others involved in their care have important implications for intervention. A skillful interpretive conference, including recommendations for treatment, is a prerequisite to further intervention. The history of the presenting problem(s) must be obtained for the clinician to formulate a diagnosis and possible treatment plans.

The mental status assessment starts with the clinician's first observations of the patient, including general appearance, manner, and attitude. It continues throughout the evaluation interview. Other areas to be explored include psychomotor activity, body movements and speech, mood and affect, intellect, association and thought processes, perception, judgment, and insight. Assessment of the patient's mental status is obtained by skilled observation, general conversation, and specific questions. Information suggesting psychiatric symptoms, provided by reliable informants but not supported by the evaluating clinician's observations, is to be considered important but not made part of the mental status report.

The personal, medical, and psychiatric history of the patient is to be obtained from the patient whenever possible. Only the patient can tell you how he or she has experienced life. As mentioned earlier in this chapter, patients may be reluctant to share their personal histories in depth until a therapeutic relationship has been developed. Previous psychiatric treatment may be a sensitive area. Also, many patients are poor historians for a variety of reasons, even when they want to share information. The limited time element of the evaluation interview has to be recognized. The most skillful clinician and the most cooperative patient will find it difficult to cover a lifetime in an hour or two.

While the patient talks about his personal and family history, the clinician begins to form a picture of his past family and social relationships. The facial expression and tone of voice will tell as much as the words themselves about the patient's feelings of acceptance or rejection by his family and friends. Information pertaining to both past and present levels of social functioning is important. If his past relationships were satisfying and supportive but are presently inadequate, the patient may be able to reestablish some of the former ones and also build new ones. If the patient has operated on the fringe of family and community for most or all of his life, however, he is not apt now to develop an extensive social network.

Information about the patient's coping and adaptive patterns is not easy to obtain. First it must be determined what life changes and difficult situations have been experienced by the patient. Was the patient profoundly or only moderately disturbed by these past experiences? How did the patient cope with disruptive adversities? Did he use massive denial, consider the change a challenge, find comfort in religion, or find new roles to replace old ones? An understanding of past coping and adaptive patterns will allow the clinician to encourage the most positive coping patterns in the present.

Clinical Evaluation Interview

After a short break I invited Mr. Johns to return to my office. As he moved into the office and to a chair, he was again unsteady on his feet. I asked if he had considered using a cane. He smiled. He said he had been thinking about that. The physical therapist had made the same suggestion.

He then let me know that he was not sure he was to return for another appointment after this one. I assured him that he was and described what would be done before he returned. His medical records would be requested from the hospital and, with his permission, one of our staff would talk with his physician. Mr. Johns seemed relieved. His face and body posture relaxed. I saw that he wanted someone to take care of him and to take charge of his situation.

During the assessment interview, when he was questioned about his living arrangements and his ability to cope with the tasks of daily living and who he had to help him, he had become distressed. He had answered, "That's why I'm here." Now I returned to that incident to ask him if he needed help prior to his stroke. He said he had not. Although he ate out frequently before the stroke, he could cook at home when he chose. He continued by talking of how things had been different then: he walked a lot, drove his car, bowled with his friends. As he talked of the recent past, his facial expression was sad, until he began talking of his hope of continuing to improve and becoming independent again, when his face eased. Just as quickly, he became irritable when he spoke of his need to have someone with him. Evidently, he had given the possibility a lot of thought. I asked what he considered the chances were of having someone with him.

Continuing to be irritable, he discussed his situation. He did not want to live with any of his relatives. Because he was upset and steadily defensive, I did not ask whether any of his family had invited him to live with them. He told me that his son had suggested having someone come in to help him during the day, but Mr. Johns was more afraid of being alone at night, which was the time he wanted someone with him. He thought he would have to store his furniture at his brother's place, where he also parked his car, and live in a boarding home. When I asked if he needed help to find a place, he told me that his sister was taking the next day off from work to help him, adding that he would appreciate any suggestions I could make. I gave him names and phone numbers of people to call at the Council on Aging and the Department of Social Services. (I was not sure what would be the best temporary living arrangement. It seemed that he and at least one member of his family had decided that he could not continue in his present apartment.)

At this point I returned to the reason his physician had referred him to the clinic and asked him if he was ready to talk about that now.

"Oh, yes," he responded, "he thinks I'm kind of depressed."

"What do you think of that?"

His expression was again sad, as he admitted that he felt "low." He had understood, from his doctor and family, that after a stroke, feeling low was to be expected. He said that he had been sleeping all right but "had not felt much like eating." When asked if he ever thought of suicide, he answered, "Perhaps I should do that, but no, I would not shame my children or my brother or sister."

He reported that when he feels weak and alone, he becomes more depressed. He worries about the future and feels he "isn't any good to do anything." Despairingly, he said, "I am taking some medicine, but it isn't helping." The only helpful thing was being with people. He smiled. He said he was glad he had come to the clinic. I reaffirmed what his doctor had told him, that some depression is to be expected after a stroke. His life, after all, had been turned upside down. I reassured him that I was glad his being with other people helped and that I hoped my team members and I would be able to help through our suggestions and recommendations. He then wanted to know more about the clinic and what would happen next. I told him that after we had completed the interview, I would present the information he had shared with me to a team conference. The team would include a nurse, a social worker, a psychologist, and a psychiatrist, as well as graduate students affiliated with the clinic. The team would then decide on the best recommendations for him, which I would discuss with him at our next interview. Mr. Johns was pleased with the explanation and attention.

I brought Mr. Johns back to the discussion of his depression and asked if he had had any similar times of "feeling low" prior to his stroke. He looked thoughtful, then told me about other times "life had been bad."

He told of two extremely difficult times, in 1947 and again about 20 years later, just before and after his wife died. I asked what he remembered about the time in 1947.

He could not remember much except that he became extremely nervous and could not do his job. He had been a salesman at the time, selling building supplies while construction was booming. The trouble was that despite the boom, he had not been able to sell. His doctor had told him that he "needed treatment." He had agreed to being admitted to a psychiatric ward. Not being able to remember, after the lapse of years and precipitating events, the treatment or his feelings prior to or during his hospitalization, he concluded that he must have "gotten too nervous" to sell. His problem, he was certain, had nothing to do with his wife or children. Although he could remember having been given medication, he could not remember what it was. He did recall that he was not taking medication when he left the hospital and that he did not continue therapy after his three- or four-week hospital stay. After his release, he was able to return to his job and do his work well. He remembered that his employer had been good to him during his hospitalization and afterward.

After talking about his difficulties in 1947, he began talking of the second "bad time" in his life, which he had mentioned earlier. He said he "got along just fine," until about 11 years ago, when he again became "nervous" and was unable to work. He developed an ulcer, and his wife became ill with cancer. Eventually, she entered a nursing home. At the time, their children were ages 12 and 14. "Debts began to pile up, and I had to sell my business. Mary died. I had to keep a home going some way for the children. That was a very bad time." He recalled taking tranquilizers but could not remember the name of the drug.

I asked how his life had been for him these past 10 years. He smiled sadly and said that life had not been good since Mary died, but that he had managed and had been able to put the children through school. As for his needing tranquilizers during this period, he remembered sometimes needing Librium. Not being able to remember when he was first given Librium, he imagined that it was several years ago, while he was managing a building supply store. He pointed out that although managing a store was not as difficult as managing one's own business, it was still very stressful for him. I wondered how his having been a single parent added to the other stresses he had felt. He said that it had been difficult, especially to find time for everything and to continue missing Mary. Last year, after deciding to retire and take early Social Security benefits, he found himself a part-time job in an office supply store to supplement his income.

When I turned our conversation to his early history, he shifted his weight in his chair, smiled, and said, "Well, I was in the middle. I have one older brother and a younger sister. We had a good time growing up. My father was pretty strict, but mother was always taking up for us. My folks got along just fine." His story disclosed that his father had owned a sawmill at which he and his brother had worked after school and in the summers. Before starting school, he had followed his father and brother around the sawmill. He would have liked to study engineering but had not had the money to stay in school. Asking about when he met Mary, I learned that they met in grade school. She had always been his "best girl." She had not worried as he had and always made him "feel better."

"I have some good friends now, and my brother and sister, but it is not the same." When I asked him if he had been able to grieve for his wife and talk with family and friends of his loss, he appeared very sad and told me that he had grieved, and guessed that he still was grieving. Hearing that he had never found it easy to talk of Mary's illness and death, I suggested that it would be helpful if he could put into words some of the pain he felt, and that I hoped he would be able to talk more about Mary in our other sessions together. He nodded, but his face was expressionless.

Again he started to talk of how frustrated he felt, because he was so weak that he could not cook for himself or drive his car. Depressed, he wondered if he had left the hospital too soon. Remembering that his sister was to help find him a place the following day, he said he needed a place where he would not have to cook or go out for meals, as though such a place were the nearest remedy for having left the hospital too soon. I supported Mr. Johns, telling him that it would be good either to have someone come to his present apartment to help with cooking and transportation or to find a boarding home situation. I suggested that he think of the new arrangement as temporary, because I was hopeful that his strength and morale would improve. He smiled and said he hoped so, too.

Although we had many more areas to explore in relation to his marriage, children, and work, our time and his energy were running out. Before ending the session, however, I asked about his medical history. I asked him to sign release-of-information forms, which I would later send to the hospital and to his physician. He dated the beginning of his medical problems to a time about 10 years ago. He remembered himself as healthy during childhood. "Nothing but measles and a cold or two." I wondered if he remembered developing any medical problems in 1947, when he was hospitalized. He did. He had had a "nervous stomach" about that time and had been treated for an ulcer while in the psychiatric ward. Over the ensuing years, the ulcer had flaired from time to time but had not bothered him recently. He had had some angina about five years earlier but had hardly been bothered since.

After thanking him for his patience, I reminded him again that I would be talking with the other team members and reviewing his medical records before our next appointment. He wanted to know when his next appointment would be. We agreed on a week from that day. Although Mr. Johns was tired after the two-hour session, his mood seemed slightly improved, and he did not seem as unsteady on his feet while leaving the office as he had been on entering. Instead of asking me to call a taxi for him, he made the call himself. So that we could check the exact amount of his prescriptions, I asked him to bring his medicines to our next appointment.

INTERDISCIPLINARY TEAM CONFERENCE

The team conference is the main formal arena in which to demonstrate and experience the interdisciplinary team approach. Team members may need immediate consultation and support during the intake process or immediately after the first interview. Informal consultations when needed—in the hall or over lunch, any place, any time—are part of a good working team. However, the backbone of the interdisciplinary team is the regularly scheduled team conference, where the evaluating clinicians present new intakes and continuing cases to other team members.

As cases are presented in this book, the authors have tried to remain practical and realistic. Time is often a factor in team conference presentations, as it is in the evaluation interviews. Every aspect of each case cannot be explored in detail. Often the clinician prepares the case presentation after only one interview and before medical records have arrived. The advantages of early comments and suggestions by other team members at times seem to outweigh the disadvantages of having incomplete information. Team members may ask questions or make observations that will be helpful in the continuing evaluation and treatment of the patient.

During the intake conference, each new intake is usually discussed as follows: (1) the evaluating clinician presents a summary of assessment and a tentative treatment plan; (2) the team members ask questions and discuss available information and implications for further evaluation and treatment; (3) the team leader summarizes the discussion and confirms or amends the assessment and treatment plan.

The clinician's summary that follows reviews the information and impressions gained from the assessment and evaluation interviews. The summary may seem repetitious. However, the presentation of Mr. Johns's story within the respective contexts in which it was first reported—in the assessment interview, the evaluation interview, and team conference—is necessary to demonstrate the initial multidimensional and interdisciplinary approach to assessment and intervention.

Evaluating Clinician's Summary

Presenting Problem

Mr. Johns is a 65-year-old, white widower who was referred to the clinic due to his recurring depression and for help in adjusting to disabilities resulting from a recent stroke.

His stroke occurred four weeks prior to his coming to our clinic. He had collapsed while at work. He spoke of having felt warm and of falling down. He remembered feeling weak and of being only vaguely aware of the people helping him, of the ambulance, and of the emergency room. During his two-week, two-day, stay in the hospital, Librium and meprobamate were prescribed. His opinion now is that neither helped.

He described himself as continuing to feel "weak all over." His left leg sometimes "gives out" on him. However, he has not fallen again. He sometimes uses a walker but did not have it with him on the day of the evaluation. He seemed unsteady on his feet and walked slowly. Sometimes he held on to a chair, desk, or door. According to the patient, he did see a physical therapist while in the hospital but was not given a follow-up appointment. Now that he is regaining his strength, he becomes increasingly frustrated when he cannot do the things he likes to do—cook, take care of his shopping, and drive his car. He does not like to be alone and described his mood when alone as "low." Prior to our interview he decided not to continue living in his apartment and made plans with his sister to look for a boarding home for himself.

In the interview the patient described his recurring depression. It began during his wife's illness and after her death 10 years ago. Earlier, when in his thirties, he was admitted to a psychiatric hospital for anxiety, but as we talked, he denied having been depressed at that time.

Mental Status

Mr. Johns was dressed carelessly but appropriately. His hair was combed neatly and his face clean shaven. His movements were slow and his walk unsteady. At the beginning of the interview, his speech was deliberate and soft, with a marked lag between question and response. Little by little he warmed up and, before the end of the session, became voluble and spontaneous. His affect was depressed. Often during the interview, his face was fixed in a sad expression regardless of the topic. Occasionally, he smiled, weakly but appropriately. He reported sleeping well but complained of loss of appetite.

He had no difficulty with the short mental status exam. His responses to the questions in the mental health section of the MFAQ gave additional evidence of his depression and anxiety. Most of the time, he is unhappy—at times, feeling useless. His daily life is not full of things that keep him interested. When asked directly about suicidal thoughts, he replied, "Perhaps I should do that, but, no, I would not kill myself. I wouldn't want to shame my children or my brother or sister." No additional psychiatric symptoms were reported by his physician in our brief phone conversation.

Personal, Psychiatric, and Medical History

Mr. Johns was the second of three children. His older brother and younger sister are now living in the same area as he. He remembers his father being strict and his mother, protective. His love and respect for them were evident as he talked about them. When he was a child, his father owned a sawmill, where he and his brother worked during the summers and after school. He considers working there to have been a privilege, not a hardship. After completing high school and two years of college, he married his childhood sweetheart. In his late thirties, a boy and girl were born to them. The children were aged 12 and 14 when, after a long illness, their mother died of cancer. He described his marriage as "good." He continues to miss his wife. After her death he was able to maintain a home for his two children, each of whom is now married and living out of state.

Mr. Johns's work history seems to be connected to his medical and psychiatric history. He identifies himself as a salesman. He sold construction supplies for many years, owning a building supply store for almost 20 years. Regarded as a good salesman and valuable employee, he was able to return to his previous job after his psychiatric hospitalization in 1947. He continued in that position until he started his own business, which he eventually lost because of debts incurred through his own and his wife's illnesses. After selling his business, he took a job managing a store, which he kept until he retired last year. Within a few months after retiring, he took a part-time job as a clerk in an office supply store.

Otherwise vague about his psychiatric hospitalization in 1947, he said that he became "too nervous to work." He denied any problems with his marriage at the time. He had agreed to go to the hospital only upon his doctor's advice. While there, he was also treated for an ulcer. After one month, he had been able to return to work. He does not remember the name of any medication or the details of his treatment. Once released, he did not continue to see a psychiatrist.

Not until the year his wife became ill did he have any other "nervous trouble." At that time he became so "nervous" that he had difficulty working and developed another ulcer. For several months before her death, his wife was in a nursing home. He referred to this period of his life as "a bad time." During the last 10 years, he has been on and off tranquilizers and has not needed hospitalization for psychiatric or medical reasons until his recent stroke.

His medical history includes the following: (1) ulcers, 1947, 1969; (2) angina, 1974 and continuing; (3) arthritis; and (4) the stroke of four weeks ago.

Family and Social Relationships

The important family members are his older brother, younger sister, and his two children. He named his brother as the person in whom he can confide. His sister is helping him find a temporary place to live. His children indicate their concern by visits and phone calls. He became defensive when asked if any of his relatives could do more for him. He mentioned "good friends," but I did not ask about specific friendships. He continues to grieve the loss of his wife.

Coping and Adaptive Patterns

Mr. Johns seems to have two basic adaptive patterns: trying to be an achiever and retreating through illness when the going gets too rough. One source of his past distress was his own expectation for achievement as a salesman, a businessman, and a store manager. One way of finding relief was through being "too nervous" or "developing an ulcer."

Summary

Mr. Johns appears moderately impaired in all five dimensions. Although he has some meaningful family relationships, none is able to provide help with his daily needs regularly or to meet his present emotional needs. His mental health, as he would say, is "pretty low." Although some of his depression may be related to the stroke, he has a history of "nervousness" since 1947. He acknowledges feeling low, off and on, since the death of his wife 10 years ago. From that time forward, a process of life review has probably been going on, reducing his sense of self-worth.

His income is inadequate, and he has no reserves. His physical problems currently include weakness following his stroke, angina, and some arthritis. He regularly requires assistance with shopping, meal preparation, housework, and walking. I suspect his depression is a chronic condition, compounded by the aftereffects of his stroke and his inability to function well in daily activities.

I suggest the following be Mr. Johns's treatment plan: (1) a psychiatric evaluation to prescribe appropriate medication, (2) supportive psychotherapy geared to problem solving and to increasing his sense of self-worth, and (3) consultation with his family physician.

Team Discussion

Psychologist: Have you thought of involving Mr. Johns's sister or other family members?

Evaluating Clinician (Social Worker): As you know, we usually ask for a family member to come with the patient for the evaluation. Mr. Johns came alone and was defensive and intimidated when asked if any of his family could help him more with his daily needs. I think it would be helpful to talk with his sister. I may suggest we do in my next session with Mr. Johns, but I'll not insist.

Nurse: What side was affected by his stroke?

Evaluating Clinician: He spoke of his left leg being weaker. His arms, hands, face, speech did not seem to be affected.

Nurse: What medication did you say he is taking?

Evaluating Clinician: He is taking Librium and meprobamate, but he wasn't sure of the dosage. I asked him to bring the medicines with him the next time he came.

Psychologist: Psychological testing may be helpful to differentiate between organic impairment and depression. The results could be helpful in setting realistic goals for psychotherapy.

Evaluating Clinician: I think psychological testing could be helpful, but I think we should wait for a few weeks, because he will see a psychiatrist for medication and see me weekly. What do you think about Mr. Johns, Dr. Whanger?

Psychiatrist: Mr. Johns's life story seems to be one of struggling, but never quite making it. While he has had more than his share of psychological and physical distress, in the losses of his wife and business and in his heart problem and stroke, he nevertheless seems to have difficulty in coping with adversity in an effective way. Whether this is due to a basically limited capacity which he has been pushing to or beyond the limit, or whether this is more likely a characterological problem that interferes with his adjustment is not completely clear.

Evaluating Clinician: Do you see similarities between the 1947 problems, the time around his wife's death, and now?

Psychiatrist: He seems surprisingly vague about his psychiatric illness in 1947 and that surrounding the death of his wife, but there may have been many similarities to his present problem. There may be a recurrent cluster of problems with vague depression, rather severe diffuse anxiety, and difficulty with effective functioning, whether it be social, psychological, or physical. He has components of depression, but I get more the sense of a characterologic depressive stance rather than a clear-cut reactive or post illness depression.

He has somatized his problems before, and he may be doing it now. I have a feeling that he has strong dependency needs, which he has not been able either to satisfactorily accept or deny, so that he tends to flounder in the middle ground. We will need psychological testing and a psychiatric evaluation, as well as ongoing observations to see how this picture fits together. We may get a good idea about the extent of the organic mental impairment left from the stroke. We need to be sure to get the medical records and to have physical therapy evaluate his potential needs. It is very likely that he has not resolved the grief over the loss of his wife. Perhaps it might be well for him to have a primary therapist who is a woman, and then see one of the geropsychiatrists to evaluate the depression and manage the medications that would be necessary. After he has gotten himself better organized and the depression is better, he might benefit by joining the weekly group to help ventilate his feelings and get some feedback and support.

Evaluating Clinician: You mentioned both anxiety and depression earlier. How would you describe the diagnoses?

Psychiatrist: While only time, treatment, and the tests may tell us how much of his problem is of organic origin and how much is functional, I would think that his diagnoses are as follows: primarily, a depressive neurosis, or what is now called a dysthymic disorder; next, he has a generalized anxiety disorder of a moderate degree; there is some organic mental disorder of the multiinfarct dementia type of a mild degree; all of this is complicated by a somewhat atypical dependent personality disorder which has become more manifest because of his multiple losses.

Let us have a follow-up report in six weeks to review our findings and his progress.

Evaluating Clinician: The revised treatment plan, then, is: (1) obtain medical records, (2) schedule a psychiatric evaluation, (3) request physical therapy evaluation, (4) consult with family physician, (5) individual therapy with possible referral to group therapy later, (6) psychological testing, and (7) follow-up report in team conference in six weeks.

COMMENTARY

Three separate components of initial assessment and intervention have been demonstrated in this chapter by following one person through the assessment process. The multidimensional functional assessment (OARS questionnaire), the clinical evaluation, and the interdisciplinary team conference were all discussed in the context of case material pertaining to Mr. Johns.

One purpose for presenting Mr. Johns has been to provide a realistic view of both patient and clinician working within the constraints of time and with limited initial information and impressions. Clinicians, teachers, and students may see sections of the interviews that they would handle differently. Some may notice comments and observations in the first interview that were not followed up as intended in the second. Others may arrive at different conclusions. With the available information, they may have preferred to present Mr. Johns differently in the team conference. If such thinking is stimulated, one purpose of the presentation has been accomplished.

The second purpose for presenting the process in detail has been to provide an understanding of the method of initial assessment used. Subsequent cases are not provided in such detail, because they are presented to illustrate the assessment of, and intervention for, specific disorders instead of the process of assessment itself.

NOTES

1. The OARS instrument has been completed for Mr. Johns and appears in Appendix A. Copies of the instrument may be purchased from the Duke University Center for the Study of Aging, Box 2914, Duke University Medical Center, Durham, N.C. 27710.

2. The OARS Geriatric Evaluation and Treatment Clinic is an outpatient clinic at the Duke University Medical Center. It was established and sponsored by the Duke University Center for the Study of Aging to provide evaluation and treatment services for older adults and their families who are experiencing problems related to growing older. The OARS instrument and subsequent research were developed through the clinic, which also serves as a training site for professionals from many disciplines.

3. Formal training in use of the OARS instrument is strongly recommended to assure reliable and complete data gathering for research purposes. Such training is available through the Duke University Center for the Study of Aging.

Part II

Working with Older Adults

Chapter 3

Organic Mental Disorders

Mary Ann Matteson

NOSOLOGY

Organic mental disorders (OMD) and organic brain syndromes (OBS) are psychological or behavioral abnormalities associated with transient or permanent dysfunctions of the brain. In the *Diagnostic and Statistical Manual of Mental Disorders (DSM-III)*, a distinction is made between organic brain syndromes and organic mental disorders in terms of etiology.[1] The former (OBS) is described as a constellation of psychological and behavioral signs and symptoms without reference to etiology; the latter (OMD) indicates that the etiology is known or presumed. The six categories of organic brain syndromes are (1) delirium and dementia, (2) amnestic syndrome and organic hallucinosis, (3) organic delusional syndrome and organic affective syndrome, (4) organic personality syndrome, (5) intoxication and withdrawal, and (6) atypical or mixed organic brain syndrome. Organic factors that are often precursors to organic mental disorders are primary brain disease, systemic illness, substance or toxic agents, and withdrawal of a substance on which the individual is psychologically dependent. Thus the term *organic mental disorder* can be used for delirium, dementia, and so forth, if the precipitating factor is known. One would use the term *multiinfarct dementia* or *alcohol withdrawal delirium* and the like to characterize a particular disorder.

Organic mental disorders are among the most prevalent psychiatric disorders of later life. The majority of epidemiologic surveys find definite organic mental disorders in 4 to 6 percent of persons over age 65 and in 20 percent or more of those over age 85. If people with mild organic mental disorders are included, the prevalence rate is even higher.[2]

In the Older Americans Resources and Services, Geriatric Evaluation and Treatment (OARS-GET) Clinic, the majority of patients with organic brain disease have a disorder in the category of delirium and dementia. Delirium is most often due to overuse or misuse of drugs, infections, alcoholism, and other medical conditions. Dementia typically results from primary brain disease or vascular insufficiency or disruption. These disorders are differentiated by their mode of onset, progression of symptoms, precipitating factors, and prognosis.

DELIRIUM

Symptomatology

Persons experiencing a delirium may exhibit a clouded sensorium, ranging from drowsiness to stupor or coma. They may also experience illusions or hallucinations, which are usually visual in nature. Disturbances in psychomotor behavior may be manifested as shifts from agitation to sluggishness. Other associated features include anxiety, paranoia, depression, anger, irritability, euphoria, or apathy.[3]

A major symptom of this syndrome is disorder of attention, which includes disorganized thinking, a short attention span, and the inability to reason. There is also a deficit in short-term memory due to difficulty in registering new information; long-term memory deficits may occur as a result of difficulty in focusing attention on past events.

Etiology

Causes of delirium include brain lesions, infectious disorders, metabolic and nutritional disorders, circulatory and pulmonary diseases, medications, and sensory disturbances. A primary brain disorder that may result in delirium is subdural hematoma (a blood clot in the brain secondary to head trauma). Subdural hematomas are often overlooked because a fall resulting in head injury either was not observed or was forgotten. Infectious disease in the elderly can be elusive because elderly persons may not necessarily show an elevated temperature or typical pain. It is important to look for sources of infection, such as pneumonia or abscesses or urinary tract sepsis, when older patients appear withdrawn, lethargic, or disoriented.

Circulatory and pulmonary diseases, including congestive heart failure and chronic lung disease, can precipitate changes in mental status. Nutritional and metabolic disorders can also produce alterations in mental status, especially hypo- and hyperthyroidism, diabetes, electrolyte imbalance (hyponatremia, hypokalemia), vitamin deficiencies, and general malnutrition. Changes in life style with advancing age can affect diet and exercise patterns, so social factors can strongly influence nutritional and health status.

Older persons are extremely sensitive to all types of medications—both prescription and nonprescription. They are very likely to have untoward reactions to multiple prescriptions, high doses, and self-medication. Drugs that are especially dangerous to older adults are psychotropic medications, diuretics, digitalis, antihypertensive preparations, and insulin.

Psychiatric disorders in older adults can produce symptoms similar to those of dementia. Depression, anxiety, paranoia, schizophrenia, and mania can reduce cognitive performance; and it is important to attempt to distinguish these diseases from organic disease. Auditory and visual senses can diminish with advancing age, so it is necessary to determine whether or not confusion or inappropriate responses are due to these psychiatric illnesses or to misperceptions due to sensory losses.[4]

Prognosis

The prognosis of the disease depends upon its underlying cause and the promptness with which it can be treated. Dramatic improvements can be made in cognition and mental status when drug regimens are modified, diets are improved, or when systemic diseases have been treated. Generally, the longer an acute illness that impairs brain tissue function continues, the more likely it is that irreversible damage will be done.

DEMENTIA

Symptomatology

All dementias are characterized by one or more of the following symptoms: memory loss, impairment of intellectual function and abstract thought, confusion, disorientation, personality changes, and visual hallucinations.[5] These symptoms must be severe enough to interfere with occupational or social function and so represent disease states, and not be normal concomitants of the aging process.

Memory

Memory is the ability to register, store, and retrieve information. Loss of memory is often the earliest and most noticeable sign of organic brain disease. Recent memory seems most affected, especially memory of events or names. Remote memory is thought to be retained longer because it has been continually reinforced through the years, or because new information is difficult to process and retain.[6] Organically impaired older persons may confabulate in order to substitute information lost in memory gaps. The confabulations may be colored by wishful thinking and are more likely to occur when there is direct questioning or confrontation.

Cognition

Organic brain disease produces intellectual decline, impaired abstract thinking, and impaired judgment. An early sign of impaired intellectual decline is a decreased ability to make unfamiliar sequential numerical calculations. This is especially devastating to bookkeepers or mathematicians, whose livelihoods depend on the ability to use figures. Later in the disease, intellectual decline can have an effect on the ability to carry out the activities of daily living. The thinking involved in putting together a meal, bathing and dressing, or dialing a phone can become too complicated for an impaired older person.

Judgment and Insight

When limited by dementia, judgment and insight impairment are often manifested through an inability to recognize and accept limitations. For example, the realization that intersection traffic causes confusion and anxiety may call for exercise of the *judgment* that driving is dangerous; willingness to discontinue driving can be a manifestation of *insight*. Organically impaired older people may be unable to recognize that they no longer have the cognitive ability to carry out activities such as driving, cooking, or dressing.

Confusion and Disorientation

Disorientation to time, place, and person is frequently symptomatic of organic brain disease, and it is usually found in that order of appearance. The individual may begin to be confused about the day and date and, next, about where he is. In cases of insidious onset of senile dementia, the family may first begin to notice that something is wrong when the impaired older person becomes lost, especially in new situations, such as on vacation trips. More severely demented persons have difficulty remembering other people and eventually can lose the sense of who they are themselves.

Personality Changes

The personality and behavior of an organically impaired older person may change drastically, either through an exaggeration or "caricature" of the former self or through a blunting of affect. There is usually decreased social interaction, resulting in progressive withdrawal and isolation. The impaired person frequently becomes agitated and may wander inside or outside of the house. At times, this becomes more pronounced in the late afternoon and evening—a phenomenon known as "sundowning." Impulse control may be impaired, and family members may report attempts to act out anger, sexual wishes, and other aggressive acts. Attention span may become progressively shortened, and there is difficulty in concentrating on activities such as reading or conversation.

Hallucinations

Hallucinations are more frequently associated with acute brain disease, but they can also be seen in chronic disorders. The hallucinations are almost always visual rather than auditory. This phenomenon can help distinguish organic disorders from functional psychoses in which auditory hallucinations predominate.

PRIMARY DEGENERATIVE DEMENTIA

The disease known as senile dementia, or Alzheimer's disease, is a chronic, nonreversible disorder that affects 50 to 70 percent of all persons with dementia.[7] It has an insidious onset with a gradually progressive course lasting from 5 to 10 years. Alzheimer's disease of the presenile type is more commonly found in women than men, and the age of onset is usually between 45 and 65 years.

Symptomatology

It has been observed that persons with Alzheimer's type dementia pass through three distinctive stages. The first stage of the illness lasts approximately two to four years and is characterized by memory loss, disorientation to time, and lack of spontaneity. The changes are often so subtle that the symptoms are not recognized as a disease but are usually attributed to stress or old age. The second stage usually lasts for several years—as long as 5 to 10—with characteristic symptoms of aphasia, wandering, repetitive movements, agitation, confusion, and changes in appetite. Early in the second stage the appetite may be voracious, while later there may be a marked disinterest in food.

The third or terminal stage of Alzheimer's disease is often the shortest, lasting from one to two years. The person may become emaciated, incontinent, and unable to communicate and may have grand mal seizures. There may be frequent outbursts of temper, the only evidence of emotion in an otherwise vacuous personality.[8]

Etiology

The etiology of senile dementia is unknown; however, the disease can be identified through characteristic pathological changes in the brain. These changes consist of extensive senile plaques, neurofibrillary tangles, and degeneration of neurons. Diagnosis is difficult because the disease may mimic symptoms of other diseases, such as depression or delirium. A definite diagnosis can be made on autopsy by identifying the neurofibrillary tangles and senile plaques.

Treatment

Because there is no known curative treatment for the disease, care of the patient centers on daily management and working with the family. Each disease stage brings its own significant problems, including management of activities of daily living, financial burdens, decision making regarding nursing home placement, and grief. Families can obtain help from the Alzheimer's and Related Diseases Association, a national organization that provides a network of information and support from families in similar situations.

MULTIINFARCT DEMENTIA

Unlike the Alzheimer-type dementia, which has a neurological origin, multiinfarct dementia is a vascular disease affecting the vessels of the brain. The disease is found more frequently in men than women, but it is generally less common than senile dementia. The onset may also be earlier than that of senile dementia. Hypertension and arteriosclerosis are the major causes of multiinfarct dementia, which is often accompanied by signs of other vascular disease, such as carotid bruits, an enlarged heart, or diminished pulses.

Symptomatology

The disease is characterized by an abrupt onset, with rapid changes rather than a uniform progression of symptoms. There is a stepwise deterioration in intellectual functioning, presumably due to damage resulting from multiple small strokes. The affected person may experience disturbances in memory, abstract thinking, judgment, impulse control, and personality, with possible emotional liability. Characteristic focal neurological signs include weakness in the limbs, reflex asymmetries, dysarthria, and a small-stepped gait.

Management

Diagnosis of multiinfarct dementia is made through careful history taking, a brain scan, a physical exam, and possibly an arteriogram. Treatment can be as simple as regulation of blood pressure through diet and drugs and vasodilator medications or as sophisticated as major bypass surgery. Prognosis depends on the patient's age, number of risk factors, and progression of the disease.

ASSESSMENT OF ORGANIC MENTAL DISORDERS

Organic mental disorders can be complicated disease states in the elderly, which makes diagnosis difficult. Frequently an older patient can experience a mix of diseases, such as multiinfarct dementia with an overlay of delirium or other psychiatric disorders, so the clinician must make a thorough assessment to attempt to determine the etiology of the disease. A thorough assessment includes a chronological health history, a mental status exam, a physical exam with laboratory studies, and a home assessment.

Health History

A health history should begin with a life medical history in chronological order obtained from the patient, family, and medical records. This can help to determine causal and influential relationships among events, thus helping to prevent certain types of mismanagement, such as overprescribing medications. From the chronological history, the clinician should determine the baseline state of the patient's health. A determination should also be made about present problems or symptoms and their duration. A careful drug history should be taken, including all prescription and nonprescription drugs and home remedies. Nutritional information may be vitally important and should include not only what the patient eats but also where, how often, with whom, and how much. A review of body systems should be made in a systematic manner and must take into account the changes in physiological functioning due to the aging process. Psychosocial aspects of the health history are another important aspect of the assessment, for social supports such as family, friends, or social agencies are often crucial in determining a plan of care for an organically impaired older person.

Mental Status Exam

The mental status exam is a crucial component of the health assessment when one attempts diagnosis of an organic mental disorder. It is an objective observation of the patient's behavior and appearance during the interview that can be carried out by most health care professionals. During the mental status exam, the patient should be observed for general appearance, manner, and attitude; psychomotor activity; movements and speech; and mood and affect. Information should be obtained through verbal questioning about intellectual functioning, orientation, and abstract thinking.

Appearance, Manner, and Attitude

Organically impaired patients' appearance may or may not indicate the extent of the disease process. In some cases they may appear disheveled, dirty, or sloppy; in others, they may have received help with personal care from family members or caretakers, especially in preparation for clinic visits. Inability to take care of personal appearance may be manifested in various ways: a woman may be wearing two slips, buttons and zippers may not be fastened, or an item of clothing may be on backwards. Patients frequently do not bathe, or they may put on dirty clothes after bathing. These problems are usually caused either by impaired memory or shortened attention span; however, patients in later stages of the disease process may retain skills with which they are most familiar, such as those involving care of the body, hair, and face.

People who experience the cognitive decline associated with organic mental disorders often use defenses to attempt to handle the stress associated with decreased intellectual function. Patients may seem to become an exaggeration or caricature of their former selves as they attempt to handle the decline in a direct manner. For example, ambitious persons may become more aggressive and controlling; compulsive persons, more rigid and set in their ways. This attempt to control directly the decline and stress allows more chance for failure, often resulting in anxiety, frustration, shame, or anger. When this happens, auxiliary defenses may come forth, such as rejection of others or withdrawal or paranoid thinking.

Psychomotor Activity, Movements, and Speech

An unsteady or shuffling gait may be seen in many organically impaired people. They may be thin because of wasting of muscle tissues, which can cause an emaciated appearance; and their skin may be thin, atropic, and wrinkled. The tone of voice may be harsh; the speech, slow. Aphasia can occur in later stages of the disease.

Mood and Affect

Patients may demonstrate a generalized indifference to, or lack of interest in, the interview, or there may be a superficial compliance characterized by overpoliteness. Social graces may be intact initially, but may break down with prolonged questioning. Some patients appear sad, unhappy, or afraid, which may be manifestations of the depression that frequently accompanies dementia when patients realize their cognitive decline.

Cognition

Loss of memory, intellectual functioning, orientation, and abstract thinking is assessed through direct verbal questioning. Impaired patients are frequently disoriented to time and place, other persons, and situations; loss of identity usually occurs only in later stages of dementia or in acute delirium. Calculations are often difficult, as are interpretations of proverbs, which are frequently concrete rather than abstract. Patients with dementia may confabulate—that is, make up answers to questions or answer in a roundabout way—to hide their cognitive decline. This response is different from that of depressed patients, who may simply answer "I don't know" to questions.

Physical Examination and Laboratory Studies

A physical examination should be done as part of the health assessment of an older person with organic mental disorder to try to determine precipitating factors. It is important to include such things as a rectal and genital exam, as well as pulses (including auscultation for bruits) and blood pressure readings in both supine and upright positions. Supine bilateral blood pressure readings in the upper and lower extremities may reveal early occlusive arterial disease before irreversible damage takes place. Necessary baseline measurements include electrocardiogram, chest x-ray, hemoglobin, hematocrit, creatinine, and a clean-catch midstream urine for urinalysis.[9] Other data may be obtained from computed cranial tomography (CT brain scan), from electroencephalography (EEG), and from various other tests, such as thyroid function studies, serological studies for syphilis, and vitamin B12 and folate levels, which can aid in the diagnosis of various types of dementia.

Home Assessment

A home assessment enables the clinician to assess the urgency of the presenting situation; to identify factors contributing to the disease, such as malnutrition or alcoholism; to identify physical barriers at home; and to determine the relationship between the patient and his family or friends.[10] It is important to look at the home for safety, mobility (proximity of transportation), water supply, heating, cooling, and cleanliness. Assessment of personal care and functional capabilities within the home setting should be carried out, as well as of the availability of family and social supports to assist in personal care. The degree to which a patient can keep his home in order and can manage his personal care is often a good measure of the extent to which the disease has progressed—especially in the dementias.

TREATMENT OF ORGANIC MENTAL DISORDER

Because delirium and reversible dementias usually result from physical factors and somatic illnesses—such as endocrine, metabolic, or nutritional disorders; drug intoxication; and so forth—treatment is centered on diagnosing and curing the precipitating disease process. In irreversible dementias, treatment frequently centers on palliative relief of symptoms and prevention of further deterioration. Drugs used for the treatment of primary degenerative dementia are major tranquilizers such as haloperidol (Haldol) and thioridazine (Mellaril), which help control wandering, agitation, and the emotional lability. There is no clear evidence that Hydergine helps the dementia process, but it is frequently used to relieve behavioral manifestations of the disease and the concomitant depression. Medications used for multiinfarct dementia are aimed at treatment of the precipitating factors such as hypertension or arteriosclerosis. There is controversial evidence that aspirin and other drugs that reduce the adhesive qualities of platelets may help maintain better circulation to the brain.

Counseling and support for both the patient and family are another form of treatment for the dementias. Patients may need counseling in the early stages of the disease for the stress and depression it produces. Families need support and counseling for the loss, grief, guilt, and anger they may experience as the disease progresses. Families are also encouraged to seek respite from the 24-hour-a-day care they eventually must provide the patient. Clinicians can be extremely helpful in arranging for services—including institutional care—as needs arise.

Milieu therapy and environmental manipulation are the most effective therapies for promoting the safety and well-being of a patient with organic mental disorder. Because cognitively impaired patients have difficulty learning new concepts, they usually function better in a structured, familiar environment surrounded by family and friends. They need constant verbal and nonverbal reassurance to reduce their anxiety and fear. Expectations for self-care and functioning should directly relate to cognitive ability, for asking patients to do more than they are capable of doing can cause frustration, anger, and hostility.

Clinicians must continually reevaluate dementia patients and their families as the disease progresses in order to provide the appropriate type of care. Needs constantly change as new behaviors and problems arise, and clinicians can act as resource persons, teachers, supporters, and counselors. In many cases they are the only people to whom families can turn in times of crisis, because other supports may drift away.

CASE STUDY—DEMENTIA

History of Presenting Complaint

Miss R. is a 75-year-old, white, single female who was referred by her sister because of increasing disorientation, hallucinations, and wandering. The problem was first noticed about three years ago, when the patient became somewhat forgetful, began losing things, and had difficulty making mathematical calculations. On a vacation with her sister approximately one and one-half years ago, Miss R. became extremely disoriented and confused in her new environment. During the past six months she has started to look for her mother and other persons who have been dead for many years. She has become afraid to stay at home alone and follows her sister around the house constantly. Visual hallucinations regarding babies in knitting baskets and flower arrangements preoccupy her thoughts but are not frightening or repugnant. About four in the afternoon the patient becomes agitated and says she wants "to go home to Mama"; this lasts until about eight or nine at night. She reads well at the present time but has not been able to write during the past few months.

Medical History

The patient is in excellent physical health. Her only history of hospitalization is a recent admission for tests to determine whether or not there was a specific cause for her disorientation and confusion. There was no evidence of infectious disease or vascular problems; all tests were negative. She does not smoke and drinks only sherry occasionally.

Psychiatric History

The patient has no known psychiatric history.

Social and Family History

Miss R. has never been married. She has often worked throughout her life as a bookkeeper in an accounting office. She has lived with her mother and her younger, unmarried sister most of her life. Her mother died approximately 20 years ago, and the two sisters worked and maintained their own home until their retirement. When the younger sister retired, they moved to an apartment and enjoyed their leisure time by traveling, playing bridge, and attending church activities. The sisters have no other known living relatives except for several cousins whom they rarely see. As Miss R.'s disorientation and confusion have increased, the two sisters have curtailed their travel and social activities. Friends continue to visit, however, and they participate in church activities. The burden of care has fallen on the patient's sister, and while she willingly does all that she can, she has become overwhelmed at times by the enormous task she is undertaking.

Physical Examination

The patient was well nourished and in apparent good health; she looked younger than her stated age. She walked with a steady gait without the aid of a cane or walker. Her eyesight was impaired because of forming cataracts, but she was able to read with her glasses. Her hearing was slightly impaired. Her vital signs were within normal limits.

Mental Status Examination

Miss R. was well dressed and neat in appearance, due chiefly to her sister's diligent care. She had a charming social facade initially, but as the interview progressed, it was evident that her cognition was grossly impaired. She was unable to answer any questions on the mental status examination except her birth date and her mother's maiden name. During the interview she became somewhat agitated and had difficulty staying seated. She was unable to answer factual questions on the questionnaire and frequently answered subjective questions with long confabulations. She referred to the babies at home in the baskets but did not claim to see them at the clinic. There was no evidence of a depressive affect or paranoid thinking.

Assessment

The patient is a 75-year-old, white, single female who is living with her sister and who has become increasingly confused and disoriented during the past two to three years. She appears to have visual hallucinations and sundowning syndrome at present. Her problem list includes organic mental disorder, instrumental activities of daily living (ADL) impairment, inability to accomplish self-treatment and medication, and inability to transport herself to needed services.

The OARS questionnaire ratings reflected Miss R.'s excellent social and economic resources and her impaired mental health and ability to carry out the activities of daily living. She was given a 1 in social and economic resources because of her satisfactory social relationships, her sister's willingness to care for her indefinitely, and her ample income with reserves. She was rated a 2 for her good physical health. Her mental health rating was a 5, or severely impaired. Activities of daily living were also rated 5, for she needs help each day with many of these activities because of her impaired judgment and cognition. The patient appeared to be in the second stage of primary degeneration dementia of senile onset of the Alzheimer's type.

Discussion

The two sisters were charming, attractive, and intelligent. They were devoted to each other and were determined to continue living together in their own home. This was becoming increasingly difficult for the patient's younger sister, however, because of the constant demands made upon her. Although they had many friends, the sisters had no close relatives upon whom they could depend for aid and respite. The patient's sister was the sole care giver and attempted to cover up Miss R.'s unusual behavior and "crazy" actions. She did not confide her problems and needs to friends or neighbors.

Treatment Plan and Intervention

As is often done in cases of Alzheimer's disease, treatment was centered in family support and day-to-day management of the patient. The tranquilizer Mellaril (10 mg. twice a day) was prescribed to attempt to minimize the patient's sundowning, agitation, and hallucinations. This was somewhat helpful and noticeably diminished the agitation. An attempt was made to find a homemaker aide to assist with Miss R.'s personal care and to provide some respite for her sister. An aide who was able to work a few hours every weekday morning was found through the local council on aging. Unfortunately, the patient resisted any efforts to help her and even became hostile and violent toward the new helper. The arrangement lasted only one week and was mutually terminated by all parties involved.

Miss R.'s sister was most interested in the Alzheimer's support group and participated actively in all the activities and programs. She found a friend and neighbor who was well known to the patient who would stay with her during the meetings. The other participants provided support for Miss R.'s sister by offering suggestions for day-to-day care and by providing acknowledgment of the burden she was carrying.

The patient's cognitive abilities and behavior quickly began to deteriorate to the point at which institutional placement was indicated. Initially the idea was abhorrent to Miss R.'s sister, but the burden of care and lack of respite were beginning to affect her health and well-being adversely. Fortunately, she sought help from her primary clinician at the OARS-GET Clinic and received counseling, support, and suggestions for institutional placement. Members of the Alzheimer's support group also did much to relieve the sister's guilt and anxiety regarding admission to a nursing home. A suitable facility was found, and Miss R. was admitted with no major problems in adjustment. As a matter of fact, she thrived on the structured environment and social interaction. This was fortunate indeed; many persons with Alzheimer's disease do not adjust as easily to the nursing home environment, especially when there is a history of agitation.

Follow-up and Comments

A six-month evaluation using the OARS questionnaire was carried out by the primary clinician. The ratings showed deterioration in all areas of functioning except for economic resources and mental health. The patient's mental capacities continued to be severely impaired, and this condition had adverse effects on her social resources (rating of 2) (i.e., no one was able to care for her indefinitely), physical health (3), and activities of daily living (6). Her ADL functioning ability became completely impaired, and she was totally dependent on the nursing home staff to carry out these activities throughout the day and night. This rapid deterioration in her capacity to carry out activities of daily living could be a result of the nursing home staff's inability to promote independent self-care, or, most likely, it represented a preterminal decline in her progressive illness. At the time of the six-month evaluation, Miss R.'s sister was concerned and caring about the patient, but she was also relieved to be free of the daily care and management. She continued to be active in the Alzheimer's support group and was able to support others and share her experience with them.

CASE STUDY—DELIRIUM

History of Presenting Illness

Mrs. R. is an 84-year-old, white female who was referred to the OARS-GET Clinic by her daughter for evaluation of memory loss, confusion, crying, depression, and lack of interest in activities of daily living. The patient had been active, independent, and well oriented until approximately six months ago, when her daughter noticed that she was becoming forgetful, anxious, and withdrawn. She lost interest in housework and cooking and ate a complete meal only when taken out to a restaurant. Her mental status deteriorated to the point where her daughter took her to a physician for evaluation. At that time, two months ago, the physician's assessment was that Mrs. R. was "troubled by old age," and she was given a diagnosis of senile dementia. The physician prescribed diazepam (Valium; 10 mg., three times a day and at bedtime) and recommended that the patient be placed in a rest home. During the past two months Mrs. R.'s daughter has been looking for a suitable rest home placement for her mother; in the meantime, the patient has become increasingly agitated and "paranoid" toward her daughter. She says that her daughter is trying to put her away, and she refuses to go to an "old folk's home."

Medical History

The patient has been in relatively good health all her life. She has never been hospitalized, even when she gave birth to her only child. For the past several years she has been treated with a reserpine and diuretic drug combination for hypertension; however, available medical records did not note blood pressure readings. She has also been taking a cough suppressant for a cough that developed during the last month. There is no history of smoking or drinking alcohol.

Psychiatric History

There is no known history of psychiatric illness or treatment.

Social and Family History

Mrs. R. was born in a small town in central North Carolina, the youngest of four children. Her parents owned a tobacco farm that was a successful business, engaging the help of the entire family. The patient completed high school and went to work as a sales clerk in a local dress shop. She married her high school sweetheart at the age of 19. The couple had a daughter two years later, and Mrs. R. devoted her time to keeping an immaculate house and caring for her husband and daughter. Mr. R. had a small business and provided well for his family. The marriage was a good one, and when Mr. R. died in 1956, the patient had difficulty adjusting. She managed to continue living in her own home, however, and to keep an active social life. She stayed in close contact with her brothers and sister until they died in the 1960s and 1970s. Her daughter and family live nearby and are in contact with Mrs. R. every day.

Home Assessment

A home assessment was made by a physician/social worker team from the OARS-GET Clinic. The house is a small, neat, and well kept two-bedroom dwelling in a middle-class neighborhood. A choreworker was in the home at the time of the visit. Both she and Mrs. R.'s daughter help with the cleaning, cooking, shopping, and personal care.

The patient appeared somewhat disheveled and unkempt; she was dressed in a housecoat and slippers. She was pleasant and cooperative but was easily distracted and confused. She was willing to show the clinicians her kitchen, which was well stocked with nourishing items. She said that she did not eat any salt or foods with sodium because of her high blood pressure. Her medicine cabinet revealed no drugs besides the three noted. Mrs. R. moved around easily in her own environment, and except for her confusion and disorientation, she appeared to be in a secure situation.

From data gathered at the home assessment, it was decided that Mrs. R. should have full medical and psychiatric examinations as well as functional assessment at the OARS-GET Clinic.

Medical Examination

The patient was found to have a basically normal physical exam. Her cardiovascular exam revealed normal heart sounds and pulses and the absence of jugular venous distention or carotid bruits. Her radial pulse was 84 and regular, and her respiration rate was 20. Her blood pressure was 185/78 left supine and 175/84 left standing. Her lungs were clear to auscultation except for some wheezing in the posterior fields. Her abdomen was soft and tender with no organomegaly. A neurological exam showed normal reflexes, intact cranial nerves, and normal cerebellar findings. There were no focal neurological symptoms suggestive of cerebral vascular disease. The patient's gait was normal except for some widening and unsteadiness.

Laboratory studies included a CT scan, a chest x-ray, a complete blood count, folate and vitamin B12 tests, and urinalysis. The chest x-ray and CT scan were normal and gave no evidence of focal disease process. The urinalysis was negative, as were the blood studies, except for lower serum sodium and chloride levels, which were 132 meq/L and 89 meq/L respectively (normals are 135–145 and 95–105).

Mental Status Examination

Mrs. R. was surprisingly well oriented, according to the mental status exam. She could answer all but four questions on the OARS MFAQ exam, missing the date, her telephone number, her age (she had recently had a birthday), and calculations. When she was asked to name 10 towns, colors, fruits, and animals, she started by naming 10 towns; but she could name only five fruits and could not name any colors or animals. She seemed to lose interest in the questioning and became easily distracted.

The patient appeared well nourished, neat, clean, and well dressed during her clinic visit. She was pleasant and cooperative but had difficulty concentrating and had trouble sitting still in her chair. When discussion centered on her daughter or rest home placement, Mrs. R. became angry and agitated. She stated that she wanted to stay in her own home and was "perfectly capable to take care of myself." There was no evidence of hallucinations or delusions. The patient showed an appropriate affect, although she became tearful at times, especially when talking about her family.

Functional Status

The patient had a good social support system from her daughter and community services. According to the OARS rating, she was given a 2 in social resources—adequate social resources and someone who would take care of her indefinitely. Economically, she received a rating of 1 because her income was ample and she had reserves. In terms of physical health, Mrs. R. was rated 3 (mild impairment) because of her history of hypertension. She was most impaired in mental health and her ability to carry out activities of daily living, which, in this case, were closely linked. A rating of 4 (moderately impaired) was given for both mental health and ADL because she needed help with cooking, cleaning, shopping, and performing personal care.

Assessment and Discussion

Mrs. R. was a warm, outgoing, attractive woman until she began to show insidious impairment in cognition and judgment. Because these changes became so striking, her concerned daughter sought help as soon as she recognized that there was a problem. When her private physician diagnosed the problem as senility and old age and recommended rest home placement, the daughter sought a second opinion at the OARS-GET Clinic because of her mother's resistance to moving and their deteriorating relationship.

When the case was presented to the team conference, it was decided that there was a good chance that the patient was suffering from a combination of delirium and dementia due to drug toxicity. The physician noted that reserpine can frequently cause depressive symptoms, while Valium, an antianxiety drug, can cause confusion and paradoxical agitation in older persons. The nurse noted that the patient had an electrolyte imbalance, which could account for the confusion and disorientation as well. The social worker also voiced concern over the deteriorating social and family relationships that Mrs. R. was experiencing because of her altered mental status.

Problems identified included loss of memory, paranoia, and agitation with possible dementia; refusal to go to a rest home; and possible drug toxicity. Goals included a return to a former level of functioning; appropriate living arrangements—staying at home, if possible; and maintenance of an appropriate drug regimen.

Treatment Plan and Intervention

The Valium and reserpine-containing drug were immediately discontinued; Haldol (0.5 mg. at bedtime) and hydrochlorothiazide (a diuretic; 50 mg. every morning) were started. The patient was instructed to drink plenty of fluids and to refrain from limiting salt and sodium intake in order to resolve and prevent further electrolyte imbalances that could result from taking the diuretic. The social worker gave supportive counseling to the patient and her daughter regarding their relationship and appropriate living arrangements.

Follow-up and Comments

Two weeks after the medication changes, there was a dramatic improvement in Mrs. R's mental status and outlook. She became completely oriented; was able to function independently in her personal care, cooking, and shopping; and was less agitated and anxious. Her improvement was so dramatic that placement in a rest home was ruled out, and she was able to live in her own home in safety. Her relationship with her daughter improved, and with counseling, both patient and daughter were able to realize that the problems were due to an external cause rather than a deteriorated emotional relationship.

A 6-month evaluation showed the following functional assessment: social resources (S) were rated 1 or excellent; economic resources (E) were rated 1 or excellent; mental health scale (M) was 2 or good mental health; physical health (P) was 3 or mildly impaired; and activities of daily living (A) were rated 2 or good. Mrs. R. was able to function independently in her home and had resumed her previous social relationships and activities. She responded well to the medication—so well, in fact, that the Haldol was discontinued after she achieved a complete absence of confusion, agitation, and disorientation. Her electrolytes returned to normal, and her blood pressure remained well regulated with her new medication. Thus in retrospect, this patient had a mild delirium complicated by depression secondary to medications, which cleared virtually completely, indicating the importance of thorough assessment in all cases of organic mental disorders.

NOTES

1. *Diagnostic and Statistical Manual of Mental Disorders (DSM III)* (Washington, D.C.: American Psychiatric Association, 1980), pp. 101-102.

2. Ewald W. Busse and Dan G. Blazer, *Handbook of Geriatric Psychiatry* (New York: Van Nostrand Reinhold, 1980), pp. 249-271.

3. Adriaan Verwoerdt, *Clinical Geropsychiatry*, 2nd ed. (Baltimore: Williams & Wilkins, 1981), pp. 46-78.

4. Carl Eisdorfer, Donna Cohen, and Richard Veith, *The Psychopathology of Aging* (Kalamazoo, Mich.: The Upjohn Company, 1980), pp. 8-18.

5. Ewald Busse and Eric Pfeiffer, *Mental Illness in Later Life* (Washington, D.C.: American Psychiatric Association, 1973), p. 91.

6. Robert Butler and Lyrna Lewis, *Aging and Mental Health* (St. Louis: C.V. Mosby, 1977), p. 77.

7. Carl Eisdorfer and R.O. Friedel, *The Cognitively and Emotionally Impaired Elderly* (Chicago: Yearbook Medical Publishers, 1977), p. 108.

8. Jean Hayter, "Patients Who Have Alzheimer's Disease," *American Journal of Nursing* 78 (1974): 1460-1463.

9. Theodore Reiff, "The Essentials of Geriatric Evaluation," *Geriatrics* 35 (1980): 59-68.

10. F.I. Caird and T.G. Judge, *Assessment of the Elderly Patient*, 2nd ed. (Philadelphia: J.B. Lippincott, 1979).

Chapter 4

Affective Disorders

Mary Ann Matteson

NOSOLOGY

Affective disorders are among the most common psychiatric disorders in older age. The *Diagnostic and Statistical Manual of Mental Disorders (DSM-III)* divides affective disorders into three categories: (1) major affective disorders, (2) other specific affective disorders, and (3) atypical affective disorders. Major affective disorders include bipolar disorder (mixed, manic, or depressed) and major depression (single episode or recurrent).[1] Bipolar disease and major depression are the most severe of the affective disorders and are diagnostically differentiated by whether or not there has ever been a manic episode.

Other specific affective disorders include cyclothymic disorder, which is a less severe form of bipolar disease, and dysthymic disorder, which is a milder form also called depressive neurosis. Atypical affective disorders include atypical bipolar disease and atypical depression. These diseases represent variations of bipolar disorder and major depression that cannot be strictly classified into the first categories.

SYMPTOMATOLOGY

Bipolar and Cyclothymic Disorders

Bipolar disorders, frequently referred to as manic-depressive illnesses, are manifested by periods of depression alternating with manic episodes. Manic phases of the illness may be identified by symptoms such as an elevated, expansive, or irritable mood; hyperactivity; loud, rapid speech; flight of ideas; a decreased need for sleep; inflated self-esteem; distractibility; and excessive involvement in activities that may have a potential for painful consequences.

In the elderly, manic episodes are frequently characterized by hostility and paranoid ideation. *Hypomania* is a term used to describe symptoms similar to, but less severe than, those found in a manic episode and would usually be characterized as a cyclothymic disorder. It is important when making a diagnosis to be sure that the symptoms of mania are attributed to bipolar or cyclothymic disorder rather than other causes, such as drugs, disease states, or organic brain disease. This is especially true in older persons, who are particularly prone to unusual side effects of drugs and disease or who may be in the early or late stages of dementia.[2]

In bipolar disorder, the initial episode is often manic and usually occurs before age 30. The alternating manic/depressive phases of the disease tend to be more frequent and shorter than the depressive episodes in major depression. Approximately 0.4 to 1.2 percent of the adult population have had bipolar disorder. In a study of 220 older persons hospitalized for affective disorders, 13 percent had predominately manic symptomatology.[3] Bipolar disorder is equally distributed among men and women, and it is more common among family members than in the general population.[4]

The prognosis for bipolar disorder in older age was generally poor until treatment with lithium carbonate began. The drug is very effective in relieving symptoms associated with mania; however, in many cases people in the manic or hypomanic state are so euphoric that they see no need for medication and refuse to comply with the physician's prescription. Because of their increased sensitivity to medications, it is important to watch for electrolytic imbalance in older persons taking lithium. This is especially true in persons with cardiac or renal problems.[5]

Major Depression and Dysthymic Disorder

Depression is the most common psychiatric disorder in late life. According to Kolb, depression is defined as an affective feeling toned with sadness.[6] It may vary from mild downheartedness or a feeling of indifference to a feeling of despair beyond hope. In the milder depressive syndrome, people are quiet, restrained, inhibited, unhappy, pessimistic, and self-deprecating; they have a feeling of lassitude, inadequacy, discouragement, and hopelessness. They are unable to make decisions and experience difficulty with usually easy mental activities; some depressed persons are petulant, querulous, and distrustful.

In deeper depression there is a constant, unpleasant tension, and every experience is accompanied by mental pain. Conversation may be difficult; dejection and hopelessness characterize attitude and manner. Depressed people feel rejected and unloved. They may be so preoccupied with depressive ruminations that attention, concentration, and memory are impaired.

ETIOLOGY

Occurrences of major depression may begin at any age; approximately 50 percent of those who have one depressive episode will have recurrences. Older people are particularly prone to depression, possibly because of the social, psychological, and physiological changes of older age. Changes in self-image and identity, as usual social roles are gradually taken away, necessitate major adaptational tasks with advancing age. Many changes are viewed as losses, such as declines in physical vigor and stamina, decreased mental agility, decreased income and economic stability, and loss of loved ones.[7] The elderly person is often unprepared for these losses and has not developed alternate ways of maintaining security and self-esteem. Isolation, loneliness, and depression may follow, especially in association with the loss of a spouse or with physical illness.[8]

Depression that occurs as a reaction to loss is more common late in life than at an earlier age. Losses and changes in older age often occur in rapid succession, without adequate recovery time. Each loss can increase vulnerability to the next loss or even precipitate another loss. At earlier stages of life this rapid succession of losses rarely occurs. In addition, losses in younger age may be outweighed by gains realized at the same time; for example, loss of a job may precede new and better employment. In contrast, losses experienced in older age are more numerous and more visible, and the gains are fewer and less apparent.

ASSESSMENT

When assessing an older person for depression, it is important to keep in mind the following questions:

1. What is the history of the presenting symptoms?
2. How do depressed older persons present?
3. How is the illness affecting his or her life?
4. How is depression distinguished from other illnesses?

History

When assessing the patient for depression, it is important first to obtain an accurate psychiatric and medical history. A chronological life review can reveal past medical illnesses or previous episodes of depression that may have an influence on the present situation. A number of physical illnesses, such as hypothyroidism, Cushing's disease, cancer, brain lesions, and malnutrition, may be accompanied by depressive features. In addition, a number of medications can produce symptoms of depression in older adults. It is important to rule out or find and treat these physical causes of depression before attempting to treat psychiatrically.

An accurate history of the presenting complaint should be taken in order to determine the duration of symptoms and whether or not they have occurred before. For some older persons depression has been a way of life, while for others it may be a singular reactive episode. It is important to look for precipitating events that may have taken place in the lives of patients and/or the lives of those around them that could have triggered the depression. Losses and changes such as physical illness, widowhood, a new living situation, and retirement are examples of events that may precipitate depressive illness in older adults.

The history should also reflect the extent to which the present symptomatology has changed the personality of the individual. Exaggerated personality changes are more characteristic of organic processes than functional processes. It is also important to note patients' perception of themselves or the level of their self-esteem. This is reflected by their feelings of usefulness, their confidence in their ability to be active participants, and their general belief in their right to enjoy life.

Depression may engender suicidal thoughts, so a determination must be made of the extent of the older person's desire to commit suicide. The aged population accounts for an inordinately high proportion of suicides, especially among older men. When older people attempt suicide, they usually intend to die and are often successful. Elderly patients may frequently attempt a form of "passive suicide" by not eating or not taking medicine.

Mental Status

How do depressed older persons present to the therapist? They may appear sad, burdened, unkempt, drab, tired, or underweight. They may be able to express that they feel unhappy, hopeless, or rejected or that they cannot feel anything at all. On the other hand, they may not be able to articulate any of these feelings, but may be able to recognize them once they have been identified or described to them.

An older depressed person may or may not look sad but may have a number of physical complaints. In fact, the sadness may be only a nuance that is glimpsed between statements about pain, nagging discomfort, or an aggravating physical malfunction. They may deny all feelings, expressing discomfort and unhappiness only as they relate to the physical and concrete. Physical complaints commonly associated with depression include insomnia, anorexia, fatigue, shortness of breath, constipation, decreased sleeping or lethargy, increased appetite, increased sexual drive, and restlessness.

Confusion and disorientation may accompany depression in older age. When a mental status exam is conducted, the depressed older person may know the answers to the questions but may respond by saying "I don't know." This may be due to lack of interest in answering or inability to decide on an answer.

An older person suffering from a major depression may have auditory hallucinations, usually of a morbid nature, such as hymn singing or pronouncements of judgment. The mood is consistently depressed, although there may be some temporary lifting of the mood as the day wears on. The depressive mood usually returns the next morning, however.

Functional Effects of Depression

The depressed person may feel that there is no reason to get up in the morning. This can be particularly true when the depression results from losses such as retirement or widowhood. They may be disinterested in taking care of their personal appearance, dressing, keeping clean, or taking care of their immediate environment.

Depression can cause older persons to become so preoccupied with themselves, their problems, and their misfortunes that they are no fun to be around. Friends and relatives may lose patience with them, have pity for them, or feel imposed upon by them—any or all of which may tend to decrease the desire to be around them. Therefore, the depressed older person may become increasingly isolated, both physically and emotionally.

Unless closely supervised, a depressed older person's physical health can decline, especially when symptoms include insomnia and improper diet. Lack of interest and motivation in the daily effort of self-medication for chronic diseases such as diabetes, hypertension, and heart disease can be fatal. Lack of interest in personal hygiene activities may also increase the possibility of physical health problems.

The depression may decrease a person's confidence in his or her ability to manage personal and financial affairs. Older people may literally feel that they cannot do anything. Making out a grocery list and going to the store may seem to be insurmountable challenges. They may be so preoccupied with their inner turmoil that their memory, concentration, and attention span are impaired to the point of interfering with their ability to carry out their usual activities.

Differential Diagnosis

Depression can manifest symptomatologies similar to other mental illnesses, including dementia, hypochondriasis, paranoia, and adjustment reactions.

In many cases older persons may suffer from a combination of these illnesses—especially depression and dementia—making diagnosis difficult. When there is doubt about the diagnosis, medical treatment of the depression helps to distinguish the illness according to the patient's response.

Dementia

Depression is frequently concomitant with dementia, especially if the patient is aware of the cognitive losses. Although the differences between the two diseases are subtle, the following points may help to distinguish one from the other:

1. In dementia there is an insidious and indeterminate onset; in depression there is a rapid onset.
2. Dementia symptoms are of long duration while symptoms of depression are usually of short duration.
3. In dementia the mood and behavior fluctuate, and in depression the mood is consistently depressed.
4. In dementia "near miss" answers are typical, and in depression "do not know" answers are typical.
5. In dementia the patients conceal the disabilities, and in depression they highlight the disabilities.
6. Cognitive impairment is relatively stable in dementia, while cognitive impairment fluctuates greatly in depression.[9]

Hypochondriasis

Hypochondriacs avoid feelings of depression by focusing on the workings of their bodies. Extreme attention is given to the internal mechanisms and accompanying bodily discomforts. When asked, hypochondriacs will give a full, descriptive account of their ailments, which are usually multiple. They may become animated when discussing their illnesses and rarely appear sad or blue.

Conversely, depressed people usually do not want to discuss their bodily discomforts and may appear sad or tearful when pressed to do so. They usually dwell on one or two parts of the body, but they do not complain of the wide range of disabilities that are characteristic of the hypochondriac.

Late Paraphrenia and Other Paranoid Disorders

Depression may have symptoms similar to those of late paraphrenia, one of the schizophreniform disorders. Delusions or hallucinations may be characteristic of both diseases. The depressed person usually does not have loose associations, however, nor is there evidence of thought disorder, as there is with the person with late paraphrenia.

Paranoid ideation can be a feature of schizophrenic disorders, organic disorders, or depression. One theoretical explanation is that a paranoid disorder is an extension or an advanced stage of depression. It is one in which patients have moved from feeling that they are bad people to feeling that others are bad or hostile toward them. Thus, paranoid persons may not feel or look depressed; rather, their primary affect may be anxiety.

Adjustment Reaction to Late Life

Adjustment reactions can and often are accompanied by depressed feelings. However, the focus is on the adjustment problem rather than the depression itself. Usually, when the adjustment is made the depression subsides. The primary diagnosis in this situation would be adjustment reaction to later life, with depressive features.

TREATMENT

If the depression is severe enough that patients are losing weight, seeming agitated or retarded, feeling suicidal, or having delusions or hallucinations, they almost certainly need to be medicated and, often, hospitalized. Drug therapy is effective in treating depression, and tricyclic antidepressants such as imipramine (Tofranil) and doxepin (Sinequan) are frequently used for older persons. Older people are particularly sensitive to the effects of drugs, so lower doses must be used, usually about one-third that of the usual adult dose. In addition it is important to be alert to signs of side effects that frequently occur, especially the anticholinergic symptoms that are associated with tricyclics, such as urinary retention and severe constipation.

Although it is not usually used until after a sufficient drug trial, electroconvulsive therapy (ECT) may be a treatment of choice for older persons. The treatment is usually carried out in an inpatient setting and can be safer than long-term drug therapy. Major complications of electroconvulsive therapy are not frequent but do include postshock confusion and cardiac problems.

Whether or not medications, ECT, or hospitalization are used, some kind of talking therapy—either psychotherapy or supportive counseling—should be carried out. Some guidelines for working with depressed older patients follow.

1. Remember that a depressed person is very sensitive to rejection and disapproval. Therefore, formation of a therapeutic alliance is of

utmost importance. This can be done through a warm understanding of the patient's efforts to cope with daily events and problems.

2. Do not try to move too quickly toward insight or relief through goading the patient to express anger. Such can actually be dangerous, because the patient is then encouraged to reject a significant other when there is no one there to replace that person. Generally, the therapist should become an important person to the patient before trying to deal with anger and other strong feelings.

3. Encourage the replacement of lost objects through helping patients to allow other things and people to have meaning for them. One should be careful, however, not to promote this too soon or too vigorously, particularly if grieving for the lost object has not yet taken place. In fact, replacement should be introduced gently and should proceed in tandem with other therapeutic endeavors. Also, patients' ability to allow replacement to occur will depend upon their previous experience in allowing this to happen; so it may help the therapist to know how successful that prior experience has been.

4. It is always helpful to the depressed older patient to increase or strengthen the supportive environment and to ensure a good diet and promote good medical and nursing care.

If the older patient has both dementia and depression, the environmental treatment is the same. The pharmacological treatment may also be the same because it is important to treat the depressive aspect of the illness. The prognosis of the patient with depression alone is much better than if the diagnosis is both depression and dementia. The prognosis of the patient with both depression and dementia is better than if the diagnosis is dementia alone. The prognosis depends on the physical health of the older patient— specifically, the presence or absence of conditions that limit mobility or social interactions; the availability of supports; and the predepression personality of the patient, especially his or her personal resourcefulness and sense of confidence and optimism.

CASE STUDY—DEPRESSION

Mrs. S. was a 60-year-old, black female who was referred to our clinic by her physician with a chief complaint of "depression." She had been in good health until about six months prior to her referral, when she suffered a major "heart attack," or myocardial infarction, and was hospitalized for about three weeks. Her recovery was uneventful, but she was not able to resume her work as a cashier in a restaurant and was forced into an early retirement.

During the months following her hospitalization, Mrs. S. became increasingly sad, withdrawn, apathetic, and disinterested in any type of activity. This was quite a different picture from the outgoing, gregarious person she once had been. Her physician prescribed the antidepressant Elavil for her, but he decided that she should have additional psychiatric intervention.

Medical History

The patient had been followed by a physician for several years for angina pectoris and emphysema. She smoked one to two packs of cigarettes per day, and, although she expressed interest in quitting, she found it too difficult. She was occasionally bothered by angina attacks, but they were effectively relieved by nitroglycerin tablets. Mrs. S.'s physician had advised her to lose about 20 pounds and to stop smoking, but to no avail.

Psychiatric History

Mrs. S. had been treated once before for depression after the death of her husband approximately 10 years ago. She was hospitalized and given ECT treatments; she made a full recovery and managed to grieve appropriately for her husband. There were no other incidences of depression or other mental illness in her life history.

Social and Family History

As a native southerner, Mrs. S. grew up in a warm, loving family, the oldest of three children (two boys and a girl). She finished high school and worked in various jobs, including domestic work, until her retirement. She met and married her husband in her early twenties and claims to have had a happy marriage for 26 years. The couple were childless because of the patient's inability to conceive.

The patient was active in church, but her main avenue of socialization was through work. She had many friends and remained close to her two brothers, both of whom lived nearby with their families. She spent every weekend at the home of her older brother and his wife, who made her feel welcome and accepted.

Mental Status Assessment

When initially seen, Mrs. S. was pleasant, cooperative, and articulate; she described her problems easily. However, she was clearly downhearted and sad and cried easily. She stated that she missed her social contacts at work and had no reason to get up in the morning. When asked if she ever considered committing suicide, she replied, "I want to die, but I could never kill myself."

The patient was clean and well dressed and looked lovely, with her hair freshly coiffed by a beautician. She wore her favorite fragrance of perfume, which she enjoyed buying in quantity. She was moderately overweight and smoked several cigarettes during the interview.

Mrs. S. demonstrated appropriate affect, showing no evidence of hallucinations, delusions, or paranoid thinking. Her cognitive state was intact, although she reluctantly answered questions on the mental status exam. Her recent and remote memory was excellent.

Functional Status

According to the OARS questionnaire, Mrs. S. was most impaired in her physical functioning and was rated a 4 (moderately impaired). This was due to her heart condition and mild emphysema and the degree to which they interfered with her daily activities. Her social resources were good, and she was rated a 2 because of the support she received from family and friends. For example, her niece went grocery shopping for her and cleaned her apartment for her once a week.

Although Mrs. S. received Social Security and disability payments, she experienced a decrease in income because of her job loss. She was rated a 3—mildly impaired—in economic resources, because she perceived that she was not able to maintain her previous standard of living and this was affecting her emotional state. Because of her depression, she was given a rating of 3 for mental health.

Mrs. S. was mildly impaired (3) in her ability to carry out activities of daily living. She was able to maintain her apartment with help from her family and was able to carry out personal tasks such as dressing, bathing, and eating. Her greatest impairment in activities of daily living was her inability to return to work, and this had the greatest impact on her life.

Assessment and Discussion

Mrs. S. was a warm, outgoing person who seemed to be depressed because of the many losses associated with her "heart attack." She was used to her social role as an employed cashier and counted on her coworkers for her socialization and friendship network. When she was unable to work, her economic status was severely reduced. She had enjoyed buying clothes, perfume, and furnishings for her apartment in the past and had given no thought to any restrictions on spending. It was extremely distressing to her to have to deny herself the small luxuries she formerly took for granted.

The patient found it difficult to adjust to a new pattern or routine in her life. When she was working, she would wake up early in the morning, dress, and eat breakfast in the restaurant with friends. When she stopped working, she would stay in bed until mid-morning and, perhaps, skip breakfast altogether. That, coupled with her depression, caused her to have difficulty in falling asleep at night. She also felt fatigued and unable to "get going" in the morning. It was felt that her fatigue was due not only to her depression but perhaps also to poor sleep patterns, poor eating habits, and decreased oxygen from her mild case of emphysema.

Diagnosis

In the case conference, Mrs. S.'s problems were discussed. In contrast to many older depressed persons, Mrs. S. had rather good insight and awareness of her emotional difficulty. One might wonder, however, whether she had a mild or masked depression prior to the onset of her heart attack, as she stated a wish to die but did not feel she could kill herself. In spite of several years of obvious and distressful signs of cardiac and pulmonary disease, she was unable to quit smoking or to diet despite an apparently good relationship with a physician who advised her directly about these matters. While overeating and smoking are extremely common problems in our culture, she may have had an unconscious wish for a passive suicide. The geropsychiatrist pointed out that many elderly depressed people have a strong bias against active or overt suicide, although elderly white males are the group at highest suicidal risk. Many depressed older persons act in ways that increase their likelihood of dying by doing such things as refusing to get medical examinations, not taking medications correctly, not eating, or overeating. Basically, Mrs. S. has a number of ego strengths that would help in her recovery, but she has several major risk factors as well. She has lost her husband and has no children. In addition, she has a life-threatening illness that very often leads to a subsequent depression. In fact, depressions—often of an atypical or masked type—follow major illness or surgery in the elderly so frequently that they should be expected and sought by those who care for older people. Not infrequently, the depression may delay recovery so the individual appears much more impaired than is really the case from a physical standpoint. Whether this was a factor in the early and abrupt retirement of Mrs. S. is not completely clear. In addition, it was noted that she was treated with the antidepressant Elavil by her family physician. Because of its high level of anticholinergic side effects, this is probably the least desirable antidepressant for use in an elderly person with heart disease. It is not apparent that it actually did her any harm, but the side effects and hazards might well prevent it from being used in a high enough dose to be effective.

Her diagnosis by *DSM-III* would be as follows: major depression, recurrent, with melancholia.

Therapeutic Plan

A tentative plan of therapy was proposed at the case presentation conference. It featured individual, supportive-type psychotherapy with an emphasis on restructuring the life style and resocialization. One team member suggested that Mrs. S. be encouraged to attend a senior center sometime in the near future. The social worker suggested that group psychotherapy provided by the clinic might be another appropriate intervention. The nurse suggested that breathing exercises might alleviate some of the shortness of breath associated with the emphysema. She added that health counseling in terms of diet and smoking could be helpful to prevent further cardiac and respiratory problems. Team members generally felt that the patient had excellent resources for a full recovery, including her loyal family and friends and her own attractive personality.

Intervention

The nurse who was the evaluating clinician was designated the primary clinician. One-to-one supportive therapy sessions were scheduled on a weekly basis for approximately 45 minutes each. Discussion centered on problem solving, family, friends, alternative life styles, and health teaching. Throughout each session, strengths were emphasized and an attempt was made to build up self-esteem, especially as new roles evolved. Early in the therapy, Mrs. S. continued to be unable to join social groups, such as volunteer organizations or senior centers, because of her depression. After several weeks, however, she appeared ready to begin group therapy, which was offered in the clinic by two other clinicians.

The patient adapted well to the group therapy setting and promoted group process by openly sharing her problems and concerns with other members. Mrs. S. continued to have weekly sessions with her primary therapist until she decided that she could not afford to pay for both individual and group therapy at the same time. The decision was made that, therapeutically, the group was the best mode of intervention for her in her present situation. An abrupt termination was made with the primary clinician, which proved too traumatic and too great a loss for the patient. It was then decided to ease the transition gradually by scheduling visits weekly, then biweekly, then every three weeks, and so on. This proved successful. In hindsight we learned again that it is often unwise to terminate abruptly with depressed patients, since this represents yet another loss in their lives.

As Mrs. S. progressed in group therapy, she was gradually able to reach out socially. She attended a senior center only once—she did not enjoy being with "so many old people." She finally found her niche in a volunteer job that required her presence once a week. There was an unexpected bonus for Mrs. S. in her new role as a volunteer: she ran into many childhood friends who had not joined the paid work force but had channeled their energies into community service. The opportunity for renewal of old friendships was a great boost to her morale and self-esteem.

After approximately nine months of therapy, Mrs. S. planned a long visit to a friend. It was the right time to plan for termination, and several therapeutic sessions addressed the issues of separation and grief. She has made an excellent transition to mental health and continues to be in contact with the clinic periodically when problems build up and short-term counseling is needed. She continues to smoke and is several pounds overweight, but she is always trying to improve by dieting and cutting down on the number of cigarettes per day.

NOTES

1. American Psychiatric Association, *Diagnostic and Statistical Manual of Mental Disorders*, 3rd ed. (Washington, D.C.: APA, 1980), p. 205.

2. Ibid., pp. 206-207.

3. M. Roth, "The Natural History of Mental Disorder in Old Age," *Journal of Mental Science* 101 (1955):281-301.

4. American Psychiatric Association, *Diagnostic and Statistical Manual of Mental Disorders*, 3rd ed. (Washington, D.C.: APA, 1980), pp. 215-216.

5. M. Shou, A. Anderson, and J. Trap-Jensen, "Lithium Poisoning," *American Journal of Psychiatry* 125 (1968):520-527.

6. Lawrence Kolb, *Modern Clinical Psychiatry* (Philadelphia: W.B. Saunders, 1977), pp. 169-175.

7. Ewald Busse and Eric Pfeiffer, *Behavior and Adaptation in Later Life* (Boston: Little, Brown, 1977), pp. 158-160.

8. Ewald Busse and Eric Pfeiffer, *Mental Illness in Later Life* (Washington, D.C.: American Psychiatric Association, 1973), p. 117.

9. D. Blazer and S.W. Friedman, "Depression in Late Life," *American Family Physician* 20 (1979):91-96.

Chapter 5

Anxiety Disorders

Steve Herman

Anxiety plays a dual role in psychiatry as both a symptom and a syndrome. As a symptom, its central feature is a distinctive emotional experience of a "direful terror of imminent catastrophe."[1] This subjective quality of anxiety is typically accompanied by a variety of psychophysiological manifestations indicative of autonomic arousal, such as palpitations, tachycardia, hyperventilation, respiratory distress, trembling, and dizziness. At times, anxiety may reach brief but unbearable levels of intensity; such conditions are referred to as "panic attacks." More frequently, it is present as a chronic condition of physical and psychological tension, which is differentiated from the similar state of "fear" by its lack of association with a realistically dangerous situation or stimulus. As a symptom, anxiety is a component of almost every psychiatric disorder; indeed, some observers have proposed that it is the central emotional experience of mankind.[2, 3]

NOSOLOGY

As a syndrome, anxiety has recently been granted the status of a separate class of mental disorder under the *DSM-III* classification system. This group of disorders, the anxiety disorders, are distinguished by the predominance of the experience—or the attempt to avoid the experience—of anxiety in the clinical disturbance. Under this heading there are four subgroups of disorders: phobic disorders, panic disorders, obsessive-compulsive disorders, and generalized anxiety disorders. Briefly, the distinguishing features of these conditions are as follows: *Phobic disorders* are defined as conditions of "persistent avoidance behavior secondary to irrational fears of a specific object, activity, or situation." Three subgroups of phobic disorder are differentiated on the basis of the type of stimulus that elicits the anxiety. Agoraphobia involves an irrational fear of leaving the home or other familiar setting. Social phobias involve fear of situations in which the patient may be exposed to scrutiny by others, or where there is a possibility of behaving in a manner that may be regarded as shameful. A common example is the avoidance of public speaking. The third subgroup is simple phobias, a residual category for specific fear of objects or situations other than those already described. Examples are snake phobias, claustrophobia, acrophobia, and so on.

The second category of anxiety disorder, *panic disorder,* is characterized by recurrent attacks of intense anxiety involving feelings of extreme apprehension or terror, coupled with marked psychophysiological activation. Such attacks are not linked with specific situations or stimuli, as are the phobic disorders, and there may be an associated residuum of chronic nervousness or free-floating anxiety that prevails between panic attacks. This category is new in *DSM-III,* along with the related category, *generalized anxiety disorder.* In the latter condition, a chronic state of generalized anxiety predominates, without evidence of panic attacks, specific phobias, or obsessive-compulsive symptoms. Features of generalized anxiety disorders include motor tension, autonomic hyperactivity, and an attitude of apprehensive expectation coupled with increased perceptual vigilance.

The final class of anxiety disorders is *obsessive-compulsive disorder,* in which the identifying feature is the presence of obsessions and/or compulsions. Obsessions are unwelcome and recurrent ideas, thoughts, images, or impulses that the patient experiences as ego-alien and outside voluntary control. Compulsions are senseless behaviors that are likewise experienced as outside voluntary control and that are accompanied by both a sense of subjective compulsion and a desire to resist. If the patient attempts to resist a compulsion, however, there is always a sense of mounting tension and anxiety that can immediately be relieved by performing the behavior.

In the elderly, the most commonly observed forms of anxiety disorder are generalized anxiety disorder and panic disorder, and it is on these that we put primary focus. Phobias and obsessive-compulsive disorders seem relatively underrepresented in the elderly population, for reasons that are open to speculation.

ORIGIN AND SIGNIFICANCE OF ANXIETY IN THE ELDERLY

Various theories exist as to the origins of anxiety, but in general, it is agreed that anxiety constitutes an emotional and bodily response to a felt danger or threat. Freudian theory has stressed the role of internal psychological threats in the form of forbidden instinctual drives that threaten to elude conscious control.[4] Social learning theorists have emphasized the role of prior conditioning, with anxiety linked to expectations of negative outcome.[5] Other theorists, including Rank, Sullivan, and Horney, have linked the origins of anxiety to the fear of separation or to loss of essential sources of external support.[6-8] This latter view may be the one most relevant to anxiety as it is present in the elderly. Verwoerdt has commented that, in the elderly, anxiety pertains less often to unacceptable impulses from within and more often to the threatened loss of emotional and social supports, which he terms "helplessness anxiety."[9] Such fears may relate to the loss of important persons or other sources of outside support, or they may relate to the elderly individual's reduced personal resources for maintaining mastery, competence, and control of his or her own life.

Verwoerdt's concept of "helplessness anxiety" appears to fit well with the phenomenology of anxiety in the elderly, and given the current social status of the aged, it is not surprising that anxiety is a frequent form of psychopathology in later life. Increased isolation, dwindling opportunities for human relationships, loss of status associated with retirement—all are factors that may generate chronic or acute anxiety in the older person. Moreover, physical illness repeatedly has been found to be associated with anxiety as well as depression in middle and later life.[10,11] The relationship between physical health and anxiety in the elderly is a complex one, however; for in addition to anxiety being an emotional *response* to illness and the threat it poses, it is at times a *harbinger* of undetected organic disease.[12]

It is generally believed that anxiety disorders tend to have their onset in childhood, adolescence, or young adulthood, and that the development of anxiety reaction *de novo* in old age is a rare event. At least one recent epidemiological survey calls this assumption into question, however. Bergmann identified a group of 72 patients with a *late-onset* neurosis and found that although the majority (64 percent) of these represented depressive disorders, there was a sizable group (36 percent) that could be classified as anxiety disorders.[13] At the same time, other studies in England that contrasted depressed and anxious patients found a more marked premorbid disposition to breakdown among those with anxiety states than among those with depressions.[14,15] Further, traits of immaturity and emotional dependence, anxiety features, instability of mood, and neuroticism were more prevalent among the anxiety disorder group, and this group showed a generally less favorable outlook for clinical improvement over time than did the depressives. In sum, then, available research suggests that although anxiety states may become apparent for the first time in later life, their appearance can usually be linked to a significant, long-standing vulnerability to emotional stress. This impression is supported by our clinical experience, as in almost all cases of geriatric anxiety disorders, the patient or family members indicate that the patient has always had "bad nerves."

When it does occur, anxiety in older people may have particularly negative consequences. The experience of anxiety, especially in its extreme forms as in panic attacks, tends not only to be extremely unpleasant but also to interfere with efficient autonomous functioning and to increase feelings of helplessness. This may lead to a position of exaggerated dependency that is destructive to the individual and may also tend to turn off family members and others to whom the individual reaches out for support. Often in such situations, the family and others will back off in fear of being overwhelmed by the older person's demands, a response that only adds to the feelings of helplessness and apprehension. In this sense, anxiety tends to be self-perpetuating.

Another negative consequence of anxiety relates to its impact on physical health. The physical course of anxiety, in the form of muscular tension and its associated fatigue, weakness, muscular pain, sleep loss, and so on, is especially hard for elderly persons to bear, particularly for those who are already functioning at a lower than optimal level because of acute or chronic diseases. Such people may have insufficient stamina to endure the stresses of prolonged states of anxiety, and rapid deterioration of functional status may ensue.

Finally, high levels of anxiety tend to impair cognitive functioning and may amplify normal age-related losses in areas such as memory skills, calculations, and problem solving. An anxious young person may still be able to think and make decisions sufficiently well to get by, but an older anxious person who is already experiencing some deficit in these areas may be considerably impaired by anxiety. For these reasons, in addition to the obvious extreme discomfort that is associated with anxiety, it is most important that older people with anxiety symptoms be treated effectively and without delay.

ASSESSMENT OF ANXIETY DISORDERS

Underlying assessment of anxiety disorders are: (1) the differentiation of anxiety disorders from other conditions in which anxiety is a symptom and (2) the determination of the factors originating and maintaining the anxiety. In determining whether the anxiety is primary or secondary, one should first consider the possibility that it represents manifestation of organic disease. Hyperthyroidism, carcinoma, and cardiac failure are examples of diseases that may present in an atypical fashion in later life with anxiety symptoms. Evaluation of a person experiencing anxiety, for this reason, should always include a comprehensive medical examination.

Symptoms of anxiety are also often present in conjunction with organic brain syndrome, especially during its initial stages of development. Often persons with progressive dementia are aware of some decline and are extremely apprehensive about its significance and its impact on their functioning. A neuropsychological evaluation should be included to identify the presence and extent of brain impairment when the anxiety appears to be accompanied by signs of compromised intellectual functioning.

Depressions in the elderly are also not uncommonly accompanied by agitation, restlessness, and other anxiety symptoms. In making this differentiation, the clinician should be attentive to biological signs of depression, depressed affect and thought content, and suicidal ideation. The presence of these symptoms would incline the diagnostic impression toward an agitated depression.

Anxiety is often encountered in patients who show signs of hypochondriasis or paranoid states. In such cases, the presence of somatic or persecutory preoccupations is usually easy to elicit upon clinical inquiry. Hypochondriacal or paranoid older persons may complain of being anxious or worried, but will tend to attribute this to the objects of their somatic or persecutory preoccupations. In many cases, it may be possible for the clinician largely to bypass the delusional content and to focus on direct treatment of anxiety-related symptoms with these difficult patients.

The second focus of assessment efforts involves the identification of present life factors that may be exacerbating or maintaining the current level of anxiety. In this effort, a detailed psychosocial history is helpful, with particular emphasis on recent bereavements or other significant losses or changes in life style. Analysis of dream content and other projective fantasy materials also is often helpful in identifying the source of psychic disturbance, particularly when the patient makes extensive use of repression as a defense mechanism.

Additional factors to be considered in assessing anxiety states include those that differentiate types of disorders within the category. One should determine the stimuli, if any, that elicit anxiety and pay attention to the presence or absence of panic episodes. If periodic panic attacks are part of the clinical picture, the degree of functional impairment is likely to be markedly increased. In the elderly, panic attacks are by no means uncommon, and they often include a significant degree of confusion in addition to the usual affective and psychophysiological disturbances. The occurrence of a panic attack in an older person may be enormously disturbing, and even when it has subsided, there may be a lingering dread that the experience will return. In this way, a panic attack may generate a secondary source of anxiety for the older person, a fear of overwhelming anxiety and acute defenselessness. Under such conditions it becomes of paramount therapeutic importance to control panic attacks.

APPROACHES TO TREATMENT

There are four general avenues for treatment of anxiety symptoms: environmental manipulation, pharmacotherapy, behavioral modification, and psychotherapeutic approaches.

Environmental manipulation is the attempt to alleviate the external sources underlying feelings of helplessness and anxiety on the part of the older person. In some situations, interventions with family members may help in raising their awareness of increasing dependency needs on the part of an older person. In other instances, social support services may be provided in the home, or the patient may be helped to relocate to a more protective and supportive environment. Where environmental factors play a large role in generating and maintaining anxiety, such efforts may be critical from a treatment standpoint.

Drugs of various types have long been used for treatment of anxiety states. Historically, alcohol has been the rather universal (often self-prescribed) tranquilizer, although it has considerable limitations, including the associated frequency of behavioral problems, disruption of sleep in chronic use, and the risk of habituation. For a number of years barbiturates and bromides were also used for this purpose, but their use has largely dropped off since it has been recognized that their action is sedative rather than tranquilizing, and that significant addictive and toxic risks are involved.

Currently a group of drugs called the minor tranquilizers or anxiolytic drugs have assumed prominence, as they are much more specific in affecting the lower brain centers involved in the anxiety process. Of these, the group most frequently used are the benzodiazepines, which include the popular drugs chlordiazepoxide (Librium) and diazepam (Valium). While these drugs are widely prescribed for anxiety symptoms, they tend to accumulate in older people, leading rather often to undesirable effects such as unsteadiness or even confusion. For this reason it is better to use the newer drugs, such as lorazepam (Ativan) or oxazepam (Serax), which are shorter acting and less inclined to cause side effects in older patients.

In some cases, especially if the patient's anxiety is very severe or disorganizing, one of the so-called major tranquilizers, such as trifluoperazine (Stelazine) or thioridazine (Mellaril), may be used in very small doses. If panic attacks complicate the anxiety or if a depressive component is present, one of the tricycli~ antidepressants such as imipramine (Tofranil), doxepin (Sinequan), or amoxapine (Asendin) may be helpful. In some cases of panic attacks, the drug propanolol (Inderal) has been used successfully. All of these drugs are potent and may have significant side effects. For elderly patients it is usually safe to start at about one-third the usual adult dose and increase the amount gradually, watching for side effects (especially low blood pressure).[16]

Behavioral treatments for anxiety states are many and varied, and include procedures such as systematic desensitization, progressive muscle relaxation, implosive therapy, hypnosis, and biofeedback. While many of these techniques are best suited for specific phobias, there are some, including progressive relaxation and biofeedback, that may be suitable for use with patients suffering panic attacks or generalized anxiety reactions. For the most part, these procedures have been developed and applied to younger people, although recent evidence suggests that they may also be of use with the geriatric population.[17] Group training in relaxation procedures has been offered through the OARS Clinic with some success.

Psychotherapeutic approaches to the management of anxiety tend to emphasize a supportive relationship rather than the development of insight on the part of the patient. Cognitive approaches, in which the therapist attempts to reassure the patient that the anxiety symptoms are emotionally related and not signals of impending physical breakdown, are often very successful on an immediate basis. The availability of a caring and concerned person is often of particular value to the anxious older person, and the therapist may fill this role best by providing regular, frequent meetings and the reassurance that he or she will be on call if needed.

In formulating treatment plans for the older patient presenting with anxiety problems, especially when "panic attacks" are involved, there is a premium on immediate and decisive action to interrupt the self-perpetuating cycle of anxiety described earlier. Most often, pharmacotherapy is begun immediately to take the edge off the anxiety and to control some of the more disturbing pyschophysiological concomitants. At the same time, efforts should be made to establish a strong therapeutic relationship with the patient, and to this end, frequent brief visits at the outset are probably most appropriate. The frequency of visits may be tapered off gradually as the patient's anxiety level subsides. In cases of generalized anxiety and panic attacks, the therapeutic strategy should be geared toward returning to patients a sense of control over their own lives. Initially, this may consist only of the knowledge that they have immediate access to a reliable ally, the therapist, whenever they feel a need for such contact. Over time, it is hoped that this source of security will be superseded by more internalized strategies for coping with anxiety-provoking situations. The development and reinforcement of these alternative coping strategies represent the therapeutic work to be accomplished gradually over time, once the immediate crisis has subsided.

The approach to the assessment and treatment of anxiety disorders in the elderly just outlined above is illustrated in the following case example.

CASE STUDY—ANXIETY DISORDER

Presenting Problem

Mrs. T is a 69-year-old, married, white woman, a retired schoolteacher, who was referred to the clinic upon discharge from a county hospital psychiatric inpatient service where she had completed three weeks of treatment. Consultation was requested to secure appropriate living arrangements and other necessary adjustments, as the patient was in the process of separating from her husband of 39 years. Mrs. T's chief complaint was "lack of self-confidence," but she was also noted by the referring physician to be suffering symptoms of generalized anxiety, exacerbated by her unsettled living situation.

Medical and Psychiatric History

The patient was apparently well until 18 months ago. At that time she experienced a syncopal episode, later diagnosed as an asystolic sinus bradycardia and treated through implantation of a cardiac pacemaker. During this hospitalization the patient's husband, without consulting her, sold the family home and moved them into an apartment, presumably to be close to a favorite sister of his. According to Mrs. T, the husband intended to use the proceeds of the house sale to travel alone with this sister, who reportedly "mothered" him. Mrs. T felt furious at her husband for this move and for other past irresponsibilities but felt "trapped" in the marriage. It was at this point that she first noted signs of anxiety and depression. Two months after her cardiac surgery, the patient was stricken with acute open-angle glaucoma of the left eye, which despite treatment resulted in near-blindness. These visual problems added to her worries, and the patient experienced additional symptoms, including a 25-pound weight loss, insomnia, constipation, memory impairment, and exacerbation of what had been a chronic, benign hand tremor. Within six months the patient was back in hospital, this time for treatment of intractable headaches. While an inpatient, she displayed some psychoticlike symptoms, with evidence of aphasia and apraxia. A thorough neurological work-up was negative, however. The symptoms resolved spontaneously and she was discharged. It was not long before she was readmitted, this time to the psychiatric ward, with a provisional diagnosis of intractable depression.

As a psychiatric inpatient Mrs. T received individual, group, and family therapy with good results. Her mood improved markedly, and the intensity of somatic complaints decreased. After the husband revealed in conjoint therapy that he wanted to dissolve the marriage, the patient decided that she wanted to move into her own apartment immediately upon discharge. The large number of psychotropic medications the patient was taking upon admission, including antipsychotics, antidepressants, antianxiety agents, and pain medications, was reduced upon discharge to just 5 mg. of Valium as needed. While depressive symptomatology had largely subsided, there remained a residue of anxiety, and it was anticipated that this would increase as the patient went about adjusting to a new living situation.

Family and Social History

Mrs. T was the sixth of 10 children who grew up on a farm in near poverty. The parents both died when the patient was in her early teens, and she took a role of responsibility in the family, caring for her younger siblings. She got married rather late, at age 30, to a grocer, who appears to have been inadequate in many respects. The patient describes him as "nervous and incompetent" to a degree that she was forced to assume most of the burden of handling their family and financial affairs. The couple had two children, one of whom is now married and living near Mrs. T, while the other lives across the country. The patient worked most of her adult life as a teacher, retiring five years ago. She describes a long history of marital incompatibility but stayed with her husband out of a feeling of responsibility. The husband was reportedly very dependent and was reckless with the family's money.

Physical Examination

Mrs. T was observed to be a somewhat underweight woman who appeared about her stated age. There was some evidence of mild arthritis in the right hip and physical evidence consistent with the diagnosis of acute open-angle glaucoma. Cardiac examination revealed normal rhythm and sounds. The neurological examination was negative aside from some indications of mild dementia compatible with her age but well compensated for by verbal and social skills. Current medications included 5 mg. of Valium four times a day, as needed.

Mental Status

On interview the patient was alert, cooperative, and freely talkative. Affect was varied, with some tearfulness when describing her mental problems. The patient appeared generally quite tense, and some mild hand tremor was noted. There was a tendency to wander from topic to topic, and at times the patient became confused and could not recall the point she was trying to make. Thought content and form were within normal limits. The patient denied psychotic symptomatology and suicidal ideation. Memory function and calculation ability were mildly impaired. Insight and judgment appeared fair. Mrs. T reported being very worried about the future and indicated that she has a great deal of trouble falling asleep.

Functional Assessment

Mrs. T completed the OARS Multidimensional Functional Assessment Questionnaire without any difficulties. She was rated as unimpaired on social resources, as she continues to maintain a sizable circle of friends and would be taken care of by her daughter indefinitely if this were needed. Economically she is also unimpaired, as her Social Security, retirement benefits, savings, and other assets provide adequately for her current and future needs. She is well covered by medical insurance. Mental health is rated as moderately impaired, insofar as the patient shows definite psychiatric symptoms at the present time, primarily of an affective nature. She is able to make routine commonsense decisions but at present is unable to handle major problems in her life. Physical health is also rated moderately impaired because of the patient's severe visual limitations. Activities of daily living (ADL) are rated as mildly impaired. The patient's main limitations in ADL derive from her loss of driving privileges. She is able to carry out all of her activities of daily living without difficulty, however, and should be able to live independently.

Assessment and Discussion

Mrs. T's history and presenting symptoms were presented to the team and her problem formulated initially as follows: Mrs. T appears to be a woman who for most of her life functioned effectively and adequately, without obvious psychiatric disorder. In fact, there is evidence that she has always functioned as the "responsible one" in the family circle—a role that though difficult at times, was not without its own gratifications. In her career as a teacher, as well, there is evidence of gratification through being a support or help to others. In recent months the patient has had to adapt herself to some sudden alterations in what had become a very stable life pattern. A sudden worsening of her marital situation, compounded by serious medical problems including cardiac surgery and near total vision loss in one eye, has led to a situation in which she feels uncharacteristically weak and vulnerable. At the very time in her life when she is feeling least able to act decisively and independently, circumstances are forcing her to cope with changes and challenges. In response, Mrs. T has experienced a variety of affective symptoms, including a mixture of depressive and anxiety features. At present the patient's depression has largely abated, with a good deal of anger being directed toward the husband. The anxiety symptoms persist, however, and will probably continue until a stable new life style is developed, and therefore, warrants a diagnosis of anxiety disorder.

Discussion among team members focused on the nature of the real-life problems facing this patient, as well as the preferred therapeutic mode for helping Mrs. T adapt to her new circumstances over time.

A social worker inquired about the status of divorce proceedings and was assured that the patient was apparently being represented by her family attorney, who is looking after her legal interests. The patient's husband is filing for divorce, and there should be a favorable settlement for the patient. The social worker also wondered what steps are being taken to help Mrs. T find suitable accommodations. After some discussion, it was decided that the patient's daughter, with whom she is currently staying, would be contacted about this and offered consultation if such appeared indicated. The nurse suggested that some concrete suggestions about the selection of living arrangements appropriate to the patient's visual limitations might be helpful to the family.

There was general agreement that the patient could benefit from supportive psychotherapy. The geropsychiatrist inquired what the patient's response had been to group and individual psychotherapies conducted during her inpatient stay, and was advised that she appeared to do well in both settings. He recommended that the patient begin with individual sessions and then later be brought into the ongoing outpatient group at the clinic. It was felt that the group session might be a better long-term arrangement, one that allowed the patient to be both a giver and a receiver of help—a situation that would fulfill her need to be a "helper."

The patient was assigned to a psychology intern, who was to be her therapist and primary clinician. A geropsychiatrist was assigned as secondary clinician to provide medication checks on a regular basis.

Treatment Course

Mrs. T spent the first two months of treatment in individual weekly therapy sessions, which were then decreased to a biweekly frequency with the addition of weekly group therapy sessions. This pattern of concurrent individual and group therapy continued for eight months, until the primary therapist's departure from the clinic. At that time individual sessions were discontinued, and the patient has continued as a member of the therapy group.

During the initial stage of therapy, the patient carefully avoided any exploration of her feelings about her husband. She preferred instead to focus on her visual impairment and some difficulties she was experiencing in relation to a new neighbor. With the daughter's help, the patient had previously secured an apartment that was convenient, though somewhat isolated socially. The therapist observed that the patient's preoccupation with her bad eye served as a focal point for underlying emotional conflicts involving issues of dependency, anger, and aging, which were still too anxiety provoking to deal with directly. At the same time, the patient's grappling with her relationship difficulties with a neighbor provided an indirect means for exploring some of the problems connected with her long-standing marital difficulties. The problem with the neighbor involved the neighbor's constant requests for aid and support that the patient found herself initially unable to refuse. It became increasingly clear that the patient had long-standing difficulties with assertiveness, and these finally came to a head within the therapeutic relationship itself. Following an initial period of acquiescence and politeness, the patient was finally able to admit and work through some of her negative feelings toward the therapist. Following this, there was a dramatic improvement in the patient's affective status as she appeared to be less tense and more willing to accept responsibility for her feelings, circumstances, and actions. Whereas previously she had been unwilling to deny another person's requests or demands, she now showed an ability to protect herself from this kind of draining relationship and found a new source of self-confidence and independence. She took a number of positive steps, including rejecting her husband's manipulative attempts at reconciliation and arranging for the transfer of her severely demented sister to a nursing home rather than taking her in herself.

As these positive steps were being made, the patient became a very active member of the psychotherapy group and one who was able both to reach out to other group members for support and to provide assistance in return. She became active as a volunteer tutor in a local elementary school, and began indulging in a number of personal hobbies and interests. To enrich her social network further, she made plans to move out of her isolated apartment and into a very pleasant retirement cooperative in a nearby town.

The effect of all these positive changes, liberally supported and reinforced by the therapist and group members, was a marked reduction in her level of generalized anxiety. More aware of her usual state of emotional stress, she requested training in relaxation techniques. These were learned quickly, and soon the patient was able to sleep without medication and had significantly reduced her use of Valium.

As the time for termination with the primary therapist approached, the patient showed some return of early symptoms, including complaints of helplessness, return of tremor, and some minor confusion in thought processes. These were interpreted as an unconscious attempt to forestall the termination of therapy. This did not appear to be a lasting problem, however, as the patient soon regained her equilibrium and became a solid member of the therapy group upon the primary therapist's departure.

NOTES

1. J.C. Nemiah, "Anxiety Neurosis," in *Comprehensive Textbook of Psychiatry,* 2nd ed., eds. A.M. Freedman, H.I. Kaplan, and B.J. Sadock (Baltimore: Williams & Wilkins, 1975), pp. 1198-1208.

2. Rollo May, *The Meaning of Anxiety* (New York: Ronald Press, 1950).

3. S. Kierkegaard, *Fear and Trembling,* trans. Walter Lowrie (Garden City, N.Y.: Doubleday, 1955).

4. S. Freud, "Inhibition, Symptom and Anxiety," in *Complete Psychological Works of Sigmund Freud,* standard ed., vol. 20 (London: Hogarth Press, 1959).

5. O.H. Mowrer, *Learning Theory and Behavior* (New York: John Wiley and Sons, 1960).

6. O. Rank, *The Trauma of Birth* (New York: Harcourt, Brace, 1929).

7. H.S. Sullivan, *The Interpersonal Theory of Psychiatry* (New York: W.W. Norton, 1953).

8. K. Horney, *New Ways in Psychoanalysis* (New York: W.W. Norton, 1939).

9. A. Verwoerdt, "Anxiety, Dissociative and Personality Disorders in the Elderly," in *Handbook of Geriatric Psychiatry,* eds. E.W. Busse and D.G. Blazer (New York: Van Nostrand Reinhold, 1980), pp. 368-380.

10. D.W.K. Kay and K. Bergmann, "Physical Disability and Mental Health in Old Age," *Journal of Psychosomatic Research* 10 (1966): 3-12.

11. T.A. Kerr, K. Schapira, and M. Roth, "The Relationship between Premature Death and the Affective Disorders," *British Journal of Psychiatry,* 119 (1969): 1277-1282.

12. M. Roth and C. Mountjoy, "States of Anxiety in Late Life: Prevalence of Anxiety and Related Emotional Disorders in the Elderly," in *Handbook of Studies on Anxiety,* eds. G.D. Burrows and B. Davies (New York: Elsevier/North-Holland Biomedical Press, 1980), pp. 193-213.

13. K. Bergmann, "The Neuroses of Old Age," in *Recent Developments in Psychogeriatrics,* eds. D.W.K. Kay and A. Walk (Ashford, U.K.: Headley Bros., 1971), pp. 39-50.

14. M. Roth et al., "Studies in the Classification of Affective Disorders: The Relationship between Anxiety States and Depressive Illness," *British Journal of Psychiatry* 123 (1972): 147-161.

15. C. Gurney et al., "Studies in the Classification of Affective Disorders: The Relationship between Anxiety states and Depressive Illness - II," *British Journal of Psychiatry* 121 (1972): 162-166.

16. A.D. Whanger and A. Verwoerdt, "Management of Anxiety," in *Clinical Geropsychiatry,* 2nd ed., ed. A. Verwoerdt (Baltimore: Williams & Wilkins, 1981), pp. 189-202.

17. R.G. Riedel, "Behavior Therapies," in *Annual Review of Gerontology and Geriatrics* 2, ed. C. Eisdorfer (New York: Springer Publishing, 1981), pp. 160-195.

Chapter 6

Paranoid and Schizophrenic Disorders

Alan D. Whanger

INTRODUCTION

The most fascinating and the most feared mental disorders of the elderly are those in the paranoid-schizophrenic spectrum. It would be difficult to determine how many elderly women with these strange types of thought disorders were diagnosed as witches during the Dark Ages and were treated with burning or drowning. While our diagnostic and treatment methods have improved considerably, our basic knowledge about these disorders is still incomplete.

The term *paranoia*, which literally means "a mind beside itself," was used by the ancient Greeks to refer to mental illness in general. The present concept of paranoia was first introduced in 1818 by Heinroth, who interpreted the delusions as disturbances of the intellect. There has been astonishingly little research or original thought about these disorders in the United States.[1,2] Various European investigators, who have been much more productive, have nevertheless held widely differing views.[3,4] The new *Diagnostic and Statistical Manual of Mental Disorders (DSM-III)* improves the conceptualization of these disorders, but it still does not deal adequately with the wide variety found in these problems among the elderly.[5] This chapter does not attempt to review the various viewpoints on these disorders or to reconcile the discrepancies. Rather, it presents a clinically relevant and useful view for those dealing with mental illness in an older population.

NOSOLOGY

Paranoid Disorders

The core feature of the paranoid disorder is the presence of persistent delusions of a persecutory or jealous nature *(DSM-III)*. A delusion is fundamentally a false belief based on mistaken assumptions about external reality; it is not amenable to the ideas of others or to obvious evidence to the contrary. According to *DSM-III*, there are several paranoid disorders; and to be so classified, they must not be due to any other type of mental disorder, such as organic, affective, or schizophrenic mental states. The other criteria include illness duration of at least one week, absence of major hallucinations, and reactions appropriate to the control of the delusional system.

Paranoia

By the new criteria, paranoia is the gradual development of a fixed delusional system, in a setting of otherwise clear and orderly thinking, that has continued for at least six months. This category includes the chronic forms of involutional paranoid state, as well as conjugal paranoia (pathologic jealousy).

Acute Paranoid Disorder

Acute paranoid disorder is distinguished basically by a duration of less than six months. Many such disorders are reactions to situations of threat or drastic change.

Shared Paranoid Disorder

Shared paranoid disorder has also been called *folie à deux*, since its principal feature is the development of a joint delusional system through close contact of a relatively well person with one who has an established persecutory disorder.

Atypical Paranoid Disorder

Atypical paranoid disorder serves as a catchall category for paranoid disorders not otherwise classifiable.

Classification of Felix Post

The authority on paranoid disorders of the elderly is Dr. Felix Post, who in his monumental study, *Persistent Persecutory States of the Elderly*, identifies three types of clinical pictures.[6] He describes them as follows:

1. *simple paranoid psychosis* in which the patient experiences only one or two commonplace delusions and the personality functioning is not seriously disrupted
2. *schizophrenia-like illness* in which there is much more general destruction of ego functioning with hallucinatory experiences and more bizarre types of delusional ideas
3. *paranoid schizophrenic states* which have characteristic features to be described in the next section

Schizophrenic Disorders

The schizophrenic disorders are a group of major mental diseases sharing certain common phenomena, although there is more confusion and controversy about these disorders than any other in psychiatry. The new classification in *DSM-III* does little to clarify the matter, since it states that when such disorders start after age 45, they should not be called schizophrenia at all, but rather atypical psychoses.[7] This view seems quite unhelpful, so a more clinically useful outlook, and one more relevant to the elderly, is developed. While the average life span of people with schizophrenia is shortened, most people with early-onset schizophrenia still will simply grow old with their disease. There may be modifications in the disease secondary to aging, but these are discussed later.

The widely split views on functional psychotic disorders with late-life onset are almost schizophrenic in themselves. The great nosologist Kraepelin devised the word *paraphrenia* to describe the late onset of illness characterized by paranoia and hallucinations, but he felt the illness was distinct from dementia praecox.[8] Roth reintroduced the term *late paraphrenia* to describe late-onset schizophrenia.[9] At another point, Post suggested the term *functional paranoid psychosis*, a concept he later altered.[10] Currently, Post prefers to use the term *persistent persecutory states of the elderly* but uses *late paraphrenia* and *late schizophrenia* interchangeably "to avoid monotony."[11] Eisdorfer, on the other hand, feels that a distinction between paraphrenia and paranoid schizophrenia seems warranted.[12] Since paraphrenia is not a *DSM-III* option, however, the term *schizophrenia* will be used.

Whatever name is given to this disorder, its essential features include the presence of psychotic features such as hallucinations or delusions during the acute phase; deterioration from the patient's previous level of functioning; characteristic psychologic processes or thought disorders; duration of at least six months; and absence of causation by organic or affective illness.

Paranoid Schizophrenia

When a schizophrenic disorder begins in later life, it is almost always of the paranoid type. While the symptoms vary widely, they always include at least one of the *DSM-III* criteria: bizarre delusions, auditory hallucinations, or disordered thought manifested by looseness of associations, incoherence, markedly illogical thinking, or poverty of speech content associated with altered affect or grossly disorganized behavior. In addition, patients are almost always "Schneiderian positive"; that is, they have one or more of Schneider's first-rank criteria of schizophrenia: ideas of passivity or influence, intrusion or withdrawal of thoughts, thought echoing, depersonalization, somatic hallucinations, or voices discussing the patient in the third person.[13]

Other Functional Psychoses

In the large central area of the paranoid-schizophrenic spectrum are a number of disorders of varying nature and terminology. Following are these categories of *DSM-III* and their essential characteristics, although their applications to the elderly are delineated elsewhere in this chapter.

Schizophreniform Disorders

The essential features of schizophreniform disorders are the same as those of schizophrenia except that the total duration of the illness—including its prodromal, active, and residual phases—is more than two weeks but less than six months.

Brief Reactive Psychosis

The symptoms of brief reactive psychosis are also similar to those of schizophrenia, but duration is less than two weeks, and the psychosis always follows a major psychosocial stress of some type.

Schizoaffective Disorders

Schizoaffective disorders are presently an indefinite diagnosis, made in conditions in which there has been a major affective component with persistent mood-incongruent psychotic features.

Atypical Psychosis

Atypical psychosis is a residual category for psychotic disorders that do not meet the criteria of any other, more specific disorders.

SYMPTOMATOLOGY

Paranoid Disorders or Simple Paranoid Psychoses

In addition to the criteria for diagnoses of these disorders already mentioned, a variety of clinical appearances and syndromes exist. On the mild end of the spectrum are what might be called paranoid personalities, which are characterized by rigidity, unwarranted suspiciousness, hypersensitivity, exaggerated self-importance, jealousy, and a tendency to blame others and attribute evil motives to them. These are moderately common conditions, but many people who suffer from them are never seen by mental health workers because they are often seclusive and secretive or merely are viewed as neighborhood eccentrics or as senile. Many experience periodic feelings of undue attention from others; these feelings are called ideas of reference. Many consider them to be puzzling or improbable, and some find them very persistent. Post calls these "over-valued ideas."[14] To evaluate the significance of paranoid symptoms better, it may be of help to understand the paranoid mode of thinking as noted by Swanson.[15] No single characteristic or symptom is either sufficient or essential in determining the presence or absence of a clinically important paranoid state; rather, the significance depends on the relative amounts and influence of all of the characteristics. They are as follows: projective thinking, suspiciousness, hostility, great focus of attention on the self, delusions, grandiosity, and fear of loss of autonomy.

Persons with simple paranoid psychosis usually have only one or two rather humdrum delusions, such as having things stolen, having their food altered or their houses watched, or their mates being unfaithful. These delusions may be associated with auditory hallucinations of related content, such as hearing the neighbors plotting to break into the house or hearing bedsprings squeeking in the next room. Their general personality functioning is not usually disrupted seriously, but there may be an occasional crisis, such as when the individual calls the police about the neighbor or stops eating properly or begins threatening the supposedly erring mate. These symptoms can often be improved rapidly by social and medical intervention, as occurs in acute paranoid disorders.

The delusional system in cases of paranoia tends to be rigidly fixed, and the rest of the personality is relatively intact. Paranoid individuals often believe they have unique or superior abilities, or they may spend considerable effort trying to gather evidence and support to prove their mates' unfaithfulness.

Rather frequently there is an affective component to the illness, usually a depressive type.

Schizophrenialike Illness

The symptoms of schizophrenialike illness, a mid-range group of disturbances, represent a partial breaking down of ego boundaries and control. The paranoid delusions are still of a commonplace nature, generally in keeping with the patient's social and educational background, but they tend to proliferate and become less loosely structured. In addition, there is an increase in hallucinatory experiences. A rather common symptom cluster is for an elderly single woman to be convinced that there are gangs outside who talk about her and accuse her of various sexual indiscretions. In addition, she is sure that they are digging a tunnel into her basement, and she hears sounds from there. The person is usually frightened by this and may seek help, or barricade the doors, or get weapons to fire at the persecutors. As in the simple paranoid psychoses, the symptoms often improve rapidly on intervention or on removal to a more secure environment.

Paranoid Schizophrenia

As already mentioned, a schizophrenia starting late in life has some of the characteristic features and symptoms of the disease with early onset, although the type is almost always paranoid. There is always a *prodromal* phase and a *residual* phase in addition to the acute episode, in which at least two of the criteria of *DSM-III* are manifested. These symptoms include social withdrawal, deterioration in role functioning, markedly peculiar behavior, deterioration of personal hygiene, altered affect, strange speech patterns or content, bizarre ideation and magical thinking, delusions, and unusual perceptual experiences. As Verwoerdt points out, there are generally two subtypes of late-onset schizophrenia.[16] The first is the *hostile* subtype characterized by delusions of injustice and persecution: a network of interrelated projections and delusions, as well as auditory hallucinations of a threatening or violent nature. Second is the *grandiose* subtype in which there are delusions both of persecution and of grandeur, regression to infantile omnipotence, and incorporation of delusions and hallucinations involving supernatural powers.

Some of the symptoms commonly seen in early-onset schizophrenia are much less common when the onset is late in life. Post notes that there is little obvious affective incongruity, and that depressive affect is common in the early stages.[17] Many elderly patients are quite upset by their abnormal thoughts and perceptions. Verbal incoherence or thought blocking or other gross speech disorders are infrequently seen. Odd movements and behaviors are not common, and one must keep in mind that many elderly may have various movement disorders, such as akathisias or dyskinesias, that occur quite independently of schizophrenia.

Mixed Disorders

Paranoid, delusional, and hallucinatory symptoms are frequently found in association with other functional and organic psychiatric disorders, as well as various physical problems, but these are discussed in the sections headed "Etiology" and "Differential Diagnosis."

ETIOLOGY

To presume to give a comprehensive explanation of the causes of these disorders would be unwise. The abundance of speculations, theories, and research underscores our very incomplete knowledge, and no attempt is made here to summarize or synthesize this area. Some observations and speculations may be helpful, however.

Dynamics

In many cases, the dynamics of paranoid syndromes go back to early childhood and primitive defense mechanisms. Cameron has speculated that those who develop functional paranoid psychoses are those who were not able to develop basic trust in early childhood, so they tend to view people and the world as basically unfriendly and hostile.[18] During the often long prodromal phase, these people respond to loss, threat, or frustration by withdrawing interest from the environment; because of this isolation, they undergo regression. In attempting to understand the uncomfortable things happening to them, they restructure their world so as to conform to the basic delusion about it being a dangerous and untrustworthy place. This assumption increases anxiety, and they perceive this growing anxiety as a growing danger from the environment. Like anyone in danger, they become uncertain, watchful, and hyperalert, often finding small things in the environment that have some sort of special meaning. In attempting to seek some explanation of what is going on, potential paranoid persons come to the wrong conclusions because of the rigidity of their denial and projections, and because of their often poor ability to communicate and objectively evaluate. These people increasingly feel they are part of a scheme in which others are watching them or trying to harm them. The final step in the paranoid reaction is to find an answer to who "they" are and what "they" are up to. This involves the formation of a "pseudocommunity" of real or imagined people intent on harming the person's reputation or being. Thus the fears and uncertainties are replaced by a delusional reality in light of which everything else is interpreted. Of course, most of the paranoid person's actions worsen the situation and either drive people away or stimulate counteraggression, thus confirming the person's fears of being attacked or persecuted.

Personality Disorders

It is very likely, though not clearly proven, that certain personality traits and disorders predispose an individual to a more serious illness later in life, or at least color the symptoms and manifestations shown when the person is under psychologic distress. Those relevant disorders in *DSM-III* are as follows.

Paranoid Personality Disorder

The individual with paranoid personality disorder tends to have pervasive unwarranted mistrust and suspiciousness, hypersensitivity, and a restricted affectivity.

Schizoid Personality Disorder

The person with schizoid personality disorder tends to be emotionally cold and aloof, with indifference to the feelings of others, a lack of humor, a tendency to be seclusive, and an inability to form close relationships.

Schizotypal Personality Disorder

A person with schizotypal personality disorder has various oddities of thought, perception, speech, and behavior that are not severe enough to be diagnosed as part of another condition. These criteria include magical thinking, ideas of reference, social isolation, illusions, odd speech, poor interactions, suspiciousness, and hypersensitivity to criticism.

Social Factors

There are many factors that could make an older person's outer world seem more threatening or less comprehensible, or could evoke within the person unacceptable or painful feelings that might be projected. The world may seem harder to contend with, and an elderly person's coping mechanisms may be less effective. Busse and Pfeiffer point out that the elderly belong to a minority group that is frequently excluded from positions of power and authority, and may be treated with active discrimination.[19] Social interaction also is important for older persons to develop and sustain mental capacities; as Weinberg points out, the worst form of segregation of the elderly is rejection by others, especially by their own families.[20]

Physical Illness

A wide variety of physical states and illnesses have been noted to correlate with various paranoid disorders.

Sensory Impairments

The diminution or alteration of sensory input has frequently been implicated as a contributory, if not causative, factor in the development of paranoid disorder, with hearing loss having the highest correlation. Cooper noted that paranoid and schizophrenic patients had a greater conductive hearing loss than that found in patients with affective disorders or in controls.[21] This would imply a long-standing loss of hearing such as might be found in people with middle ear infections. On the other hand, the affective patients showed a significantly greater sensorineural hearing loss, such as that found with aging changes or noise trauma. In another study, Cooper and Porter found that paraphrenic patients had significantly more cataracts and far vision problems.[22]

Toxic Agents

A wide variety of toxic substances have been associated with paranoid disorders in the elderly, and these have been well summarized by Bridge and Wyatt.[23] Among the common offenders are alcohol, amphetamines, barbiturates, antiparkinson agents, cortisone, Dilantin, digitalis, bromides, minor tranquilizers, tricyclic antidepressants, and lithium. The hallucinogenic drugs are common offenders, but are not in wide use by the elderly. One wonders what effect these drugs might have later on in the lives of those who used them in younger years.

Metabolic, Nutritional, and Infectious Disorders

There is an increased incidence of paranoid symptoms with several states more commonly found in the elderly, including hypothyroidism, hyperthyroidism, uremia, hypoxia, vitamin B12 deficiency, and pellagra. Several infectious diseases may include paranoid reactions as part of their acute phase or its aftermath; these may include influenza, infectious hepatitis, syphilis, typhoid fever, and tuberculosis.[24]

Neurologic Diseases

A number of neurologic diseases that afflict the aged may present with paranoid ideation. Among these are Alzheimer's disease of the presenile and senile types; temporal lobe epilepsy; brain tumors, especially of the frontal lobes; subdural hematoma; hypertensive encephalopathy; Parkinson's disease; and any disease causing an organic mental syndrome, including multiinfarct dementia. In the postseizure phase of grand mal epilepsy, the person may demonstrate paranoid delusions and an excited state, which may result in marked aggression.

In his fascinating studies correlating symptoms with postmortem findings, Corsellis noted an incidence of paranoid ideas in about 20 percent of patients who had had organic brain syndrome caused by either senile dementia or multiinfarct dementia; in contrast, those with mixed senile dementia and cerebrovascular changes had a 35 percent incidence, and those with psychoses associated with other organic cerebral diseases had an incidence of about 3 percent.[25] In general, those with schizophrenia had less evidence of cerebral changes than those with paranoid symptoms.

Genetics and Heredity

The role of heredity in paranoid disorders is unclear, both because of widely discrepant ideas about the nature of the disorders and because of the difficulty of separating out genetic contributors from the influences of early environment. The Scandinavian investigators, such as Retterstol, generally have emphasized the reactive nature of the disorders.[26] Others, such as Kay, feel that the etiology of the paranoid psychoses is complex, with genetic and other more general constitutional factors interacting with various exogenous ones to produce the mental illness.[27] The contribution of heredity is easier to see in the clearly schizophrenic states; here Kay reports a significantly increased likelihood of a patient's immediate relatives also developing schizophrenia.[28] The risk of late-life-onset schizophrenia in a patient's immediate family was about midway between the risk of the general population and that of early-onset schizophrenia, indicating either a particular type of heredity for late-life schizophrenia or, more likely, a multifactorial etiology with less of a genetic component; thus, it manifests itself later in life.

Some increased incidence of paranoid disorders is found in individuals with such genetic disorders as Turner's syndrome, Klinefelter's syndrome, and the XYY syndrome.

Schizophrenia

The etiology of schizophrenia is still unknown and is certainly complex. This is reflected in a recent issue of the *American Journal of Psychiatry;* in a single month it contained eleven articles dealing with the nature of schizophrenia.[29] The theories run from heredity to cerebral processing dysfunction to early maternal deprivation to left-handed dominance caused by early brain trauma to a wide variety of biochemical and hormonal alterations involving various neurotransmitters (such as norepinephrine, dopamine, and GABA) to faulty learning. How these relate to the conditions we see in old age remains to be determined. An interesting observation by Saccuzzo and Braff compares the markedly similar, associative cognitive dysfunctions found both in schizophrenia and in old age. They speculate that relatively normal aging changes, especially when intersecting with the effects of institutionalization, may produce mental disorders similar to schizophrenia.[30]

EPIDEMIOLOGY

The variability of terminology and the frequent mixing of different disorders makes studying them difficult; but the epidemiology of mental illness in late life helps us to identify cases, determine their distribution, clarify etiologic factors, plan services, and measure outcomes, as described by Blazer.[31]

Incidence and Prevalence

The incidence of mild paranoid symptoms in the community elderly is uncertain, but Savage et al. report that about 11 percent of their community sample indicated by their answers to a paranoid scale that they were perturbed.[32] Extrapolation from surveys that have shown an incidence of about 15 percent of significant psychiatric disorder among the community elderly would indicate that probably 1 to 2 percent of the community elderly have major paranoid disorders. The incidence is much higher in those sick enough to be institutionalized. Our own studies agree generally with those of Lowenthal and her group in San Francisco, who noted that about 40 percent of those elderly admitted to a mental hospital had, on close questioning, some paranoid symptoms, although these were often associated with some other disorder.[33,34] Of their patients with paranoid psychoses, fewer than 10 percent were admitted because of actual harmful behavior. In half their patients, symptoms had been present for less than two years. Among hospitalized patients, our experience was rather similar to that of Fish, who noted that about 5 to 10 percent of the elderly were admitted for late-life paranoid disorders.[35]

It has been estimated by Kay that about 4 percent of all schizophrenic illness in males and 14 percent in females occurs after age 65.[36]

Sex Distribution

After age 35 more women than men are diagnosed as having paranoid and schizophrenic illnesses, so that by age 65 this shift probably yields about a 3:1 ratio of women to men. This is significantly greater than the sex ratio in the general population.[37] The figures on paranoid reactions are much less clear, but women are predominant there as well. How much of the increased incidence in women is related to biologic factors and how much to sex-linked factors is certainly not clear.

Social and Other Factors

The highest incidence of paranoid disorders is found in the lowest socioeconomic classes, although this "downward drift" was true for late-life schizophrenia only in divorced and never married patients.[38,39] Among those who are married, there are many more who get late-onset illness than those who got sick earlier in life, but there is a very high incidence of marital and sexual discord. Paranoid disorders are much more common in urban populations and among the foreign born and the isolated.

ASSESSMENT

In assessing patients with paranoid or schizophrenic disorders, a number of points should be looked for and steps taken. The concern is not only to diagnose the conditions accurately but also to understand patients in their settings, so that the best possible treatments can be given, and to establish a working relationship with patients and their support groups.

Approach

Paranoid or schizophrenic patients are different from most other patients in that they often do not see the problem as being within themselves, so they do not seek out help in the usual ways. They are more likely to call the police, or write a government official, or be reported by their families or neighbors than they are to show up on their own in a mental health clinic. Because of their delusional systems, they see things in markedly different ways; so the history must be obtained both from the patient and from some other informed individual. In her study of factors leading to hospitalization of people with paranoid disorders, Lowenthal noted that observers classified the precipitating factors as potentially harmful behavior in 46 percent, actual harmful behavior in 8 percent, and environmental factors in 46 percent. The patients themselves classified their precipitating causes as disturbances in thinking or feeling in 15 percent, physical factors in 15 percent, and environmental factors in 70 percent.[40]

Rather often the paranoid patient will be brought in under considerable pressure from some family members or will have been committed by them. This usually generates considerable suspicion and hostility on the part of the patient, and the skill of the therapist is tested to make effective contact with the patient in these circumstances. It is best to be honest with such patients, letting them know that you are examining them to get an understanding of them and the reasons they were brought in, so they may be helped in whatever ways seem best. Many paranoid individuals are hypersensitive and alert, and will pick up on the therapist's discrepancies or fears or reactions to their behavior, and will throw these up at the therapist. The patients are often defensively offensive, as they frequently fear losing control or being dominated by someone they do not yet know. The delusions are often obvious, but generally it is best to avoid a confrontation with the patient at this point, since that is more likely to result in the therapist being included in the delusional system than in the patient believing it any less. The therapist should be identified as the patient's own therapist or evaluator, but some contact with the family will be necessary to understand the patient and his or her predicament better. If the patient is already hospitalized and upset, then a more gradual approach, allowing the patient to set the time for history taking, may help. It is often difficult to sort out many parts of the history into what is true, half truth, or delusion. Even paranoids have enemies, and they may indeed be within the family. If there is concern with this, it is helpful to talk to at least two family members or to some knowledgeable outside observer. With the less severe paranoid disorders, symptoms may disappear almost immediately on hospitalization or the person may be consciously hiding them, so outside information is important.

History

A thorough history, as has been explained previously, is essential as a preliminary step. Since the patient may be frightened or hostile or fatigued, it may be necessary to get the history in several sessions.

Many of the points to be sought will be apparent from previous sections. The presenting complaints must be understood, along with the duration and development of the symptoms. The previous personality style needs to be understood, as well as previous bouts of illness. It is of importance to assess how much the disorder is affecting various areas of life, such as sleeping and eating patterns, medicine taking, personal hygiene, paying bills, and relationship with the family. Behavioral problems need to be inquired about, such as peculiar behavior that will alienate others, actions such as calling the police or writing to public officials for inappropriate reasons, and especially responses to supposed environmental threats that are actually delusions. The danger of the condition needs to be determined in terms of physical violence; access to weapons, especially guns; and history of impulsive actions. If the patient is living in a family or institutional setting, it is helpful to inquire about behavior that places demands on the caretakers, such as loss of sleep, temper outbursts, or demands for care that strain the family's life style or ability to tolerate peculiar behavior further.

Psychological Testing

In many acute paranoid or schizophrenic disorders, the disease will be blatantly obvious. When the disorder is not obvious, or when it is mixed with other problems, or when the therapist needs an evaluation of how well the patient's ego is functioning, formal psychologic testing may be helpful. As Dinello points out, most paranoid patients are rather threatened by psychological tests because they are very defensive, they like a very structured situation, and they are very suspicious of what will be done with the information.[41] The Minnesota Multiphasic Personality Inventory (MMPI) is probably one of the best test measures, as it has both a paranoia scale and a schizophrenia scale. If the results of the MMPI are positive, one has a good degree of confidence; but there are many false negatives since an intelligent, fairly well compensated, paranoid person can succeed in covering up symptoms well. As the level of severity of the paranoid disorder becomes less, even the projective tests will become more normal, with fewer clues presented. The Rorschach inkblot test may show a meager, guarded response, but more often it will show content about being spied on or scrutinized or even attacked, and many people get extremely anxious during the test. The Thematic Apperception Test (TAT) often reveals themes of oversuspiciousness of motives, distortions of sexual identity, or manipulation of the central figure by others. The Draw-a-Person Test may show a large, grandiose figure in the center of the paper, with a rather characteristic large head and ears and prominent eyes. In more severely troubled individuals, sexual identity confusion is again often present. The late-life-onset schizophrenias generally have much less disintegration and florid symptomatology than those with early-onset disease.

Differential Diagnosis

In addition to the previously listed diagnostic categories, paranoid ideation and thought disorders may be found in several other conditions in the elderly, and a differential diagnosis is important for correct management.

Organic Mental Disorder

A wide variety of symptoms may be seen in organic mental disorder, and the delusional ideas may be more prominent than the organic content. Unless the schizophrenia or paranoid disorder was known to be present previously, these diagnoses should not be made in the presence of organic impairments. The usual types of drugs, such as amphetamines or hallucinogens, that cause either the organic delusional syndrome or organic hallucinosis are not commonly used by the elderly; but the possibility of an alcoholic causation should be kept in mind.

Depression

In major depressive episodes, in the elderly both paranoid ideation and delusional ideation are moderately common, but they are usually mood-congruent, such as ideas of being persecuted for sinfulness or of being in poverty or of having delusions of being cancer ridden. Hallucinations are not prominent and usually are of voices berating the individual for sins or shortcomings. Very depressed persons may not verbalize all of their thought processes because of depressive apathy, and so may seem to have a looseness of association or thought blocking that is not actually the case.

Manic State

Delusional and even hallucinatory phenomena, especially paranoid ideation, are moderately common in manic episodes in the elderly. The stream of thought may be so rapid that only part of it is verbalized and hence may lead to the impression of illogical thought and loosening of associations. Occasionally in the elderly person with bipolar affective disorder, both manic and depressive symptoms may be present simultaneously, giving rise to a rather disorganized appearance that may suggest schizophrenia.

Obsessive Compulsive Disorder

Older compulsive, perfectionistic individuals may find their usual defenses overwhelmed, and may develop symptoms and overvalued ideas that are difficult to differentiate from delusions. Their speech may become so tangential that it seems disorganized.

COURSE OF THE ILLNESSES

Effects of Aging

The development of effective treatments has rather markedly changed the course of these illnesses, but that is discussed in the next section. Herein we should examine the more natural courses and the effects largely age-related changes have on them. There is frequently a gradual intensification of pathologic personality traits over the years, both because of long practice and because of a decrease in the effectiveness of various high-energy defensive mechanisms, such as obsessive-compulsiveness, as described by Taylor and Verwoerdt.[42] This may lead to disengagement from external objects and relationships and withdrawal into the self, with atrophy of social and personal skills. This may lead to a hypochondriacal or compulsive stance, but these brittle adjustments may not hold up and may deteriorate, with a loss of reality testing into a paranoid or thought-disordered state.

Paranoid Disorders

The frequency of paranoid disorders tends to increase with age and is related to both external and internal losses and to an increase in vulnerability. These may be of an acute, more reactive nature or of a more chronic variety. As Post notes, there tends to be a persistence of the symptoms in the more severe varieties, which would now be called paranoia.[43] People with this problem are often surprisingly healthy physically, and occupational and intellectual functioning is usually preserved. Marital and social functioning tend to deteriorate, however.

Schizophrenia

Those schizophrenias with onset early in life tend to have a relapsing course, with increasing residual impairment between the episodes, although there are those with a good prognosis.[44] Factors contributing to a good prognosis are an adequate level of premorbid personality and social functioning, an abrupt onset with precipitating events in mid-life, a clinical picture involving confusion, and a positive family history of affective disorder. Paranoid schizophrenia tends to have a later age of onset than the other types and leaves the overall personality more intact. In whatever type of schizophrenia, aging often has several effects on the course. Among others, Molchanova noted that schizophrenia is often episodic, with sustained improvement in old age.[45] It has been noted that hallucinations often become less frequent and upsetting; psychotic motor activity tends to decrease with age, and there are often alterations in the delusions. It was noted by Muller that in about half of aged schizophrenic patients, the delusions disappeared or altered markedly.[46] This might occur through suppression, conversion into depression, restructuring the milieu, regression because of organic mental disorder, development of a physical illness that allows focusing of distress on body malfunctions, or switching from a persecutory to a grandiose delusion. This phenomenon of "burnout" in older schizophrenics was reviewed by Bridge and associates.[47] Much of the improvement began to occur in the involutional period, although it is often overlooked in the chronic patient. Schizophrenia with true onset in late life usually seems to be a more benign type of disease than that with early-life onset.

TREATMENT

Drug Therapy

Until the development of the major tranquilizers and antipsychotic drugs, the outlook for the major paranoid and schizophrenic disorders was generally rather grim. Many patients were institutionalized for long periods of time, until they died or until the disease modified because of intercurrent physical illness or aging changes. With the advent in the early 1950s of effective drugs, such as chlorpromazine (Thorazine), marked changes in responses occurred, as documented by Post, who observed that of 24 patients treated before the major tranquilizers, all remained psychotic; while in a sample of 37 similar patients treated with drugs, only 11 percent remained unchanged while 22 percent had partial remissions and 67 percent had complete recoveries.[48]

A large number of antipsychotic drugs have been marketed, and a list of these with their usual dose ranges appears in Appendix B. The effects of most of these drugs is similar in that they inhibit certain sites in the central nervous system and reduce the irritability of the part of the midbrain called the reticular activating system.[49] Their principal differences are in the various side effects that occur. These side effects are often of major consequence to older people, because they may involve drops in blood pressure, drowsiness, unsteadiness, and various movement or extrapyramidal disorders. The drugs most useful with the elderly are the so-called high-potency drugs, such as haloperidol (Haldol), trifluoperazine (Stelazine), or thiothixene (Navane). Older people vary widely in their responsiveness to these drugs, but in general they are quite sensitive to them, and the drugs should be given slowly and carefully. People with chronic schizophrenia sometimes seem to require large doses of antipsychotic medication, so sometimes one of the low-potency drugs, such as thioridazine (Mellaril), is used to avoid certain side effects. The specifics of drug management are quite complicated, and those with special interest in this area are referred to some of the more technical texts for details.[50-52]

If an individual is very agitated, relatively large doses of antipsychotic medication may be needed to get the condition under control. Then the dose should be dropped quickly to a maintenance level for long-term administration. If a patient has a rather mild paranoid reaction for the first time, he or she may be left on drugs for about six months before trying to stop. If the problem is recurrent or chronic, the person may be left on drugs for at least a year. In case of schizophrenia or hazardous paranoia, the person may stay on medication for at least two years. Some may need a low dose of one of these drugs for a relatively indefinite period. If depression is a prominent part of the clinical picture, one of the antidepressants may be added to the antipsychotic. The so-called minor tranquilizers have almost no role in the treatment of these disorders. Sometimes one of the long-lasting injectable drugs, such as fluphenazine (Prolixin Decanoate), can be given once every three or four weeks.

Psychotherapy

The traditional analytic type of psychotherapy has little place in the treatment of these psychotic disorders, but a supportive, nonthreatening therapeutic relationship with the individual can be very helpful in reducing anxieties and fears and in providing an opportunity for ventilation and exploration of alternatives. Building the relationship is often difficult, especially since many of the patients come in under duress, and the therapist must be able to handle the patients' initial hostility and rejection. Many practical issues, especially those dealing with the environment, can be dealt with effectively in therapy to help the person reduce the perceived stresses and threats. At times there will be persistent delusional ideas that, with the help of the therapist, may be encapsulated so that the patient can share them in therapy but suppress them elsewhere.

Institutionalization

Hospitalization is often necessary in the acute initial phase of a paranoid or schizophrenic disorder, since the person has often decompensated and views the environment as hostile or destructive. In the milder disorders, there may be an immediate quieting of symptoms, although these will likely return if the patient is discharged to the same situation without some medication and alteration in the environment. Institutionalization has been much overused in the past; it is better to treat the person on an outpatient basis if it can be done safely and effectively. However, a number of therapies can best be initiated and carried out in an institutional setting.[53] Planned and active hospital care can be very effective, but simple warehousing of the elderly mentally ill borders on mistreatment.

Family Therapy

Since the family is almost always involved in some way with the older person who is paranoid or schizophrenic, some type of family therapy will usually be necessary, as detailed by Anderson and Janosko.[54] This may include counseling with the family if commitment is needed, since commitment often stirs up many guilt feelings or factions within the family. The family may need support to understand that the patient is sick and not just obnoxious and difficult. A home visit may help the therapist get a better idea of the patient's immediate environment and some of the stresses that may exist therein. Therapy will be needed to deal with the anxieties of both the patient and the family, but joint sessions generally are not indicated until the psychosis has subsided and the therapist has a good working relationship with the patient. Even then, confronting the delusional areas generally should be avoided by mutual contract between the family and the patient, with the therapist acting as monitor. Disagreement can be acknowledged, but intact noncontroversial areas and adaptive skills and tension relief measures should be emphasized. Since many patients are not reliable about taking drugs, some sort of family support for this should be worked out if possible. Some type of home supervision, with the cooperation of the family and the patient, will often help maintain progress and avoid hospitalization.

CASE STUDY—LATE-LIFE PARANOID SCHIZOPHRENIA

Present Illness

Mrs. J. is a 67-year-old, black, widowed woman brought to the clinic by her daughter, who said the patient had been "having delusions and fantasizing a lot" for about one year. At the time of initial examination the patient denied problems and said that all she needs is to find a job. According to the daughter, however, the patient had telephoned on a number of occasions, complaining that the police were driving around her house using radar on her that caused numbness in her face, arms, and hands, as well as pains in her chest. In addition, she had seen a red light in the window of one of her neighbors, and after looking at it for several minutes, she felt that everything became steamy looking. Shortly after that, she developed vomiting and diarrhea that lasted for several days. On a number of occasions she reported auditory hallucinations, sometimes of dead relatives telling her that they loved her, and sometimes of people around her home telling her to pack up her things and leave the neighborhood.

On closer questioning the patient did admit that many of her old neighbors had moved out, that rough younger people were moving in, and that this made the area dangerous to walk in at night. In addition, she did admit to being worried since an automobile accident two years previously in which she was knocked unconscious and apparently awoke with police cars and ambulances with flashing lights around her. She described this episode with considerable emotion and noted that she had felt increasingly nervous since the accident, had become fearful of driving, and so had quit her job as a domestic worker. She had been put on Librium at the clinic where she went, but she seldom used it and did not return for follow-up. She had called her daughter on a number of occasions in fright, and had asked to come over to spend the night. Otherwise, she became much more withdrawn, visited with her neighbors very little, and stopped going to church. More recently she got the idea that if she got away from her home more, she would be bothered less by the police and neighbors, so she had begun to think that returning to work would help. Some of the children had suggested on several occasions that she come to the clinic for help, but she was very opposed to this, saying that the doctors would decide that she was crazy and would lock her up in the state hospital. She has been calling some of the children more frequently, complaining of her fears and delusions.

Psychiatric History

Neither the patient nor her daughter, who was the informant, knew of any previous psychiatric problems of the patient or of any in the family other than the patient's deceased husband. The daughter did feel as though the patient had begun to be more reclusive since the last child had left home six years before, and said that it is usually increasingly difficult to get the patient out of the house. There is no history of drug abuse and only occasional minor use of alcohol.

Medical History

The patient had been in generally good health, but had had a gall bladder operation some 15 years previously. She had had seven pregnancies, with two miscarriages. Within the past two years, she had been noted to have occasionally elevated blood pressure, but she would not take medicine or get regular care for this. She had no apparent symptoms other than occasional complaint of headache.

Social and Family History

The patient was the third of six children born to a sharecropper family. Her father died of probable alcoholism when she was six, and two years later her mother married a rather harsh man. The patient remembered her hair having caught fire about that time, and she still has occasional nightmares about that episode. Her childhood was generally unhappy, but she managed to finish the eighth grade. She married a man seven years her senior when she was 17, but he turned out to be a heavy drinker who frequently abused her and the children when he was drunk. He had died about 11 years previously. She subsequently worked, first as a nurse's aide in a rest home, then in a cigarette factory, and then as a domestic. She has five children, the two daughters living nearby, and the relationships seem fairly good.

Examination

Mental Status

The patient was a thin, neatly dressed woman who looked several years younger than her age. She was quite restless and tense during the interview, opening and shutting her pocketbook frequently and crossing and uncrossing her legs repeatedly. She appeared to be rather suspicious and guarded and spoke in a rather rapid, rambling way. She had difficulty sticking to the point of a question and would then often say that if she could only get a job, her problem would clear up. She admitted to some nervousness, but generally tried to hide things or resist talking about certain subjects, so most questions had to be repeated several times. She was fully oriented, and her memory was intact. On questioning, she denied having hallucinations and delusions, but seemed especially restless at this point. She was quite tense, but denied depression. Her affect was constricted but not inappropriate. Her proverb interpretation was rather concrete. Her insight was very limited, and she seemed to be attempting to cover up her problems. It was felt that her judgment was significantly impaired.

Physical Examination

The general examination was within normal limits except for a mildly elevated blood pressure and a slightly enlarged thyroid gland.

Functional Status

The OARS Multidimensional Functional Assessment Questionnaire (MFAQ) took longer than usual to administer because of Mrs. J.'s defensive tendency to talk off the point and avoid answering questions, which necessitated repeating many of the questions several times. She made no errors on the preliminary questionnaire. It was noted by the MFAQ administrator that the patient was very alert, extremely tense, quite suspicious, and excessively talkative during the whole procedure.

Her rating on the Social Resources (SR) scale was 3, or mildly impaired, as she had lost contact with many of her friends and had become isolated. However, she still has available children who can take care of her even though they expressed hesitation about this because of her peculiar behavior and ideas. Economically, she was moderately impaired and was given a 4 rating. She had managed to buy her small house, but she has little money saved, and the area in which her house is located seems to be deteriorating in values. On the Mental Health (MH) rating scale she scored a 5, because—while she was intellectually intact and actually gave no positive answers in the mental illness screening scale—she was obviously very paranoid and had a marked change in her life style because of her mental illness. It was noted during the interview that she took several long pauses while answering the questions about wanting to leave home, about being understood, about being happy, and about being plotted against, although she denied the problems. It was a case in which her behavior during the test belied some of her answers. On the Physical Health (PH) rating scale, she was given a 2, indicating being in good health except for a mild labile hypertension. The Activities of Daily Living (ADL) rating scale was scored a 2, as she can perform all the activities without assistance. It was felt that she has to labor at some of these because of her psychiatric problems, as during three of these questions she rather inappropriately volunteered that getting a job would help all her problems.

Assessment and Discussion

When Mrs. J.'s case was presented to the intake conference, several interesting problems were discussed. This is a case in which the patient is trying desperately to look and act normal to avoid a presumed diagnosis of being "crazy" and uses verbal denial of illness fairly successfully. The MFAQ interviewer's observations, the therapist's interview, and the family information help to establish the illness and its duration. One of the geropsychiatry fellows did the clinical interview of the patient, and she again displayed the same type of behavior as she did on the MFAQ, with repeated denial of illness, suspiciousness, and elaborate, rambling, tangential answers. The patient obviously was trying to hide her pathology, and at the end of the interview, when it was suggested that she come again so that a more complete history could be obtained, she refused to return to the clinic, stating that she was not "crazy" (although this had not been mentioned), that she did not have any problems that a job would not take care of, and that she would not take any medicine even if it were given to her.

The attending geropsychiatrist commented that Mrs. J. presented a very fascinating problem because of the rather florid psychotic symptoms reported by the family but denied by the patient in the interview. There were some first-rank symptoms of schizophrenia with auditory hallucinations extending over a period of time. In these, "they" talked about the patient in the third person. In addition, she had rather bizarre hallucinations and delusions of radar and red lights being beamed at her and causing strange physical symptoms. In spite of the history of these psychotic symptoms, she was able to hold herself together fairly well during the interviews, albeit with massive denial and a compulsive stance. Although this woman experienced several early psychologic traumas, she seems to have done rather well, except for a bad marriage, until about six years ago, when her last child left home. It is likely that she was able to have a sense of ego integrity in her role as mother until there was no one left to mother anymore. How large a role the accident had in precipitating the illness, or even whether the incipient illness may have caused the accident, is hard to tell at this point.

The psychologist brought up the issue of getting a clear-cut diagnosis on this woman since there is a marked conflict between what the patient says and what the family says. For a person with as bizarre a history as she has, she appears surprisingly intact. He suggested a battery of tests, especially the projective tests, to clarify the diagnosis and to get an idea about her ego strength. While organic mental syndrome hardly seems a possibility here, it would be well to document this in light of the head injury.

The nurse suggested that a home visit be made, both to get an accurate idea about whether the neighborhood is really as dangerous as it seems to the patient, and to find out how well she is actually able to function at home.

The social worker indicated the probable desirability of working with the family on a regular basis to help in their adjustment to the problem, since they were giving signs of fatigue and hostility because of the patient's delusions.

Diagnosis

It was felt that this woman has a schizophrenic disorder of the paranoid type, with onset in late life. At this point she is fighting off ego decompensation and is using gross suppression to try to handle her illness and hide it from her therapists.

Therapeutic Plan

The recommendations of the intake conference were that the patient be engaged in treatment if at all possible in spite of her statement that she would refuse to come back or take any medicine, since her hold on reality is so weak. A clearer idea of the home and family situation is needed, and further family interviews should be arranged, as well as a home visit if the patient will agree at a later time. Because of the psychosis, it was felt by the geropsychiatrist that she should be placed on an antipsychotic tranquilizer. Because of her extreme suspicious and uncooperative stance, it was felt desirable to use one with likely minimal side effects and to build up the dose gradually. The recommendation was to use haloperidol (Haldol) concentrate—0.5 mg. at bedtime for five nights and then to increase the bedtime dose to 1.0 mg. It will be necessary to see her on a rather regular basis, but probably for short visits for the time being to allow a relationship to build gradually at the patient's own speed.

It was felt that ongoing family counseling would be needed both to guide the family as well as to follow the patient's progress, since her reporting was obviously inaccurate.

Obtaining medical records would be helpful to see how much problem she has with hypertension as well as to get observations of her at the time of her accident and subsequently. Unfortunately, she does not presently have regular medical care; it might be well to offer her this, since she might be better able to relate in physical terms than in psychological ones.

Psychologic testing was recommended to evaluate the extent of her pathology and to test her ego strengths and suitability for going back to work.

Intervention and Follow-up

Problems developed rapidly. Two days after the initial visit Mrs. J. called to cancel her appointment for the following week, stating she wants her name "off the list" since she is now "okay" and is going to get a job and this would take care of her problems. A call from the daughter shortly afterward indicated that the problems are persisting as before, and are probably even a little worse. This put us in a dilemma often encountered with paranoid patients who are so suspicious that they refuse medication or any other treatment. It was suggested that the Haldol be supplied to the daughter, who seemed to have a fairly good relationship with the patient, to see if she could prevail upon the patient to comply with the treatment program. Often, after a patient starts antipsychotic medication, the paranoid ideas and delusions calm down and the patient becomes more approachable and cooperative. The family was advised that the delusions might otherwise become worse, and that if she began retaliating at the supposed persecutors, she might need to be legally committed to treatment to avoid harm to herself or others.

Fortunately, the patient did agree to take the medicine from her daughter. The geropsychiatrist sent a brief letter to the patient and followed up on this with a friendly phone call a few days later. The patient was still somewhat suspicious but agreed to take the medicine and come back for another visit in two weeks. She returned for two visits and then refused to come in again, stating that she was better and had no need to come. Consultation with the daughter indicated an improvement, so the case was left open.

In about four months, the family called back to say that the symptoms had recurred, with auditory hallucinations of an accusatory nature and with strong sexual overtones. The patient, who had stopped the Haldol after one month, did agree to come back in. The previous findings were again present, but she was more guilty and upset. She had met a man a few weeks before who was expressing some interest in her, and she was very confused and afraid over this situation. She agreed to go back on the Haldol, and was put on 2.0 mg. twice a day. Within two weeks the hallucinations and delusions were gone, and she was feeling better. Unfortunately, in about three weeks she began getting extrapyramidal symptoms to the Haldol, with pulling of her neck muscles, slurring of her speech, and an inability to sit still (akathisia) that did not respond well to antiparkinson drugs. She was therefore shifted to thioridazine (Mellaril), 25 mg. three times a day. About seven days later she apparently had a cross reaction of some type and became very anxious. She developed the idea that there was something that was connecting a small skin lesion on her forehead to her brain, and she worried that this would cause a deterioration in her functioning. It was felt that she was still having residual extrapyramidal symptoms from the Haldol but had not had enough time or dose with the Mellaril to cover the symptoms. The Mellaril was increased to 50 mg. three times a day, and within a week she was feeling rather normal. She began to be involved in outside activities, and has continued to do fairly well over a period of a year, with no more gross evidence of the schizophrenia and requiring only brief bimonthly checks. She developed a much more positive outlook toward her therapist and the clinic. It may work out that she can eventually get a part-time job, as her cognitive functioning is good and she is generally free of paranoid ideas.

Commentary

When Mrs. J. finally got into therapy and would take her medicine, the symptoms were well controlled after a dose of a suitable antipsychotic medicine was established. She has functioned well and shows the frequent good response of late-life schizophrenia to treatment. She will need to be followed indefinitely at intervals. It may be that after two years, the medication can be tapered and stopped to see if her schizophrenia has gone into prolonged remission.

CASE STUDY—PARANOIA IN THE SENIUM

Present Illness

Mrs. T. is a 70-year-old, white, married woman from a small town who was referred into the clinic by a daughter who was concerned about the patient's fears and nervousness. The patient complained of nervousness and expressed the concern "I may be under a spell." There had been a problem for almost two years, starting shortly after her husband was found to have cancer of the rectum. He had surgery for this and a colostomy followed by radiation treatments. He had been rather sick for several months but has been in stable condition for the past year. The patient had a marked loss of hair during the previous three years and felt quite sensitive about that. She held up fairly well during the acute phase of her husband's surgery, but within a few weeks after his return home, she began to worry at night about people talking about her not being a good wife. At first these seemed to be nightmarelike dreams, but more recently she had begun to hear her relatives talking about her failure as a wife. The couple had been sexually active until the time of the husband's surgery, but there has been no further intercourse since then, as he had become impotent. She would sometimes think that she heard a baby crying in the next room. More recently, she began to have ideas about her husband and accused him of having sex with their grandson; she also had some other bizarre ideas. She was worried about these thoughts and told her husband and daughter about them, which led to her coming to the clinic.

Psychiatric History

No history of psychiatric problems could be elicited from the patient or her family. A few months after the problems began, she went to her local mental health clinic, where she was given a minor tranquilizer, which did not help at all. She chose not to return after the second visit there. One of her sisters had been hospitalized in another state many years previously for a nervous breakdown and had recovered, but the details of this were not known.

Medical History

In general the patient's health had been good; she had had an ovarian cyst removed many years previously. For the past four years she had had mild hypertension and was getting a reserpine-containing diuretic for this, with no apparent problems. She apparently has a good relationship with her family doctor, and it was he who initially suggested that she go to the mental health clinic when she had mentioned the earlier thoughts about people talking about her.

Social and Family Life

Mrs. T. was the oldest of nine children born to a farm family. They had had to work very hard to make ends meet, but she remembered her early life as being generally good, although she had had to look after her younger siblings to such an extent that she felt like she was the mother in the family. Because of the pressures of the family and farm and her own difficulty in school, she dropped out in the sixth grade. She remained on the farm until age 21, when she met her present husband, who is three years younger than she, and they quickly married. They had three children in five years, and the early years of the marriage were difficult, especially since the husband drank heavily and caroused. After several years he had a conversion experience, gave up his drinking, and became a pillar of their fundamentalist church. Later they moved to town, where he became a mechanic. She feels that generally their marriage had been good since then. She worked occasionally in a fabric mill but in recent years was home most of the time, often caring for the children of her daughter who lives next door.

Examination

Mental Status Examination

The patient is a rather plump, fairly neatly dressed woman wearing a wig. She was rather anxious but cooperative and almost engaging, and fully oriented. Her speech was relevant and coherent, although her vocabulary was limited. At times it seemed as if she could be led by the interviewer, and she seemed suggestible and rather naive. She indicated that "something strange seems to be happening to me," especially because the criticism of her relatives about her not being a good wife made her feel plotted against. She was puzzled by the occasional supposed sounds of a baby crying, as well as by her husband's suspected peculiar sexual behavior. At times she had felt compelled to respond to the crying of the infant, but at other times she questioned the nature of this idea. Often she was frightened by the delusions and was afraid she might be hurt. As she had never had these ideas before—and indeed there was no indication of perceptual difficulties in other areas—she developed the notion of being under some kind of a spell. Being a religious person, she said that she often prayed to "the Lord who will show me if people are plotting against me," but she did not feel as if she had gotten any clear response. In addition, she mentioned her hair falling out, indicating that since that happened, she felt down and often stayed in the house. There were no changes in her appetite or her sleep pattern except for occasional nightmares about the same types of concerns as her delusions. She has had no crying episodes or suicidal preoccupations, but during the present illness she often has had difficulty concentrating. Her sexual interest has disappeared, and she frequently feels "nervous," meaning vaguely anxious.

Intellectually, Mrs. T. seemed to be a dull individual with limited general information. Her proverb interpretation was appropriate, but her problem solving seemed limited in complex tasks. Her calculations were poor, and she could recall only four figures forward and three backward. It was felt that there was significant impairment of judgment.

Physical Examination

The patient reviewed her four-year history of mild hypertension and complained of some joint pains, especially in her knees and ankles. She gave a history of a "weak right eye," which seems to have caused little trouble, and she denied hearing problems or recent gastrointestinal dysfunction. Physical examination was remarkable for a blood pressure of 170/94 lying and 160/98 standing, obese abdomen without enlargement of organs, varicose veins of both legs, some grinding in the knee joints, and marked thinning of her hair. Routine laboratory studies showed a marginal hemoglobin of 12.0 g., a slightly elevated blood sugar of 135 mg., and a borderline low thyroid function.

Functional Status

The patient made three errors on the preliminary questionnaire of the OARS MFAQ, getting the day of the week wrong, being unable to recall the previous president, and being unable to subtract serial 3s. The questionnaire administrator noted that Mrs. T. was pleasant and cooperative but anxious and tense as well. Her rating on the Social Resources (SR) scale was 2, indicating good resources, as she has her husband and several children who are concerned about her and are available to help in spite of her delusional ideas about them and her withdrawal from others. On the Economic Resources (ER) scale, she rated a 3, as their present income and resources are adequate for their needs but there is little in reserve. The Mental Health (MH) scale was rated a 4, or moderately impaired, with definite psychiatric symptoms that interfered somewhat with her life style. She was not defensive as in the previous case, and admitted to positive response to 11 of the 15 questions on the mental symptom checklist. She rated her own mental health as poor and was aware that it had deteriorated over time. On the Physical Health (PH) scale, she was rated a 3 because of her mild impairments and need for treatment of her hypertension and arthritic problems. As far as the Activities of Daily Living (ADL) scale was concerned, she was rated a 2, as she has a good capacity for daily functions in spite of her emotional and physical problems.

Assessment and Discussion

At the intake conference, Mrs. T.'s case was presented by the social worker who had done the intake interview, the geropsychiatry fellow who had done a psychiatric evaluation, and the geriatrician who had reviewed her medical records and done a physical examination. The patient has a variety of delusional ideas, the reality of which fluctuates in her mind. She is puzzled and distressed by these and is not particularly defensive about them. Information from the patient and her husband and daughter indicated that there seemed to be little psychopathology until the onset of symptoms following the husband's illness, in spite of her rather limited intellectual capacities and the unhappiness caused by her husband's behavior and alcoholism early in the marriage. At this point, there is predominantly paranoid symptomatology, but with a moderate depressive component and some anxiety.

In formulating the problem, the attending geropsychiatrist commented on the apparent reactive nature of the difficulties to the husband's illness. He had had the rather sudden appearance of a life-threatening illness, along with the aesthetic problem of a colostomy and post-surgical impotence. The husband seems to have been the dominant figure in the family, and—as the patient seems to have depended on him rather heavily—his illness triggered the wife's fears of abandonment and inability to cope. It is likely that she had difficulty adjusting to his colostomy as well as to their inability to continue their sexual life, which had been rather important until then. It is not clear why she adopted a projective defense for these feelings, although this may be related to her limited intellectual abilities. Her delusions are interesting in this regard, for it is the family that seems to accuse her of being an inadequate wife who is not able to take care of her sick husband happily. The spreading nature of many paranoid delusional systems is perhaps well illustrated in this case, as the focus moves from her difficulty in adjusting to her husband's illness to the accusations of the family about her inadequacy, from the husband's sexual inability to her accusations that he is ignoring her because of his homosexual involvement with their grandson, and from the realization that her relationship with her husband is threatened by his illness to the idea that someone (probably a jealous sister) has cast some kind of an evil spell on her. Many might think that the idea of being "under a spell" has a very ominous implication psychiatrically in terms of being a schizophrenic symptom, but the cultural context must be taken into consideration. The idea of magic spells and the influence of demonic powers is moderately widely spread in this area, especially among less well educated rural and older people, and so is rather readily available as an explanation for strange or unwanted feelings, especially when a paranoid stance is being developed.

It was pointed out as well by the geropsychiatrist that this is one of the rather frequent cases among the elderly in which there is a mixture of paranoid and depressive symptoms in varying degrees. Given the series of problems the patient had, one might have expected a depressive reaction rather than a predominantly paranoid one. As is the case with many paranoid reactions in late life, there is a florid sexual component, both in the idea of a baby crying when all possibilities of pregnancy except in extreme fantasy are gone, and in the rather bizarre explanation of the husband's lack of sexual activity with her because of his supposed involvement with the grandson.

The geriatrician commented on several physical problems that might be related to the patient's difficulties. Her mild hypertension is being treated with a reserpine-containing drug, which is occasionally associated with the production of a depressive state, especially in older people. Ordinarily, paranoid states are not associated with it, but it might be well to keep this possibility in mind, especially as other antihypertensives will be less inclined to cause that problem. In addition, she has had a rather marked thinning of her hair in the past three years for an unclear reason. One of her thyroid function tests was borderline low, but it is not clear whether this woman has any significant hypothyroid condition that may be associated occasionally with either depressive or paranoid or even organic phenomena.

One of the clinic nurses raised the issue of whether the husband's colostomy is still a major problem for the patient. It is not clear that the patient knows how to care for it or understands it, even though the husband apparently cares for it adequately himself. It would be well to evaluate the husband's care of it, as well as to educate the patient about it in order to reduce her fear and possible revulsion over it. In addition, the nurse wondered about evaluation of the couple's sexual practices, as some other way to express intimate and sexual feelings might be worked out between them. Perhaps the husband might be examined to see whether he is organically impotent or is reacting to his own illness by withdrawal and depression.

A visit to the patient's home was suggested by one of the social workers, both to get a better idea about the milieu and also to talk with other family members. Some family therapy might be supportive and helpful.

The chaplain suggested that it might be helpful to talk with the patient when she is somewhat improved about some of her religious beliefs in order to clarify some of her possible punitive ideas about God, and about her possible feelings of guilt about being an inadequate wife.

The desirability of formal psychologic testing was brought up by the clinic psychologist, especially in light of measuring this woman's intellectual capacities and determining whether there is evidence of recent organic impairment. In addition, it would be well to evaluate her ego strength and the possibilities of psychotic decompensation.

Diagnosis

The consensus was that, because of her having gradually developed a persistent delusional system in an otherwise clear though limited cognitive setting, this woman has paranoia. It was felt that this woman may have borderline mild mental retardation. The depressive and anxiety features are very mild and probably do not warrant a separate diagnosis.

Therapeutic Plan

The consensus of the intake conference was that one of the female geropsychiatrists should be the primary therapist, since long-term medication regulation will be necessary and since the patient may be able to deal with her sexual problems more comfortably with another woman. The psychotherapy needs to be basically of a supportive nature with only very limited insight. The secondary therapist will be one of the nurses who will provide counseling to the patient and the husband over matters relating to his illness, as well as keeping in touch with the family.

The basic goals were to treat this woman on an outpatient basis with antipsychotic medication in order to reduce her delusional and hallucinatory ideation, and with supportive psychotherapy to avoid deterioration and prevent hospitalization. Coordination with her family doctor was undertaken, especially about her hypertension. Because of her hair loss, she was referred to an endocrinologist at the medical center for a diagnostic work-up. Psychological testing was arranged. The antipsychotic medication selected was haloperidol (Haldol) in the amount of 1 mg. twice a day; it was felt she would tolerate this dose, and it was desirable to get the paranoid symptoms under control rather quickly to prevent further deterioration. She was to be seen at two-week intervals until she stabilized and then at monthly intervals.

Intervention and Follow-up

The patient returned with her husband and daughter in two weeks, with marked improvement. The symptoms and preoccupations with the delusions had disappeared during the day, but she still had occasional delusions and vague auditory hallucinations at night; she felt much less anxious. There was a minimal amount of cogwheeling in the arms, indicating some side effect from the Haldol. Therefore the medication was shifted so that she received it all at night, and diphenhydramine (Benadryl)—an antihistamine with mild antiparkinson properties that is often well tolerated by the elderly—was added (25 mg. at bedtime). When seen two weeks later, she was much better, with almost complete disappearance of her symptoms. The family noted no delusions or accusations, and they felt she was "about back to normal." She did not spontaneously mention her ideas about having a spell on her, she seemed much less anxious, and there was no indication of depression. In the meantime, endocrine studies showed a borderline low thyroid function, probably resulting from a previous thyroiditis. She was to be followed at intervals by her family doctor for this. The psychological tests showed an IQ of 81, with no indication of acquired organic impairment. Paranoid ideation was prevalent, as were indications of some depression. The projective material was low in output, and did not indicate schizophrenic decompensation. Her ego strength seemed adequate.

By the time she returned in another month, she was doing very well, and she and her family requested that her care be transferred back to the community mental health clinic serving her area because of the lengthy travel they had to undergo. Contact was made with that clinic, and records and recommendations were sent to them. About five months later, the daughter called back, saying that the patient had done well for the first three months, but then had stopped her antipsychotic medicine and refused to return to the community clinic. For the two or three weeks prior to the call, the patient had been having delusional ideas about the family again, and had been having nightmares. As she was willing to return to our clinic, another appointment was made for two weeks hence, and she was instructed to start back on the Haldol again, as it did not seem that any major problem or side effect had occurred. When she was seen two weeks later, she again was considerably improved. She continued to be seen at two-month intervals, and the Haldol dose was cut in half. She continued to do rather well over a two-year period, and the dose of Haldol was reduced to 0.5 mg. at bedtime. She continues to be followed at four-month intervals for support and evaluation. It is thought that her antipsychotic medication may be discontinued in about six months, as she has been essentially symptom free, and that she should continue to be observed at occasional intervals. The relationship with her husband improved. She has developed a good relationship with the receptionist at the clinic as well as with her therapists, and she seems to consider it a major social outing to return for her follow-up visits.

Commentary

There are similarities between this and the previous case in certain of the symptoms and in the patients' good response to antipsychotic medications. The symptoms of Mrs. T. were much less pervasive and caused less disruption of her personality, which helped distinguish her paranoia from the much more malignant symptoms of schizophrenia. These cases do illustrate the frequent problems of paranoid patients who tend to blame others for their problems and often stop taking their medications. However, they do illustrate that good therapeutic results can be obtained in elderly people with major psychotic disorders when appropriate medications are used and a working relationship is established with them.

NOTES

1. T.P. Bridge and R.J. Wyatt, "Paraphrenia: Paranoid States of Late Life. II. American Research," *Journal of the American Geriatric Society* XXVIII, no. 5 (1980): 201-205.

2. A.D. Whanger, "Paranoid Syndromes of the Senium," in *Psychopharmacology and Aging*, eds. C. Eisdorfer and W.E. Fann (New York: Plenum Press, 1973) pp. 203-211.

3. T.P. Bridge and R.J. Wyatt, "Paraphrenia: Paranoid States of Late Life. I. European Research," *Journal of the American Geriatric Society* XXVIII, no. 5 (1980): 193-200.

4. F. Post, "Paranoid, Schizophrenia-like and Schizophrenic States in the Aged," in *Handbook of Mental Health and Aging*, eds. J.E. Birren and R.B. Sloane (Englewood Cliffs, N.J.: Prentice-Hall, 1980) pp. 591-615.

5. American Psychiatric Association, *Diagnostic and Statistical Manual of Mental Disorders, 3rd ed. (DSM III)* (Washington, D.C.: American Psychiatric Association, 1980), pp. 181-203.

6. F. Post, *Persistent Persecutory States of the Elderly* (Oxford: Pergamon Press, 1966).

7. APA, *Diagnostic and Statistical Manual*, pp. 181-203.

8. E. Kraepelin, *Dementia Praecox and Paraphrenia* (1919; reprint ed., New York: Krieger, 1971).

9. M. Roth, "The Natural History of Mental Disorder in Old Age," *Journal of Mental Science* 101 (1955): 281-301.

10. F. Post, *The Clinical Psychiatry of Late Life* (Oxford: Pergamon Press, 1965).

11. Post, "Paranoid, Schizophrenia-like and Schizophrenic States," pp. 591-615.

12. C. Eisdorfer, "Paranoia and Schizophrenia Disorders in Later Life," in *Handbook of Geriatric Psychiatry*, eds. E.W. Busse and D.G. Blazer (New York: Van Nostrand Reinhold, 1980) pp. 329-337.

13. K. Schneider, *Clinical Psychopathology* (New York: Grune & Stratton, 1959).

14. Post, *The Clinical Psychiatry of Late Life.*

15. D.W. Swanson, P.J. Bohnert, and J.A. Smith, *The Paranoid* (Boston: Little, Brown, 1970).

16. A. Verwoerdt, *Clinical Geropsychiatry*, 2nd ed. (Baltimore, Williams & Wilkins, 1981), p. 90.

17. Post, "Paranoid, Schizophrenia-like and Schizophrenic States," pp. 591-615.

18. N.A. Cameron, "Paranoid Reactions," in *Comprehensive Textbook of Psychiatry*, eds. A.M. Freedman and H.I. Kaplan (Baltimore: Williams & Wilkins, 1967) pp. 665-675.

19. E.W. Busse and E. Pfeiffer, eds., *Behavior and Adaptation in Late Life* (Boston: Little, Brown, 1969) p. 2.

20. J. Weinberg, "Geriatric Psychiatry," in *Comprehensive Textbook of Psychiatry*, 3rd ed., eds. H. Kaplan, A.M. Freedman, and B.J. Sadock (Baltimore: Williams & Wilkins, 1980) pp. 3024-3042.

21. A.F. Cooper, R.F. Garside, and D.W.K. Kay, "A Comparison of Deaf and Non-deaf Patients with Paranoid and Affective Psychoses," *British Journal of Psychiatry* 129 (1976): 532-538.

22. A.F. Cooper and R. Porter, "Visual Acuity and Ocular Pathology in the Paranoid and Affective Psychoses of Later Life," *Journal of Psychosomatic Research* 20 (1976): 107-114.

23. Bridge and Wyatt, "Paraphrenia: Paranoid States of Late Life," pp. 193-200.

24. Whanger, "Paranoid Syndromes of the Senium," pp. 203-211.

25. J.A.N. Corsellis, *Mental Illness and the Aging Brain* (London: Oxford University Press, 1962).

26. N. Retterstol, *Paranoid and Paranoiac Psychoses* (Oslo: Universitetsforlaget, 1966).

27. D.W.K. Kay and N.J. Roth, "Environmental and Hereditary Factors in the Schizophrenias of Old Age ("Late Paraphrenia") and Their Bearings on the General Problem of Causation in Schizophrenia," *Journal of Mental Science* 107 (1961): 649-686.

28. D.W.K. Kay, "Schizophrenia and Schizophrenia-like States in the Elderly," *British Journal of Hospital Medicine* 8 (1972): 369-376.

29. *American Journal of Psychiatry* 138, no. 8 (August 1981): 1045-1056.

30. D.P. Saccuzzo and D.L. Braff, "Associative Cognitive Dysfunction in Schizophrenia and Old Age," *Journal of Nervous and Mental Disease* 168, no. 1 (1980): 41-45.

31. D.G. Blazer, "Epidemiology of Mental Illness in Late Life," in *Handbook of Geriatric Psychiatry*, eds. E.W. Busse and D.G. Blazer (New York: Van Nostrand Reinhold, 1980), pp. 249-272.

32. R.D. Savage et al., *Personality and Adjustment in the Aged* (New York: Academic Press, 1977).

33. Whanger, "Paranoid Syndromes of the Senium," pp. 203-211.

34. M.F. Lowenthal, *Lives in Distress* (New York: Basic Books, 1964).

35. F.J. Fish, "Senile Paranoid States," *Gerontological Clinics* 1 (1959): 127-131.

36. Kay, "Schizophrenia and Schizophrenia-like States in the Elderly," pp. 369-376.

37. Post, "Paranoid, Schizophrenia-like and Schizophrenic States," pp. 591-615.

38. Swanson, Bohnert, and Smith, *The Paranoid.*

39. Post, "Paranoid, Schizophrenia-like and Schizophrenic States," pp. 591-615.

40. Lowenthal, *Lives in Distress.*

41. F.A. Dinello, "Psychological Testing of the Paranoid Patient," in *The Paranoid*, eds. D.W. Swanson, P.J. Bohnert, and J.A. Smith (Boston: Little, Brown, 1970), pp. 169-194.

42. W.M. Taylor and A. Verwoerdt, "Thought Disorders and Paranoid Phenomena," in *Clinical Geropsychiatry*, ed. A. Verwoerdt (Baltimore: Williams & Wilkins, 1981), pp. 79-97.

43. Post, "Paranoid, Schizophrenia-like and Schizophrenic States," pp. 591-615.

44. APA, *Diagnostic and Statistical Manual*, pp. 181-203.

45. E.K. Molchanova, "Episodic Schizophrenia with a Regressive Course with Marked and Sustained Remission in Old Age," *Neuroscience and Behavioral Physiology* 9, no. 1 (January-March 1978): 45-48.

46. C. Muller, "The Influences of Age on Schizophrenia," in *Processes of Aging*, eds. R.H. Williams, C. Tibbits, and W. Donahue (New York: Atherton Press, 1963), pp. 504-511.

47. T.P. Bridge, H.E. Cannon, and R.J. Wyatt, "Burned-out Schizophrenia: Evidence for Age Effects on Schizophrenic Symptomatology," *Journal of Gerontology* 33 (1978): 835-839.

48. Post, *Persistent Persecutory States*.

49. A.D. Whanger and A. Verwoerdt, "Psychopharmacology: Some Theoretical and Practical Considerations," in *Clinical Geropsychiatry*, 2nd ed., ed. A. Verwoerdt (Baltimore: Williams & Wilkins, 1981), pp. 156-169.

50. Ibid., pp. 156-169.

51. J.I. Walker and H.K.H. Brodie, "Neuropharmacology of Aging," in *Handbook of Geriatric Psychiatry*, eds. E.W. Busse and D.G. Blazer (New York: Van Nostrand Reinhold, 1980), pp. 102-124.

52. R. Hicks et al., "Geriatric Psychopharmacology," in *Handbook of Mental Health and Aging*, eds. J.E. Birren and R.B. Sloane (Englewood Cliffs, N.J.: Prentice-Hall, 1980), pp. 745-774.

53. A.D. Whanger, "Treatment within the Institution," in *Handbook of Geriatric Psychiatry*, eds. E.W. Busse and D.G. Blazer (New York: Van Nostrand Reinhold, 1980), pp. 453-472.

54. C.N. Anderson and R.E. Janosko, "Family Therapy in Paranoia," *Current Psychiatric Therapies* 18 (1978): 107-116.

Chapter 7

Somatoform Disorders

Steve Herman

The group of disorders newly classified in *DSM-III* as somatoform disorders all involve physical symptoms that give the appearance of being caused by some underlying physical disorder. In such cases, however, there is a lack of organic findings supporting the existence of an underlying disorder, coupled with positive evidence to suggest that the symptoms are linked to psychological factors or emotional conflicts. In these disorders the somatization of emotional conflict is viewed as occurring outside voluntary control, and also generally outside of conscious awareness. This differentiates them from the more deliberate condition know as malingering.

NOSOLOGY

Under the *DSM-III* classification system, there are four distinct categories of somatoform disorder.[1] The first of these is *somatization disorder* (Briquet's syndrome), which is a common and chronic disorder involving multiple somatic complaints. The second disorder is *hypochondriasis*, the essential feature of which is preoccupation with the fear or belief that one has a serious disease. The third disorder is *psychogenic pain disorder*, where the primary feature, complaints of pain, appears to be attributable to psychological factors. Finally, there is *conversion disorder*, which nowadays is a relatively rare disorder involving the loss or alteration of physical function, again attributable to psychological conflict. An additional category, *atypical somatoform disorder*, is reserved for those somatoform disorders that do not fit the criteria for any of the categories already described.

All of these categories of somatoform disorder are well represented in the elderly medical and psychiatric population, and a familiarity with their clinical presentation is essential, not only to the psychogeriatrician but to other geriatric health care professionals as well. Let us begin by examining in

125

more detail the varieties of somatoform disorder identified by the *DSM-III* classification system.

Somatization Disorder

The essential feature here is a long-standing pattern of multiple somatic complaints that may involve a variety of organ systems and types of symptoms. Patients manifesting this disorder often present their complaints in a markedly dramatic, vague, or exaggerated manner. It is typical in such cases that medical attention is repeatedly sought without any positive organic findings emerging to explain the presentation of symptoms. Such patients are usually persistent in their pursuit of medical attention, and may be receiving medical care from many physicians, either sequentially or concurrently. This disorder typically begins early in life, most often during adolescence. The course of the disorder tends to be chronic, though fluctuating. It involves essentially a lifelong adjustment pattern that rarely remits spontaneously. The disorder is much more common among women than among men, and, according to *DSM-III* manual, it is estimated that approximately 1 percent of females have this disorder. Anxiety and depressive symptoms are often accompanying features, although there is generally little willingness on the patient's part to recognize any underlying emotional conflicts. Such symptoms are generally attributed to physical problems by the patient.

Hypochondriasis

Hypochondriasis, or hypochondriacal neurosis, is similar to somatization disorder in that both involve a preoccupation with somatic symptoms. In hypochondriasis, however, it is not the symptoms themselves that are of most concern to the patient but rather the belief that these symptoms are indicative of an underlying serious and perhaps life-threatening disease. In such cases the fear of having a disease is resistant to medical reassurance and persists despite negative findings on medical examination. The individual's preoccupation may be with normal bodily functions, such as heartbeat, bowel functions, perspiration, and the like, or with minor physical abnormalities. Even mild symptoms will take on a major significance to the patient when they are interpreted as signs of a serious disease process. The hypochondriacal patient will often narrate his medical history with excessive attention to detail. There is often a history of doctor shopping, associated with generally poor doctor–patient relationships. Such patients, with their fixed notions of an underlying disease process, typically feel that they are not getting proper care, and they often express bitterness toward previous physicians who failed to diagnose them "properly." Unlike somatization disorder, hypochondriasis may appear for the first time in the middle or later years. It is also noted to be equally common in men and women.

Psychogenic Pain Disorder

The primary feature of this disorder is the complaint of pain in the absence of adequate physical findings to explain the pain and in association with direct or indirect evidence suggesting a psychological basis for the development or maintenance of symptoms. In some cases the pain symptoms are inconsistent with the known anatomical distribution of the nervous system, while in other cases the existence of organic pathology may be ruled out after extensive diagnostic evaluation. The role of psychological factors in causing and/or maintaining the pain can most often be inferred from evidence that the onset or exacerbation of pain is linked to a known environmental stressor generating psychological conflict. In other cases the pain may be recognized as an unconsicous means by which the patient fulfills needs for emotional support or avoids activities that are undesirable or feared. Patients with this disorder typically complain a great deal, both verbally and by gesture, and they tend to make frequent visits to physicians to obtain pain relief. They may make excessive use of analgesic medications despite their stated dissatisfaction with the amount of pain relief thereby obtained. Generally, patients with this disorder develop an unusually passive life style, and may eventually take on an invalid role. Psychogenic pain disorders may have their onset at any stage of life and are by no means uncommon in the elderly. They are more frequently diagnosed among women patients and tend to follow a chronic course, especially if pain behavior is positively reinforced by the environment.

Conversion Disorder

Conversion disorder, also labeled hysterical neurosis, conversion type, involves a clinical picture long recognized in the psychiatric literature. Here the predominant feature is a loss of, or alteration in, physical *functioning* that suggests a physical disorder but instead represents an expression of a psychological conflict. The most familiar conversion symptoms are those that mimic neurological disease, such as paralyses, seizures, blindness, and paresthesias. A conversion disorder is likely to focus on a single symptom during any given episode, although with continued episodes there may be a shift in the location and nature of the symptom.

The psychological mechanisms underlying the conversion symptom can be explained along two lines. The first would view the symptom as representing a symbolic expression and partial solution of an underlying psychological conflict. What is involved here is a standoff between competing impulses to express, and to inhibit expression of, a strong feeling or impulse. In such cases the impulse and the conflict about expressing it are kept out of awareness through a "compromise" solution involving a conversion symptom. For example, after an argument, an individual's conflict about the expression of anger may be symbolically expressed as a "paralysis" of the arm that might otherwise be used to strike out in anger. The other mechanism thought to underlie conversion symptoms is the achievement of secondary gain, whereby the symptom allows the individual to avoid an activity or response that is frightening or unpleasant, or enables him or her to obtain attention, affection, or emotional support from the environment that might not otherwise be forthcoming.

Conversion symptoms typically appear suddenly within a context of extreme psychological stress. Typically the onset is in adolescence or early adulthood, but it may also appear for the first time during the middle or later years of life. Compared with the other categories of somatoform disorder, it is relatively rare at present. It is thought to have been much more common several decades ago, and may continue to be more common in culturally and geographically isolated parts of the country.

In summary, the four variants of somatoform disorder all involve a reaction whereby emotional conflict is manifested by somatic complaints and symptoms. The individuals who experience these disorders tend to deny or minimize any personal or emotional problems and generally pursue treatment of their problems along medical channels. Such persons are often extremely resistant to the notion that their problems may have a psychological cause, and relatively few find their own way to mental health facilities for treatment. With the exception of conversion reactions, the somatoform disorders tend to be chronic conditions that are resistant to psychotherapeutic and medical efforts. There are a number of reasons why this group of disorders is particularly prevalent, and potentially dangerous, among the elderly population.

SOMATOFORM DISORDERS AMONG THE ELDERLY

One of the stereotypes about the elderly is that they are unusually preoccupied with bodily functions and will talk endlessly about ailments, real and imagined. As with most stereotypes, there is both an element of truth and a large degree of exaggeration in this notion. The fact is that by age 65, there is a likelihood that an individual is already suffering from one or more chronic illnesses, and this becomes increasingly more prevalent in subsequent decades. In addition, the older person tends to be surrounded by illness and death among family members and friends. Is it any wonder, then, that many older persons tend to regard the day-to-day condition of their body as a source of concern, worry, and preoccupation? In many cases chronic disease brings with it significant functional impairment, with limitations in day-to-day activities providing a constant reminder that the body is not functioning as well as it once did. From this perspective, an increased concern with bodily functioning among the elderly is understandable, and it may in a sense be thought of as adaptive. Beyond a certain point, however, the older person's preoccupation with bodily functioning may become nonadaptive, and it is here that we enter the realm of the somatoform disorders. In practice it is often difficult to differentiate normal from abnormal bodily preoccupation in the elderly. Furthermore, the high incidence of chronic health conditions in the elderly renders the task of differentiating somatoform disorders from actual organic conditions especially difficult.

How common are somatoform disorders among the elderly? Two studies compared self-perceived health status with objective evaluations of physical health among elderly community residents.[2,3] These studies found that between 10 and 20 percent of the elderly surveyed rated their physical health as poor when it was, in fact, good by objective standards. Another study, based on psychiatric interviews with community-residing elderly, concluded that 33 percent of their sample manifested hypochondriacal concerns.[4] Other studies have indicated that hypochondriacal symptoms are especially common among depressed elderly and those with actual medical diseases.[5-8]

More recently, Busse and Blazer noted the high prevalence of somatoform disorders in the elderly population, and they found the most common of these disorders to be psychogenic pain disorder and hypochondriasis.[9] The view that somatoform disorders increase in prevalence in later life is shared by Verwoerdt.[10]

What accounts for this increase in somatoform disorders in later life? One major factor has already been alluded to—namely, the increased prevalence of actual organic disease. Such diseases "can serve as the nucleus around which hypochondriacal concerns can be precipitated and crystallized."[11] In such cases an individual's somatic concerns may be labeled hypochondriacal only to the extent that they are out of proportion to the actual physical condition. It is not uncommon to come across an older person with a lifelong history of good or even perfect health who becomes suddenly hypochondriacal in response to a minor physical problem. In some instances this response may involve preoccupation with a minor symptom similar to one that has recently been observed in a seriously ill friend or family member.

Another factor that may account for the increase in hypochondriasis in later life is the so-called process of disengagement from work, family, and social life. Verwoerdt construes hypochondriasis as a withdrawal of interest from the outer world and a refocusing upon oneself and one's physical body.[12] For many (though by no means all) individuals, old age brings with it a degree of perceptual, social, and emotional deprivation that may tend to focus attention more intensely on bodily events. Furthermore, the presence of physical symptoms may involve "secondary gain" through insuring more extensive contact with family members or health care professionals. In such cases the development and maintenance of physical complaints may serve as an indirect means of fulfilling dependency needs for the older person.

Finally, there is a sense in which somatization may represent an attempt to maintain a positive self-image through abrogating responsibility for personal failures. The explanation "I am sick" can be used as a rationalization for personal short-comings, thereby salvaging some measure of self-esteem. As Verwoerdt points out, old age is a life period where some individuals must confront and come to grips with ultimate failure in their lives, and for some of these individuals a retreat into hypochondriasis represents an alternative to despair.[13]

Whatever the specific etiological factors involved may be, somatoform disorders generally represent a particular type of response to chronic or acute *stress*. In such a context somatic complaints may be thought of as a "vocabulary of stress" that allows an individual indirect expression of emotional conflict and dysphoric affect.[14] In individuals who develop somatization disorders, there tends to be a strong inhibition against direct expression of emotional concerns, and the language of somatic symptoms— being more "acceptable"—may become a primary medium for expressing personal fears, needs, and so forth. Viewed from this perspective, the somatoform symptoms may be regarded as possessing certain positive functions. Busse and Blazer have listed among these the following:[15]

- facilitating communication and interaction
- displacing anxiety
- forming an identification with a deceased or absent loved one
- providing punishment for unresolved guilt feelings
- controlling the behavior of others in the environment

While these factors may bring some degree of personal gratification to the older individual in the short run, the gains are generally more than outweighed by the negative consequences of obsessive somatic preoccupation in the elderly. These negative consequences can be spelled out along two lines. The first is the impact on the individual's pattern of health care usage and the increased risk of iatrogenic disorders. The second involves the disturbing effect of somatization behavior on the elder person's friends and family.

With regard to the first point, it has already been mentioned that a characteristic feature of somatoform disorders—particularly somatization disorder and hypochondriasis—is the patient's tendency to seek out medical care from multiple practitioners, either sequentially or concurrently. In many cases, physician consultations are initiated directly by the patient, which may result in little or no coordination among various practitioners treating the patient. In such cases it is not unusual to find that the patient is maintained on a large number of drugs, including some with overlapping or antagonistic actions. This tendency toward polypharmacy is further heightened by the somatizing patient's manipulative and demanding behavior, which often leads the physician to prescribe drugs more freely than usual. The risks of polypharmacy in the elderly are particularly great insofar as drug sensitivities may be heightened in later years. Another factor to consider is the impact that hypochondriacal behavior has upon the doctor–patient relationship. Hypochondriacal or somatizing patients are generally experienced as very frustrating to work with, and they tend to generate a good deal of resentment and hostility in the practitioners they consult. Often such attitudes become apparent to the patient, or they affect the manner in which the doctor examines or otherwise deals with the patient. These attitudes may be detected, consciously or unconsciously, by the patient, who takes them as a further indication that he or she is not getting the quality of care that is needed. There is also the danger that the physician, having grown accustomed to an endless and repetitious symptom recital, might tend to overlook or minimize certain symptoms that turn out to represent a bonafide and dangerous physical condition. The hypochondriacal or somatizing patient may thus emerge in the position of Aesop's "Boy Who Cried Wolf," a stand that is especially dangerous for the physically vulnerable elderly patient.

In addition to these effects on the quality of health care, there are equally significant implications for the quality of family relationships. Verbalization of preoccupations, or exaggerated physical complaints, often conveys a signal of helplessness or dependency that is covertly designed to elicit nurturant or supportive behavior on the part of family members. While this may be immediately effective in securing attention, in the long run it is likely to have the opposite effect. Family members will sooner or later recognize the way they are being manipulated and are likely to become resentful. These feelings may lead them to avoid the patient even more, thus leading to a self-perpetuating cycle of mutual frustration and anger.

THE DIAGNOSIS OF SOMATOFORM DISORDERS

As stated earlier, the essential feature of somatoform disorders is the presence of physical symptoms without an adequate organic basis. The primary diagnostic differential is therefore between somatoform disorders and actual organic illness. The presence of a concurrent organic condition does not rule out the possibility of a somatoform disorder, however, as there may be a large discrepancy between the organic findings and the individual's subjective experience and expression of symptomatology. The prevalence of organic disorders in later life renders this a particularly important diagnostic consideration among elderly patients.

The second general diagnostic consideration is the relationship between somatoform disorders and depression. Several studies have identified the prevalence of somatic complaints and symptoms among elderly patients suffering from depression.[16,17] According to the *DSM-III*, mild depressive and anxiety symptoms are common in the somatoform disorders and are not diagnostically counterindicative.[18] At the same time, however, where somatic complaints are one feature of a major depression, the latter diagnosis takes precedence.

Somatic symptoms are also frequently encountered in some psychotic disorders, where they take the form of somatic delusions. In such cases there is often a bizarre quality to the somatic symptoms and other indications of an underlying thought disorder.

Finally, the condition known as malingering must be differentiated from somatoform disorders. In such cases the symptomatic complaints are under the individual's voluntary control and serve a goal that is obviously recognizable given the individual's environment and circumstances.

The *DSM-III* provides very specific criteria for differentiating the various categories of somatoform disorder. The diagnosis of somatization disorder requires: (1) history of physical symptoms of several years' duration beginning before the age of 30 and (2) the presence of a certain number of complaints (14 for women and 12 for men) from a list of 37 symptoms. Somatization disorder is not diagnosed in elderly individuals unless there is evidence that the patient's tendency to report multiple symptoms was already established earlier in life, and has been a chronic adjustment pattern.

Hypochondriasis is identified as "an unrealistic interpretation of physical signs or sensations as abnormal, leading to preoccupation with the fear or belief of having a serious disease."[19] Furthermore, it is necessary that there be evidence to document an absence of organic disease, as well as persistence of the patient's belief despite medical reassurance. In contrast to somatization disorder, hypochondriacal symptoms frequently appear for the first time in later life.

In psychogenic pain disorder, the primary symptom is severe and prolonged pain. This diagnosis is based on the presence of two conditions: (1) The pain symptoms are inconsistent with physical findings; and (2) there is reason to believe that psychological factors are etiologically involved in the pain. Evidence for psychogenic factors may involve a temporal connection between the onset or exacerbation of pain and some environmental stressor, or some evidence of "secondary gain." According to Busse and Blazer, psychogenic pain disorders rarely emerge for the first time in old age but tend to have their onset in middle age.[20]

In conversion disorder, the prominent disturbance is a loss of, or alteration in, physical functioning. In such cases the symptomatology is usually rather specific and limited. Beyond this, the diagnostic criteria are similar to those of psychogenic pain disorder, and involve a lack of confirming organic findings together with evidence for psychogenic origin of the symptoms. At present, conversion disorders are the least common category of somatoform disorders.

ASSESSMENT OF THE ELDERLY PATIENT WITH A SOMATOFORM DISORDER

The immediate assessment goals in cases of somatoform disorder include the following: (1) To identify the personal and situational factors that serve to produce and maintain the symptomatic behaviors; (2) to assess the positive and negative consequences of the symptomatic behavior on the patient's day-to-day functioning (of particular importance is the impact on health care behavior and familial relations); and (3) to determine appropriate paths of therapeutic intervention.

When searching for underlying causative factors, it is very important to obtain a detailed history of the patient's symptomatology with particular emphasis on its temporal course. Very often the outbreak or exacerbation of symptoms can be linked with a significant environmental change, and thus provide an insight into underlying dynamics. It is also important to investigate whether the patient's somatizing behaviors represent a long-standing pattern of adaptation to stressful situations. Much valuable information along these lines can be obtained from a family member or friend who has known the patient for a long period of time and can place the present behavioral picture into perspective.

While it is important to understand the underlying causes of somatization behavior, it is perhaps even more important from a practical standpoint to understand the factors that tend to perpetuate this behavior. As we indicated earlier, somatization tends to function not only as a primary defense against dysphoria but also as a source of secondary gain, in the form of attention, nurturance, and support. One might attempt to answer the question: What realities would this patient have to confront if the somatic preoccupations were erased from the picture? And what sources of emotional gratification does the patient maintain through symptomatic behavior?

These questions lead us into the second major assessment area—the negative and positive effects of symptomatic behavior. Here it is important to ask not only what the patient is gaining through his or her symptom behavior but also what the costs are. Specifically, how tolerant of the patient's symptomatic behavior are family members and other significant persons? Does the patient's behavior serve to alienate individuals who might otherwise be important sources of emotional and instrumental support? What impact does the patient's behavior have on the quality of relationships with health practitioners?

Another important issue to investigate here is the individual's pattern of health care usage. It is important to identify all the physicians and other health care providers from whom the patient is currently receiving care, as well as those who have been consulted in the recent past. An attempt should be made to determine to what extent these various professionals are aware of one another's involvement with the patient. In addition, a thorough review of current medications should be conducted, preferably by examination of the patient's medicine cabinet if on a home visit, otherwise by asking the patient to bring *all* medications to the clinic. This request may often provide surprising results, as when one of our patients at the OARS Clinic showed up for an initial appointment with two shopping bags filled with over 200 separate prescription medicines spanning several decades.

Finally, in the assessment phase an attempt should be made to identify potential avenues for therapeutic intervention. A key consideration here is what steps were taken in the past to deal with the patient's problem and what the outcomes were. It is helpful to identify key health care providers and other individuals with whom the patient has come in contact and has developed rapport. It is also helpful to know who is already on the patient's "enemies list." Often, hypochondriacal or somatizing patients will be disappointed in previous health care providers, and it is a strategic mistake to direct such an individual back to someone who is no longer trusted. Finally, it is particularly important with elderly patients to consider any logistical and/ or financial constraints that might restrict treatment options. Such limitations may render an otherwise ideal treatment plan ineffective in practice.

SOMATOFORM DISORDERS: PRINCIPLES OF TREATMENT

As a rule, patients with somatoform disorders are (1) quite insistent that they are physically sick and (2) resistant to the notion that they have problems that are basically emotional in nature. From a strategic standpoint the following questions immediately present themselves: Should the patient be told that he or she is actually not sick? Should symptoms be interpreted as a manifestation of emotional disorder? Should additional somatic complaints be taken at face value and worked up medically? What should the patient's family be told? What, if any, psychiatric treatment should be initiated?

These questions are indeed problematic, and many clinicians feel that this class of patients are among the most difficult to manage successfully. Fortunately, over the years some tentative answers to these questions have emerged from clinical trial and error, and have been confirmed by the pioneering efforts of Busse and his colleagues at Duke University Medical Center, who developed a specific program of outpatient treatment for the hypochondriacal patient.[21] This approach, recently updated by Busse and Blazer, is based on avoidance of direct confrontation with the patient's defensive system, and seeks instead to establish a firm therapeutic alliance between doctor and patient which may eventually take on a psychotherapeutic cast.[22] The essential principles of this approach follow.

1. Do *not* attempt to convince patients that their symptoms or "illness" is not real. At the same time, however, do not venture a diagnosis or prognosis of the condition. Emphasize instead that the individual does have a serious problem that is worthy of the physician's attention, but that it does not appear to be dangerous or critical. This type of response can be most reassuring to the patient, and is likely to be experienced as a confirmation of being "heard." Most hypochondriacal patients do not necessarily seek a cure but, rather, seek understanding. They are not likely to be overly anxious about the absence of a definitive diagnosis.

2. Attend to, and treat, the patient's *symptoms* or complaints; do not try to "cure" the "illness." The patient's complaints should be listened to with attentiveness and inquired about with concern. Practical interventions should be offered to ease individual symptoms, without any promise of marked success or total cure. This should demonstrate to the patient that the doctor takes the problem seriously and is interested in actively helping. At the same time, the belief in an imaginary illness is not encouraged or reinforced through attempts at curing or eliminating it.

3. The patient should be offered a stable therapeutic contract with a single primary physician. The patient should be instructed to return on a regular basis independent of symptom severity. Initially the visits should be rather frequent, and these may be tapered off over time as indicated. Visits should be relatively brief, perhaps 15 to 20 minutes initially, and the patient should be discouraged from any extended contact with the physician between visits. An attempt should be made to avoid shifting the patient from one physician to another, so as to permit a deepening rapport and reliability of treatment.

4. An attempt should be made to impart a decidedly medical flavor to the treatment arrangement. Visits should take place in a medical clinic

setting, even if the primary clinician is a mental health professional. Other medical trappings, such as white coats, may reassure the patient that medical attention is being received.

5. During sessions the patient should be allowed to focus attention on physical symptoms without undue pressure from the therapist to steer the conversation toward more emotionally significant issues. The therapist should inquire about the patient's living situation, relationships, and so on, in a casual way. Over time, as the patient develops trust in the therapist, there will occur a natural and gradual shift in the content of sessions from somatic to psychological issues.

While these principles outline the general strategy behind this approach, there are many additional procedures that can be employed effectively in the treatment of somatoform disorders. For example, behavioral treatment such as biofeedback or relaxation training may be effective in alleviating symptoms of tension, pain, and sleep disturbance. Hypnosis may be used in a variety of ways to achieve symptomatic relief, as can the judicious use of mild medications. The use of placebos is not recommended, however, as this runs the risk of destroying doctor–patient rapport if it is detected. In addition, psychopharmacological agents may be used to control associated symptoms of depression and/or anxiety (see Chapters 4 and 5).

The essential thrust of this therapeutic approach is that patients be convinced that their complaints are being taken seriously and that an attempt is being made to do whatever is possible to help them. When this approach is compared with the types of response the patient is likely to have received in the past from medical consultants ("There is nothing wrong with you . . . it's all in your head"), one can appreciate why such techniques are effective in reaching this difficult-to-treat group.

The physician treating a patient with somatoform disorder will generally have to answer as well to the patient's family, who may be quite involved with the patient's symptomatology. Here great tact is called for, as the physician must provide accurate and helpful information but must also avoid saying anything that might jeopardize his rapport with the patient. Usually this can be accomplished by telling the family that there is no evidence for any critical illness, but that the patient does seem to be experiencing substantial discomfort and distress about physical problems. Family members of older persons with hypochondriacal behavior are often confronted with significant emotional conflicts that call for professional intervention. The family's needs in this respect should be carefully assessed. The treatment principles involved are beyond the scope of the present chapter, but are discussed at length by Herr and Weakland.[23]

CASE HISTORY—SOMATOFORM DISORDER

Mrs. L. is a 74-year-old, white widow currently living alone in a high-rise building for the elderly. She was referred to the clinic by her family doctor for evaluation of financial problems, prolonged grief reaction, and memory difficulties. The referral was made shortly after a brief hospitalization for complaints of shortness of breath and chest pain. A thorough medical work-up could find no organic basis for these symptoms, although the patient was noted to be quite anxious and was found to hyperventilate when stressed.

Mrs. L. was brought to the clinic by her brother who had been looking after her. Both the patient and her brother agreed that Mrs. L.'s general condition has deteriorated in the past eight months, since the sudden death of her son, and that she is currently having great difficulty in carrying out everyday activities. Mrs. L. identified as her major concern a severe, involuntary muscle twitching or "jerking" that occurs primarily at night and seriously interferes with her rest. The jerking begins with a tingling sensation in the legs, leading to jumpiness in both legs, progressing into a sudden spasmodic straightening of the spine. This has the effect of thrusting back the shoulders and pushing forward the abdomen and pelvis. When observed in the clinic, these appeared as large, truncal myoclonic tics that occurred at the rate of one to two per minute. These tics rarely occurred in the daytime but would begin when the patient lay in bed at night. In addition to the jerking, the patient complained that she is weak and fatigued, and subject to episodes of shortness of breath accompanied by fear and confusion. She also stated that she is often upset about her recently deceased son. Mrs. L. recounted a long list of other physical ailments—including arthritis, diabetes, recent disc surgery, chest pain, and "hardening of the arteries"—but emphasized that she had never experienced anything that gave her more misery than the jerking.

A detailed inquiry into the patient's symptoms was conducted through interview and examination of past medical records. The history that emerged is as follows. Mrs. L. recalls that as a young child she had often experienced prickly sensations in her lower legs upon falling off to sleep, but added that these were transitory and never a problem. She does recall that the sensations returned, accompanied by lower leg spasms, during her one pregnancy at age 23. They then again largely subsided until a particularly stressful period five years ago when the patient was 67, at which time they reemerged with renewed intensity. On this occasion the patient had been summoned to a hospital where her only child was suffering from advanced alcoholism and was in a delirious condition, close to death. Mrs. L. recalled seeing him as he lay on the bed shaking, after which she was sent out to wait for further word from the doctors. As she maintained her vigil over the following days, Mrs.

L.'s legs began to twitch involuntarily. The twitching gradually intensified and spread to her abdomen and finally involved large truncal spasms. The son survived and Mrs. L. returned home, but the spasms remained with her. Mrs. L. sought treatment for these symptoms and was initially given anticonvulsant medications, without improvement. She was referred to a university teaching hospital for a thorough neurological evaluation, which turned up no evidence of a seizure disorder or other organic evidence to support her symptoms. The impression at that time was that the spasms were psychogenic, and a psychiatric referral was recommended. This was refused by the patient, and she was discharged with a prescription for Valium. Mrs. L. reports having been very angry at the implication that she was in need of psychiatric treatment. Without further treatment her symptoms subsided over time to a tolerable level but then reemerged in full intensity after the sudden death of her son eight months ago.

Mrs. L. became quite upset and tearful as she spoke of her son's death, and it soon became apparent that he had died under most unfortunate circumstances. For many years the patient had alternatively struggled with, or stood helplessly by, her son as he became increasingly incapacitated by alcoholism. For almost three years prior to his death, Mrs. L. had been living close to her son (who was married and a father) in order to provide what help and support she could. Finally, for reasons of her own failing health and increasing inability to cope with her son's drinking, Mrs. L. decided to move back home to be near her siblings. Her son opposed this, however, and pleaded with her not to go. Amid great conflict, Mrs. L. returned to her siblings, ostensibly for a visit but with plans to stay if possible. When she arrived, she was met with the news that her son had died of a heart attack while she was enroute. As she recounted these events during the interview, Mrs. L. described with great anguish how she had been plagued by her final visual image of her son sitting on his porch begging her pitifully, "Mama, please don't go, please don't leave me." These thoughts were especially vivid at night as she lay in bed, where they represented an ideational companion to the physical torment of the muscle spasms. It became apparent that there was an intimate connection between the jerking and an intense, unresolved grief reaction to the loss of her son. Further historical data helped to place the present conflicts within the larger framework of the patient's life.

Family and Social History

Mrs. L. was the oldest of six children who grew up on a farm where her father was a sharecropper. The family was very poor, but cohesive and loving. For financial reasons Mrs. L. was forced to begin working on the farm and later in a textile mill after completion of the fourth grade. She married for the first time at age 18, but left her husband after two years because of his drinking and running around with other women. At the time she left her husband, she was three months pregnant, and she moved back to her family where she raised her son while continuing to work in the textile mill. Mrs. L. married again at age 30 to a man who subsequently became disabled with emphysema exacerbated by alcoholism. Although they were dependent on her earnings, Mrs. L. recalls that she would go to work reluctantly when her husband was drinking, fearful that something would happen to him while she was gone. The anticipated tragedy finally did occur when she was 59. Her husband, on a binge, died in a fire at their home while Mrs. L. was at work. This unfortunate event left Mrs. L. with strong, irrational feelings of guilt: If only she had done more to help her husband stop drinking; if only she had taken better care of him to ensure he would not hurt himself. Perhaps it was this guilt that led her to become more involved with her son's increasing problems with alcoholism, for over the next 15 years, Mrs. L. devoted a great deal of time and energy to caring for her son and attempting to cure his alcohol abuse—always without success. In recalling these years, Mrs. L. described the intense frustration and anger she felt as she helplessly watched her son destroy himself, and she often found herself lashing out at him in anger only to be grief stricken and remorseful later. The increasing conflict between feelings of anger and compassion, hostility and nurturance, soon made it extremely difficult for Mrs. L. to be around her son, and she began to seek solace in religion. During one particular night of prayer, Mrs. L. reportedly came to the conviction that her problems would resolve if she eliminated her anger entirely. Mrs. L. states that this represented a turning point for her, as she has from that time on been able to eliminate both the awareness and expression of anger, not only toward her son but in other situations as well. It soon became apparent, however, that this approach would be no more successful than anything previous, and she sought to remove herself physically from the situation. It was at this point that the tragedy of her son's death occurred.

At present the patient's five siblings are all still living, but close contact is maintained only with two brothers who live in town. With one of these brothers there is a strained relationship, and Mrs. L. feels that he is "critical" and "bossy." There is a very warm relationship with the other brother, who is perceived as both emotionally supportive and helpful. This brother has his own health problems, however, and is further constrained by his wife's illness, which leaves her bedridden. At the present time Mrs. L. has virtually no social contact outside of her occasional visits with her brother. Although still very religious, she has discontinued going to church and in fact ventures out from her apartment very rarely.

Medical History

Mrs. L. has received most of her medical care in a single hospital and clinical facility; thus there is a fairly complete record of medical care over time. The medical chart records no less than eight minor operations from age 38 to 50, plus a disc operation two years ago. There is a record of an evaluation in the neurology clinic for muscular twitching. An EEG at this time was normal, and the patient was referred for psychiatric treatment, which was declined.

Recently the patient had been hospitalized for five days at the county hospital, where her discharge diagnoses included hyperventilation syndrome, anxiety, anemia, adult-onset diabetes, chest pain, and possible angina pectoris. Since discharge, she has been followed at a family health clinic where she has presented multiple symptoms prompting the present referral. Current medications include Darvocet and Valium. At several points in the patient's medical chart, there are notations indicating a tendency for the patient to overmedicate herself by increasing doses of prescribed medications. There is no history of alcohol use.

Mental Status

Mrs. L. is a large-boned, somewhat obese woman, plainly dressed, who walks slowly and with some unsteadiness. Mrs. L. was quite anxious at first and asked that her brother accompany her into the consulting room. She was observed to hyperventilate periodically throughout the interview, but became noticeably more relaxed with time and began to speak freely about her problems and concerns. Mrs. L. was basically oriented to time, person, and place but did become confused and showed some memory impairment at several points. There was considerable unilateral hearing loss, which made conversation difficult at times. Mood was predominantly anxious and sad, with much emphasis on somatic problems and worries. There were no indications of delusions, hallucinations, or other evidence of thought disorder. Although quite limited in educational background, Mrs. L. showed good common sense and a capacity to grasp abstract concepts. She was observed to develop quickly a strong, positive transference toward the interviewer and freely expressed feelings of relief at being understood.

Functional Assessment

Mrs. L. completed the MFAQ with the help of her brother as informant. On the social resources scale she was rated moderately impaired, reflecting the very limited nature of her current social relationships and the availability of only short-term care from her brother. However, it was apparent that her current living situation is conducive to the development of an expanded social network, and improvement in this area was predicted. On the economic resources scale, she was also rated as moderately impaired, as there are no current financial reserves and a monthly income that just barely covers the basic necessities of life. Mrs. L. was rated as moderately impaired on the mental health rating scale, as her psychiatric symptoms are quite obvious and interfere considerably with her ability to handle major life problems. Physical health is mildly impaired. Although there are a large number of physical problems at present, none of these is sufficiently serious to require immediate treatment. Finally, a rating of mildly impaired is given to the patient's current capacity for the activities of daily living. Mrs. L. is capable of living independently at present, but requires help in handling her financial matters. In addition, she needs assistance in carrying out heavy housework.

Assessment and Discussion

The clinical impression presented by this patient was of multiple neurotic manifestations, including anxiety, depression, conversion reaction, and obsessional tendencies, that appear to have been acutely exacerbated by the trauma of losing her son some eight months previously. Of these various manifestations, the one with the longest history—and incidently the one most disturbing to the patient—is the truncal myoclonus, which presents clear evidence of being a conversion symptom. It is apparent that the patient has been unable to grieve the death of her son normally insofar as she is troubled by unrecognized ambivalence toward him, accompanied by substantial guilt.

Diagnostically the impression was of a conversion disorder in an individual with a long-standing tendency to somatize. This disorder is accompanied by a significant amount of distress including depressive, anxiety, and obsessional components. There is also evidence of a mild degree of dementia, most likely exacerbated by the patient's current emotional condition.

Team discussion of this fascinating patient was lively and multifaceted. There was much speculation regarding the symbolic significance of the patient's conversion symptoms and its progressive development over time. The phenomenon of nocturnal "jumpy legs" is frequently encountered in elderly patients, and there was some question of whether this might not form the basis for the patient's present symptoms. The geropsychiatrist also questioned whether there may not be a connection between the patient's hyperventilation and her myoclonus. In response, it was pointed out that the hyperventilation occurred primarily during the day, where it was unaccompanied by myoclonus.

Treatment

In formulating a treatment plan for this patient, several factors were of particular importance. First, it was clear that the patient identified as her chief concern the nightly myoclonic episodes, which caused extreme distress and loss of sleep. This symptom thus had much validity as an immediate focus of intervention for both the patient and the clinician. Second, it was apparent that the patient regarded psychological intervention with much ambivalence. In the past, psychiatric consultation had been rejected with much anger by the patient, and it was only out of desperation and additional pressure from family members and physician that the present referral was accepted. For this reason, it was felt necessary to move slowly in approaching treatment issues involving strong emotional content.

From these considerations the following treatment plan emerged. The immediate focus of therapy would be on relief of the jerking symptom, utilizing a direct behavioral approach that would be concrete and would involve the patient in an active way. The advantages of such an approach include the following: (1) It would establish the *relevance* of therapy through dealing with a problem that the patient immediately recognized as important; (2) it would focus therapy on an achievable, realistic goal whose progressive accomplishment could be monitored by the patient; and (3) it would provide a somatic focus less likely to arouse the patient's anxiety and/or resistance. In setting up an immediate therapy goal that is both important to the patient and likely to be accomplished, the therapist is able to consolidate rapport with the patient and at the same time provide an experience of increased self-efficacy for the patient. Such developments in the therapeutic relationship would hopefully provide a valuable foundation for gradually approaching more sensitive areas of personal conflict. It was thus hoped that the patient's unresolved grief over her son might eventually become the focus of therapy.

With minimal delay a treatment plan was proposed to the patient involving weekly meetings for the purposes of alleviating the jerking. The patient's symptoms were first "explained" to her in simple terms she could understand. She was told that the jerking was a *habit* her body had learned, a habit that seemed to occur most when she was upset. It was explained further that the worst part of this habit was that it happened when she did not want it to happen; that it was outside of her control. The therapist then introduced the "negative practice" intervention commonly used to control tics.[24] This involves the patient in deliberately producing and "practicing" the tic for periods of time each day. The patient was told that this was to teach her body how to produce the tic *voluntarily*, and that once this was accomplished, her habit would be hers either to express or inhibit as she wished.

To enhance the prescriptive nature of this intervention further, Mrs. L. was given a sheet of paper with a week's calendar on it. She was instructed to practice her jerking each night before retiring and then write down the number of repetitions performed (five repetitions were prescribed) each night. Upon arising, the patient was also to record the extent to which her symptom was troublesome during the night, and she was to bring the completed calendar with her to the next week's session.

Over the next two weeks the patient carried out her prescription faithfully on all but one night, and was entirely symptom free on 6 of the 14 nights. At this point the patient felt encouraged and elected to discontinue her Valium. By the sixth session Mrs. L. was no longer experiencing truncal tics at all, and the negative practice procedure was discontinued. Her leg twitching continued, however, and Valium was reinstituted (5 mg. at bedtime), which brought this under effective control.

As Mrs. L.'s primary symptoms improved, her mood lifted noticeably, and she began to speak spontaneously about a number of personal concerns, including her rumination over her son's death and the strained relations that existed with one of her brothers. It became clear that the therapist had successfully gained Mrs. L.'s trust, enabling her to approach previously overwhelming feelings and share them openly. The therapist responded by encouraging Mrs. L. to grieve openly. At the same time, he adopted the role of a "good son"—one who is understanding, forgiving, and appreciative. Over the course of several sessions, the "grief work" reached its completion, and the topic of the son's death faded from the therapeutic spotlight. Mrs. L. reported being free from obsessional thoughts about her son and in all respects seemed better able to cope with daily life.

Supportive therapy focusing on a variety of real-life issues continued for several months, and the patient was observed to become more relaxed and confident. She began to engage more in the social activities of her housing unit. Frequency of sessions was decreased to biweekly, and then monthly. A request to terminate treatment was initiated by the patient, and treatment ended five months after the initial contact.

NOTES

1. American Psychiatric Association, *Diagnostic and Statistical Manual of Mental Disorders, 3rd ed.* (Washington, D.C.: APA, 1980).

2. D.G. Blazer and J. Houpt, "Perception of Poor Health in the Healthy Older Adult," *Journal of the American Geriatrics Society* 27 (1979): 330-334.

3. G.L. Maddox and E.D. Douglas, "Self-assessment of Health: A Longitudinal Study of Elderly Subjects," *Journal of Health and Social Behavior* 14 (1973): 87.

4. E. Busse, R. Dovenmuehle, and R.G. Brown, "Psychoneurotic Reactions and Defense Mechanisms of the Aged," in *Normal Aging*, ed. E. Palmore (Durham, N.C.: Duke University Press, 1970) pp. 84-90.

5. N. Krietman et al., "Hypochondriasis and Depression in Outpatients at a General Hospital," *British Journal of Psychiatry* 111 (1965): 607-615.

6. T.J. Jacobs, S. Fogelson, and E. Charles, "Depression Ratings in Hypochondria," *New York State Journal of Medicine*, December 15, 1968, pp. 3119-3122.

7. D.W.K. Kay and K. Bergmann, "Physical Disability and Mental Health in Old Age," *Journal of Psychosomatic Research* 10 (1966): 3-12.

8. F.E. Kenyon, "Hypochondriacal States," *British Journal of Psychiatry* 129 (1976): 1-14.

9. E.W. Busse and D.G. Blazer, "Disorders Related to Biologic Functioning," in *Handbook of Geriatric Psychiatry*, eds. E.W. Busse and D.G. Blazer (New York: Van Nostrand Reinhold, 1980), pp. 390-414.

10. A. Verwoerdt, *Clinical Geropsychiatry*, 2nd ed. (Baltimore: Williams & Wilkins, 1981), pp. 142-155.

11. Ibid.

12. Ibid.

13. Ibid.

14. D. Mechanic, "Social Factors Affecting the Presentation of Bodily Complaints," *New England Journal of Medicine* 286 (1972): 1132-1139.

15. E.W. Busse and D.G. Blazer, "Disorders Related to Biologic Functioning."

16. N. Krietman et al., "Hypochondriasis and Depression in Outpatients," pp. 607-615.

17. Jacobs, Fogelson, and Charles, "Depression Ratings in Hypochondria," pp. 3119-3122.

18. APA, *Diagnostic and Statistical Manual*, pp. 241-252.

19. Ibid., p. 251.

20. Busse and Blazer, "Disorders Related to Biologic Functioning."

21. E.W. Busse, "The Treatment of Hypochondriasis," *Tri-State Medical Journal* 2 (1954): 7.

22. Busse and Blazer, "Disorders Related to Biologic Functioning."

23. J.J. Herr and J.H. Weakland, *Counseling Elders and Their Families* (New York: Springer, 1979).

24. F.J. Nicassio et al., "The Treatment of Tics by Negative Practice," *Journal of Behavioral Therapy and Experimental Psychiatry* 3 (1972): 281-288.

Chapter 8

Adjustment Disorders

Alice C. Myers

Adjustment disorders are often more acceptable to the patient and understandable to the therapist than some of the other disorders. The adjustment disorders are related to stressful life events or circumstances. Everyone knows something about stress! Stress is a familiar and constant companion to many well-functioning persons. Stress has received a lot of bad press, but it is not always bad news. Most individuals learn to adjust to it, or are motivated to change to a different and sometimes better way of doing things when exposed to varying amounts of stress. Stress can lead to new and more positive and healthy adaptations. Cumulative stress or stressful events in a person's life may result in a maladaptive reaction, however, such as impairment in occupational or social functioning. A maladaptive reaction to stress is the essential feature of an adjustment disorder. Symptoms such as anxiety, withdrawal, or dependence in excess of what would be a normal and expected reaction to a stressful life event are also indicators of an adjustment disorder.

The *Diagnostic and Statistical Manual of Mental Disorders (DSM-III)*, compiled by the American Psychiatric Association in 1980, does not classify the adjustment disorders according to the patient's developmental stage, as had been done previously. However, it is acknowledged that some stressful life events are associated with specific developmental stages and that the developmental stage of the person may influence the severity of the stress and the severity of the reaction.

The developmental stage of late life brings many stressful life events for the average older person in a relatively brief time. The cumulative effects of these events, combined with the older person's reduced ability to cope with stress, account for the common prevalence of adjustment disorders among the elderly.

In this chapter we continue to consider the adjustment disorders as presented in *DSM-III*, but with special attention to the significance of these disorders for the older population.

NOSOLOGY

The description of adjustment disorders in *DSM-III* clearly relates this disorder to psychosocial influences.

The essential feature is a maladaptive reaction to an identifiable psychosocial stressor, that occurs within three months after the onset of the stressor. The maladaptive nature of the reaction is indicated by either impairment in social or occupational functioning or symptoms that are in excess of a normal and expected reaction to the stressor.[1]

Stressful life event(s) or circumstance(s) may become "stressors." These stressors may be single, multiple, recurrent, or continuous. Retirement is an example of a single stressor that can produce a maladaptive reaction. More often the stressors are multiple and continuous for older persons, such as chronic illness and unsatisfactory living arrangements. The stressor may affect only the patient—for example, death of a spouse—or may affect many people—for example, a natural disaster.

A specific stressor may be mild to severe, depending on its duration and timing within the context of a person's life. However, the severity of the reaction may not be directly related to the severity of the stressor. A mild or moderate stressor may produce a rather severe adjustment disorder for individuals who are particularly vulnerable, whereas others may respond to more severe stressors with only a mild form of the disorder. Individual personality, past coping patterns, cultural or group norms, current self-esteem, and current support system are all factors that influence the severity of the reaction to single or multiple stressors.

The emotional, physical, and behavioral symptoms are varied. These are discussed in relation to specific diagnostic classifications. The *DSM-III* indicates that an adjustment disorder may begin at any age and by definition begins within three months of the onset of the stressor. The disorder will remit when the stressor ceases or when a new level of adaptation is achieved. The remission may be sudden or gradual, immediate or delayed.[2] For older persons, the remission is more often gradual and more often a result of a new level of adaptation, because many of the stressors in late life do persist.

TYPES OF ADJUSTMENT DISORDERS

Adjustment Disorders with Depressed Mood

The predominant symptoms are depressed mood, tearfulness, and hopelessness. This category should be used after ruling out major depression and uncomplicated bereavement. Depression is discussed in the chapter on affective disorders. *Uncomplicated bereavement* is a term used to refer to a normal reaction to the death of a loved one.[3] An adjustment disorder with depressed mood is illustrated in a detailed case study at the end of this chapter.

Adjustment Disorder with Anxious Mood

Nervousness, worry, and jitteriness are the predominant symptoms. This category should be used when individuals cannot be diagnosed as having an anxiety disorder. The diagnosis of adjustment disorder with anxious mood may be considered for a 62-year-old widow who reports having "a case of the worries" and being "jumpy" often. The symptoms began to occur one month after her divorced son returned home to live.

Adjustment Disorder with Mixed Emotional Features

Various combinations of depression and anxiety or other emotions would indicate that this category should be considered when the disturbance does not meet the criteria for affective and anxiety disorders. A 69-year-old married male has episodes of tearing and feelings of apprehension following his wife's heart attack and subsequent reduced activities.

Adjustment Disorder with Disturbance of Conduct

This category should be considered when the disturbance involves conduct in which there is a violation of the rights of others or of major age-appropriate societal norms and rules. The specific disorders that must be ruled out are conduct disorder and antisocial personality disorder. This category may be considered for a 72-year-old widower who begins to "drop in" to visit his son late at night and entertains anyone who will listen with sex jokes. This behavior started several weeks after a woman he had been dating for a year decided to move near her sister in another state.

Adjustment Disorder with Mixed Disturbance of Emotions and Conduct

When both emotional features and a disturbance of conduct are present, this diagnosis should be considered if the symptoms have occurred within three months after the onset of the stressor(s). Again the therapist will need to rule out disorders with similar symptoms.

Adjustment Disorder with Work (or Academic) Inhibition

This category should be considered when an inhibition in work or academic functioning occurs in an individual whose previous performance has been adequate. Anxiety and depression may also be present. The specific disorders to be ruled out are again the affective and anxiety disorders. The *DSM-III* does not suggest a specific category for older adults who may have similar dysfunctions but are not involved in the work or academic world. The older person's work may be his or her volunteer job, hobbies, or the general maintenance of home and self. This diagnosis may be considered for a 68-year-old woman who has been unable to complete her usual volunteer task of hostess and traffic director of visitors at a local hospital. She reports that she does not feel like being pleasant or patient with the visitors since her husband's minor car accident last month.

Adjustment Disorder with Withdrawal

This category should be considered when social withdrawal occurs and when a significant depressed or anxious mood is absent. The diagnosis may be considered for a 70-year-old widow who has refused to visit her daughters' homes, go to church, or call friends on the phone following a series of losses. The most apparent losses included the death of a close friend, termination of a regular babysitting job because of the child starting school, and reduced income.

Adjustment Disorders with Atypical Features

It is suggested that this category be used when the disturbance involves symptoms that cannot be coded in any of the specific categories, but the disturbance still meets the diagnostic criteria outlined for adjustment disorders.

TREATMENT APPROACHES

The importance of differential diagnosis is readily acknowledged as treatment approaches are considered. An individual receiving the diagnosis of adjustment disorder with anxious mood should have a different treatment plan from one receiving a diagnosis of anxiety disorder. For example, pharmacotherapy is most often begun immediately for someone with an anxiety disorder but is limited, if used at all, for those with adjustment disorders. For them, treatment approaches include psychotherapy, environmental manipulation, and limited pharmocotherapy. Specific treatment plans should be formulated after a careful evaluation of the patient's current level of functioning, his or her level of functioning prior to the disturbance, ego strengths, and general resources.

The goal of the treatment plan is most often to help the older person obtain a new level of adaptation and to return to the level of functioning prior to the disturbance. If the therapist chooses to set goals of a higher level of functioning or a more healthy life style than previously enjoyed for the patient with an adjustment disorder, it must be acknowledged that the therapist is seeking to treat an additional disorder. This may be intrapersonal conflict or another condition not attributable to a mental disorder. The additional goals may be appropriate and attainable, but need to be considered with care. Adjustment disorders in late life must be treated cautiously, because the choices of adjustment become fewer and the range of adjustment more narrow for the older person. Treatment should focus on bolstering adaptive strengths.[4]

Psychotherapy

Psychotherapy is one of the first choices of treatment for adjustment disorders. Verwoerdt suggests that the therapy should focus on the patient's reactions to the precipitating event or on resolving the environmental stress.[5] Patients need to verbalize their feelings about what has happened, gain perspective about possibilities, and be encouraged to use personal and other resources to enable them to make the best adjustment possible.

Environmental Manipulation

Environmental manipulation may be a very appropriate part of the treatment plan. Whenever possible, the patient should participate in finding ways of resolving or diminishing the environmental stress. Choosing to relocate to a less stressful living arrangement or accepting personal care or health services in the home are examples of environmental manipulation when the psychosocial stressor is a chronic illness. Consultation and intervention with family members are especially appropriate when intrafamilial relationships are in difficulty.

Medication

Medication may be considered as part of the total treatment plan but should be limited. The need to verbalize one's feelings may be masked by medication.[6] Also, just enough relief may be provided by reliance on drugs to keep the patient from seeking a decisive solution.[7]

The assessment and treatment of adjustment disorders are discussed further in the following case examples.

CASE STUDY 1—ADJUSTMENT DISORDER

Mrs. W. is a 66-year-old widow. She presently resides in a duplex on the edge of town. During her first interview she reported that she simply does not have an interest in anything. She does not finish projects she starts, such as sewing, cooking a meal, or writing a letter. She also reports a feeling of uselessness.

She states that she has "felt low" since her retirement earlier in the year. Approximately two months after her retirement, her only daughter and son-in-law came to visit and found Mrs. W. unable to function in her usual manner. During her daughter's visit she agreed to schedule a medical appointment and consider counseling to help her decide about future living arrangements.

Mental Status

Mrs. W. was a pleasant and cooperative woman. She was appropriately dressed, but appeared to have given little attention to her appearance. She is an obese person and displays considerable difficulty in rising from a sitting position. She used words such as "listless," "low," and "useless" to describe herself. She spoke of a "loss of purpose" in her life since her retirement. There were no indications of memory impairment.

Medical History

Mrs. W. listed arthritis as her most serious medical problem. This has become progressively worse in the past 10 years. She has had one orthopedic evaluation, with the recommendation that she lose weight. Surgery for gall bladder was performed eight years ago.

Psychiatric History

The patient does report a "difficult time" following the death of her husband, but states she did not feel the "loss of purpose" that she does now. She has not felt the need of counseling or psychiatric treatment during what she considers the normal "ups" and "downs" of her life.

Personal History

Mrs. W. is the youngest of four children. An older sister and brother died three and four years ago. Her remaining sister lives out of state. They phone and write each other often. She remembers her parents as loving and good-natured. They operated a small grocery store for most of their lives. Mrs. W. worked as a secretary until her marriage at age 23. She describes a fairly happy marriage and states she continues to miss her husband. Her work as sales manager in a department store became even more important to her after her husband's death. Her daughter was born in the second year of her marriage. She described herself as wife and mother until her daughter started to school, when she started to work for the department store where she was employed until her recent retirement.

Social and Family Relationships

Mrs. W. has not been active in church and civic groups. Social activities revolved around friends she made at work and through her husband. Mrs. W. spoke of being friendly with many people but of having made few close friends over the years. There are three women she continues to call and occasionally has a meal with one of them. Important family members include her daughter and sister, both of whom live out of state. The daughter visits once a year and writes often. Letters and phone calls keep her in close contact with her sister.

Physical Examination

The following information is from our physician's notes on her first visit to the clinic: "On physical examination, Mrs. W. is a pleasant, 66-year-old white female, moderately obese, who is alert and cooperative. Recumbent blood pressure is 140/90; sitting 130/88. Eye examination is unremarkable except for early atherosclerotic changes noted on the funduscopic examination. The chest is clear to examination; heart examination revealed no murmurs, rubs, or gallops. The abdomen is obese and soft, and there is slight lower quadrant tenderness (patient has diverticulosis). There is no guarding or rebound.

Impressions: (1) obesity; (2) osteoarthritis, right hip; (3) mild systemic hypertension (she has a history of a borderline problem with high blood pressure and is currently using a diuretic daily); and (4) history of diverticulosis. *Recommendation:* Calorie-burning athletic endeavor that would not involve use of her hip (swimming)."

Functional Status

Social resources for Mrs. W. were rated as moderately impaired. She does not have satisfactory social relationships, and only short-term help is available from her daughter. Economically she is mildly impaired. She must live on a reduced income since her retirement. She does not own a home but has some savings. On the mental health rating scale, she was rated as mildly impaired. She is having difficulty making routine decisions and completing tasks. Several of her comments indicated a depressed mood. Mrs. W. was rated as moderately impaired physically because of her arthritis, obesity, diverticulosis, and borderline hypertension. She was rated as having a good capacity for activities of daily living because she is able to perform all these for herself.

Assessment and Discussion

The evaluating clinician summarized her assessment as follows: Mrs. W. is a pleasant, obese widow who has felt listless and without purpose since her retirement of four months. Her present lack of interest in life and inability to complete her usual tasks seems directly related to her loss of work role. She also depended on work relationships for socialization.

The diagnosis of adjustment disorder with depressed mood is suggested. The initial treatment plan includes individual therapy and immediate involvement in a "purposeful" activity, such as a volunteer job of her choice. The individual therapy will focus on her reactions to retirement and her need to find meaning for her life now.

During the case conference following the presentation, other clinicians posed questions and offered suggestions. The nurse commented that it would be helpful to have more information about the onset of diverticulosis. The psychologist suggested that additional information about the patient's marriage and her relationship to daughter and sister should be obtained. The family medicine resident asked if the evaluating clinician had explored the patient's interest in diet counseling and specific weight reduction activities. The psychiatrist confirmed the diagnosis of adjustment disorder with depressed mood and responded to a student's question concerning the possible diagnosis of depression. The patient does indicate a depressed mood rather than a clinical depression, and it does seem directly related to her recent retirement. Certainly long-standing personality traits may be explored further if this seems appropriate and if the patient is willing to work on relationship issues. Part-time employment was suggested to be considered as well as volunteer opportunities.

Therapeutic Intervention

The social worker who was the evaluating clinician continued to see Mrs. W. weekly for three months. During individual therapy sessions, Mrs. W. used the time well to verbalize her feelings of loss related to retirement. She was able to reclaim her self-esteem and interest in life as she found success in several volunteer jobs and became friends with other volunteers. She also used her time in therapy to look at her past and present relationships with her daughter and sister. She then visited both on separate occasions and enjoyed the time with each. In the third month of therapy, she joined Weight Watchers and began to express her satisfaction with a more relaxed schedule and to appreciate the positive benefits of retirement. Both she and her therapist agreed on a date of termination for therapy with the understanding that she could return if symptoms recurred.

CASE STUDY 2—ADJUSTMENT DISORDER

Mr. B., a 69-year-old widower, lives in an apartment complex for senior citizens. He was referred to our clinic by his nephew, who became concerned about Mr. B. during a recent visit. The nephew lives two hours from the patient and visits for two to three hours once a month. Mr. B has been a good letter writer over the years, and the nephew usually receives one or two letters between visits. No letters arrived between the nephew's last two visits. When the nephew called Mr. B. prior to the most recent visit, he was told, "I'm fine, I just haven't gotten around to writing." During the visit, Mr. B. did not respond with his usual interest to his nephew and refused to go out for a meal or walk down the street. The kitchen had only basic food—the usual snack food and special items were missing. Before leaving town, the nephew made a few phone calls to friends, including the pastor of Mr. B.'s church. The phone calls did not reassure him. Friends and pastor reported a withdrawal pattern over the last two to four months. The patient has refused all invitations from friends and has attended only one church service.

Mental Status

Mr. B. is slim, well dressed, and neatly groomed. He walks without the assistance of a cane and does not have apparent hearing, sight, or speech problems. He was polite but gave either guarded or apathetic answers to questions during his initial interview. He did not volunteer any information. There were no problems with his recent or remote memory. He did not indicate any delusions, hallucinations, or paranoid thinking. He denied thoughts of harming himself or others. When questioned about his recent behavior, he stated that he didn't want to be around people right now.

Medical History

The patient has been in good health over his 69 years—no hospitalizations for surgery or illnesses. His family physician of many years retired three years ago, and Mr. B. has had only one clinic appointment during that time. Two years ago he was suffering some low-grade back pain. He was told to lose 10 pounds and to do some simple exercises. He did lose the pounds and has been faithful about the exercises until the last few months. He has not had any back pain for the last 18 months.

Psychiatric History

Mr. B. does not report any previous psychiatric problems. He enjoys an occasional beer or glass of wine but has never abused alcohol. He states that the year following his wife's death was a very sad time for him. At that time he did not want to be alone much and spent a lot of time with his sister, nephew, and friends.

Personal History

The patient is the oldest of two children. He grew up on a farm and did his share of farm work from an early age. He recalls those years as "good years" and reports a close relationship with his father. He finished high school and started share farming with his father. He owned his own farm at age 23 and married a year later. His wife was from the same area and also grew up on a farm. Together they managed to save enough to purchase a small feed store and move into town. Mr. B decided to continue his education by enrolling in some accounting courses. He later "kept books" for several small businesses.

He states he was a "happily married man." Both he and his wife regretted the lack of children. He did not know why but supposed it was "God's will."

His sister's only son was "like our own" and often stayed overnight and for several weeks during the summers.

The church, family, friends, and acquaintances he made through his business have been important to Mr. B. Following his retirement two years earlier, he began to do more yard work and to go fishing and hunting with his buddy Frank. Four months ago Frank had a stroke and is now in a nursing home. His speech is not clear, and it is difficult for Mr. B. to understand him.

Functional Status

The results of the OARS questionnaire were as follows:

Social Resources—a rating of 4, moderately socially impaired. Due to his recent withdrawal, his social relationships are of poor quality, and only short-term care would be available in the event of illness.

Economic Resources—a rating of 2, economic resources are satisfactory. His present income is adequate to his expenses; he owns his own home and has an undisclosed amount of savings.

Mental Health—a rating of 3, mildly impaired. He has not been able to handle the major problem of his friend's stroke and his own reaction to his friend's present condition.

Physical Health—a rating of 2, in good physical health. There are no significant illnesses or disabilities.

Activities of Daily Living—a rating of 2, good ADL capacity. He can perform all the activities of daily living without assistance.

Assessment and Discussion

Mr. B. presented as a polite but withdrawn, thin, well-groomed widower of 69. He has performed well as a son, husband, worker, uncle, and friend during his lifetime. His wife's death was sad for him, but he managed to cope with his loneliness and respond to his friends and family. However, his close friend's recent stroke and subsequent disability have been a real blow. His withdrawal from other friends and activities seems directly related to this loss.

The diagnosis of adjustment disorder with withdrawal seems appropriate. Group psychotherapy is suggested by the evaluating clinician. Individual sessions will be offered if Mr. B. is reluctant to enter a group. During treatment Mr. B. will be encouraged to talk about and grieve for the loss of his friend and the person he knew. It is hoped that through the support of therapist and group members, Mr. B. will begin to accept his loss and draw on his personal resources to develop two or more buddies to replace Frank as a fishing and hunting partner. He will be encouraged eventually to relate to Frank on whatever level possible.

During the case conference it was suggested by other team members that Mr. B. be encouraged to choose another family physician and obtain a current physical. It was also noted that the patient may not be responsive to treatment suggestions and that some environmental manipulation may be helpful. A visit to the nephew's home, more aggressive approaches for church involvement, and persistent calls and visits by friends were suggested.

Intervention and Follow-up

Mr. B. refused group therapy, but did come for three individual sessions. He was able to talk more about his feelings concerning his friend Frank and his own aging. His pastor appointed him to a small church committee to explore activity interests of retired members in the church. Mr. B. reluctantly accepted this appointment and was soon a very enthusiastic member. He found another fishing buddy on the committee. He has attempted several visits with his friend. At last report from patient and nephew, he has regained his past high level of functioning and involvement with friends and family.

NOTES

1. *The Diagnostic and Statistical Manual for Mental Disorders*, 3rd ed. (Washington, D.C.: American Psychiatric Association, 1980) p. 299.

2. Charles M. Gaitz and Roy V. Varner, "Adjustment Disorders of Late Life: Stress Disorders," in *Handbook of Geriatric Psychiatry*, eds. E.W. Busse and D.G. Blazer (New York: Van Nostrand Reinhold, 1980) p. 382.

3. *Diagnostic and Statistical Manual*, p. 333.

4. Gaitz and Varner, "Adjustment Disorders," p. 388.

5. A. Verwoerdt, *Clinical Geropsychiatry*, 2nd ed. (Baltimore: Williams & Wilkins, 1981), p. 200.

6. Gaitz and Varner, "Adjustment Disorders," p. 388.

7. Verwoerdt, *Clinical Geropsychiatry*, p. 200.

Chapter 9

Substance Use Disorders

Alan D. Whanger

INTRODUCTION

To many, the stereotype of a person involved in drug abuse is an unkempt and often antisocial young person using a variety of rather exotic substances to achieve some sort of dreamy fantasy state or a "high." It is well that *DSM-III* has changed the terminology to *substance use disorders* to help us broaden our concepts of who uses what for what purpose and with what results, so that we can better understand the nature and extent of this problem in the elderly.[1] Certainly the scope of substance abuse in the elderly has been both underreported and underappreciated. Perhaps some of this stems from the idea that drug abuse primarily involves illegal drugs; also, earlier statistics dealt mainly with narcotics. The relative paucity of known addicts over age 40 was explained in 1962 by Winick, who—after studying the active addict list of the Federal Bureau of Narcotics—noted the disappearance of many addicts between ages 35 and 45.[2] He postulated that addiction was closely related to the teens and twenties, when individuals were struggling with developmental issues of the life cycle, such as aggressiveness, sexuality, and career choices, which predisposed many to drug abuse. He felt that by the late thirties, most of these people would "mature out" by reaching a state of emotional homeostasis and thus would grow to rely less on drugs as a means of coping. This concept was altered by later studies such as that by O'Donnell, who in 1969 did a follow-up study of 266 former patients of the narcotics treatment program of the Lexington Hospital.[3] This study showed that 144 of the former patients had died; 21 were still addicted to narcotics, and a substantial number of the others were addicted to different drugs. Of those addicted, however, only 1 was still on the active addict list kept by the Federal Bureau of Narcotics. The rest were not listed; for some, there was a lack of definite proof of addiction; others had become "medical addicts," being nurtured on legally issued supplies; and some simply were unknown to the bureau.

Another illustrative study of an older addict group was conducted by Capel and Stewart in New Orleans, where a group of 38 narcotics addicts between the ages of 48 and 73 were found who were not involved in any treatment program.[4] They discovered that many of the older addicts do not outgrow their habit; rather, they hide it from official attention by such measures as switching to cheaper narcotics, decreasing their daily doses, or substituting other drugs. These and other studies suggest that there are significant numbers of older typical addicts who often manage to keep their habits hidden.

Most of the substance use disorders of the elderly do not involve illegal drugs, however. The major problems occur in the abuse of so-called recreational and legal drugs or with the misuse of medicinal drugs, prescribed either by the physician or the patient. While the elderly (i.e., those over age 65) of the United States make up only about 11 percent of the population, they receive more than 25 percent of all prescriptions; and over 75 percent of all the elderly regularly use some kind of medication, of which at least a third are obtained over the counter.[5] In a cynical mood long ago, Voltaire said, "A physician is a person who pours drugs of which he knows little into a body of which he knows less."[6] Fortunately, both medicine and practice have improved greatly since then, but as Maddox points out, a major problem still exists in the abuse of older persons by health professionals who prescribe drugs frequently without adequate information, knowledge, or surveillance.[7] The subject of geriatric medicine and physiology is just beginning to be studied and taught seriously.

References to drug use and abuse in the elderly are rather sparse, and they are difficult to summarize or even correlate because of differences in the patient populations and in the definitions and terms used, and because of the fact that many new drugs are only recently available. Some studies lump together those subjects "over age 50" or do not look at those over age 75, and these often tend to ignore or overlook important age-related changes. It is easy to forget that just 30 years ago hardly anybody knew what a tranquilizer was. Yet, as Maddox says: "We live in a society which desperately wants to believe that better living can be achieved through chemistry. Informed individuals are now less confident than they once were that their faith is well placed, but the will to believe is still there."[8] In this chapter we hope to deal with some of these problems and issues in such a way as to help practitioners understand the complexities of drug treatment, use, and abuse in the older people with whom they work, with the goals of both *primum non nocere* (first do no harm) and, indeed, to make life more healthful and gratifying.

NOSOLOGY

Introduction

It is noted in *DSM-III* that the use of substances such as alcohol or caffeine or medically prescribed drugs to modify mood or behavior is generally regarded as normal and appropriate.[9] In distinction are those conditions that are generally viewed as extremely undesirable and are considered mental illnesses, and in which behavioral changes are brought about by the more or less regular use of substances affecting the central nervous system. These disorders are distinguished from the substance-induced organic mental disorders that describe the direct acute or chronic effects on the central nervous system, such as intoxication or withdrawal; and the reader is referred to the chapter on organic mental disorders for further details. Generally, pathologic use is divided into substance abuse and substance dependence.

Substance Abuse

To distinguish substance abuse from nonpathologic use, three criteria are used. First is a pathologic pattern of use, which may involve daily intoxication, including an inability to cut down or stop use even when it may aggravate a serious physical problem; regular use of the substance for adequate functioning; or episodes of complications such as blackouts or overdose. Second is impairment in social or occupational functioning because of the substance use, so that the individual experiences difficulty in meeting obligations to family or friends; this impairment may include such things as displays of aggressive or impulsive behavior, legal difficulties because of accidents or criminal behavior, or inability to function adequately in the everyday affairs of life. Third is duration, with the requirement that the disturbance last at least one month, although signs of the problem may not be continuously present.

Substance Dependence

Substance dependence is more serious than substance abuse, because it involves physiological dependence manifested either by tolerance or withdrawal. Tolerance refers to either the increasing amounts of the substance needed to reach the desired effect or the marked loss of effect with the usual dose. Withdrawal is the substance-specific syndrome that occurs after reduction or cessation of the usual intake. The *DSM-III* does require additional evidence of social impairment or pathologic substance use to support a diagnosis of substance dependence in the cases of alcohol and cannabis (marijuana).

Classes of Substances

In *DSM-III*, there are five classes of substances that can be involved in both abuse and dependence. These major classes include alcohol, barbiturates or similarly acting sedatives or hypnotics, opioids, amphetamines or similarly acting sympathomimetics, and cannabis. Three groups of substances are connected only with abuse, since clearly defined dependence has not been demonstrated. These are cocaine, phencyclidine (PCP) or similarly acting compounds, and hallucinogens. Tobacco is included, but it is associated only with dependence. Caffeine may be associated with toxicity. It is recognized that an individual frequently uses several substances simultaneously or in rapid sequence; the listing of each specific substance is encouraged where possible. There is, of course, a category of "other specified substance dependence" to include drugs that cannot be categorized elsewhere.

Classification of Course of Illness

There are general guidelines for subclassifying the course of the illness according to patterns of use. These are: continuous use, with regular maladaptive use for over six months; episodic use, with recurrent circumscribed bouts in the past; and remission, in which the person is not presently using the substance but is felt, because of circumstances, to require continuing evaluation and treatment.

Application to the Elderly

As indicated previously, our concepts of substance use disorders must be modified considerably to make them applicable to older persons. Certain classes of drugs are so rarely used by older persons that they need not be considered here. In their careful survey of elderly substance abusers, Peppers and Stover found that the use of hallucinogens, amphetamines, and inhalants by the elderly is extremely rare.[10] There is a small group of abusers of opioids, but not of cocaine. The situation with cannabis is less clear; Pascarelli observed that many of the older opioid users also continue to use marijuana.[11] Far and away the greatest substance abuse problem is alcoholism, with Schuckit estimating that about 10 percent of the general elderly population have alcohol-related difficulties.[12] The other major problem area for the elderly is drug misuse, a complex issue that is reviewed by Petersen and his colleagues and by Eisdorfer and Basen.[13, 14] It is detailed along with the other significant disorders in the next section.

SYNDROMES—SUM AND SUBSTANCE

Alcoholism

Introduction

Mankind has had a long, intense, and ambivalent involvement with ethanol, a simple alcohol. It has been humanity's main recreational drug and has also been the prescribed treatment for many ills; yet the substance has also caused more personal and societal havoc than all other drugs combined.[15] This involvement has been described as a 5,000-year-old uncontrolled experiment by Mishara and Kastenbaum, who also point out that mankind's earliest legends dealt with old age and alcohol in the Epics of Gilgamesh in ancient Sumeria.[16] The hero attempted to use his courage and intellect to preserve youth against the onslaught of aging and death but was unsuccessful. In this human and cosmic struggle, many of the benevolent and malevolent deities fell in battle with one another, and from their bodies sprang the grapevine. While humanity, personified in Gilgamesh, failed to deter either aging or death, it was given wine or the "blood of the grapes" by the dying gods, perhaps as a solace for the privations of the human condition.

Incidence

The abundant ancient legends, folklore, stories, and teaching about alcohol being what they are, we need to look at the situation in which older Americans now find themselves. About 70 percent of the adult population use alcohol to some extent, although in the elderly this figure may drop into the range of about 50 percent.[17] There are basically two types of older alcohol abusers: those who have been drinking for much of their lives but have managed to survive into old age, and those who began their drinking late in life. As Forni points out, however, even older social drinkers are at increased risk, because of mixing (1) drinking and driving, (2) drinking and other drugs, and (3) even drinking and walking.[18] The exact rate of alcohol abuse is not clear, as there are wide variations in the reported studies; but Schuckit estimates that up to 10 percent of the older population are affected significantly by alcohol problems, while among certain groups the incidence is much higher.[19] He estimates that among the elderly, about 20 percent of medical inpatients and 15 percent of medical outpatients have serious, alcohol-related life problems. Those admitted to psychiatric facilities may have an even higher incidence; Simon reported that 28 percent of all admissions to a geriatric screening unit had serious drinking problems, while Gaitz and Baer reported that of 100 consecutive patients over age 60 admitted to a county psychiatric screening ward, 44 percent were diagnosed as having an alcohol-related disorder.[20, 21]

Pharmacological and Physiological Effects

Alcohol has a variety of pharmacologic effects on the human body, but primarily it is a depressant of the central nervous system. The results of this are generally related to the concentration of alcohol in the blood. As Woolf outlines, alcohol in low doses first depresses the inhibitory areas of the brain, giving the mistaken impression that it is a stimulant.[22] As the reticular formation is involved, behavioral changes take place. The cortex is then involved, and as the dose increases, the depression extends down the brain stem until at lethal dose the medulla is suppressed, causing respiratory arrest. Alcohol decreases the ability to perform mental or motor tasks, but intoxicated individuals may think they are doing better because they have a concomitant impairment of judgment. Some anesthetic properties are present, which may cause the individual to ignore physical or cold injury. Ethyl alcohol has a number of complex effects on the neurotransmitters of the brain, and it has been speculated that it stimulates the production of substances with a morphinelike effect, which may account for alcohol's addictive properties. Alcohol has a profound effect on sleep patterns, so excessive sleep may occur during some levels of intoxication; since it decreases rapid eye movement (REM) sleep, however, there is a REM rebound during withdrawal that results in insomnia. A number of diseases are directly related to biochemical changes induced by the metabolism of sizable quantities of alcohol: fluctuations in blood sugar, ketoacidosis, hyperlipemia, fatty liver, and gout. Alcohol is a direct hepatotoxic substance and can cause reversible fatty liver, alcoholic hepatitis (with a mortality rate of 10 to 30 percent), and cirrhosis. Various vitamin and mineral deficiencies occur in alcohol abuse, both because of limited food intake and through alcohol-related defects in absorption and storage of nutrients. Deficiencies of the B vitamins, in particular, lead to frequent neuropathies, psychoses, and some cardiovascular symptoms. The intestinal tract is markedly inflamed by prolonged alcohol ingestion, and it is often the subsequent vomiting that brings the patient to a physician. Most cases of pancreatitis occur in alcoholics. Even moderate to occasional doses of alcohol can suppress testosterone levels, and continued abuse causes an increase in estrogen levels, creating some feminization in males. Heavy alcohol intake also has a variety of effects on the cardiovascular system, including hypertension, cardiomyopathy with heart failure, irregularities in cardiac rhythm, and rapid heat loss because of vasodilation. The activity of white blood cells is impaired by alcohol, so resistance to infections such as pneumonia and tuberculosis is lowered by alcoholism.

Clinical Problems

The elderly alcohol user or abuser may come to health care professionals because of a variety of problems in a variety of circumstances. Many will present with some type of alcohol organic mental disorder, as described in *DSM-III*.[23] Simple alcohol intoxication will probably show up only if there are severe maladaptive behavioral effects, such as fighting, suicide attempts, or injuries. The length of intoxication is largely dependent on the amount ingested, since there is a relatively constant rate of metabolism—about 5 to 10 cc. per hour. There is considerable variation in individual susceptibility to intoxication. Some people show signs of it with blood alcohol levels as low as 30 mg. percent, while others may show no toxicity with levels at 150 mg. percent. The elderly are often more sensitive to the effects of alcohol, especially if there has been previous brain damage or the use of other drugs.[24] A diagnosis of intoxication is indicated when there is a history of recent alcohol intake with at least one sign of physiological changes, such as slurred speech, incoordination, nystagmus, or facial flushing; and at least one psychological sign, such as mood change, irritability, talkativeness, or impaired attention. A few individuals respond to very small amounts of alcohol with a marked reaction that has been called pathological intoxication or idiosyncratic intoxication. Those with cerebral damage or other debilitating illness are more likely to have a low tolerance for alcohol, making it more likely that the older drinkers' thinking processes will be more susceptible to the effects of alcohol than those of younger drinkers, as mentioned by Eckardt.[25]

Alcohol withdrawal usually occurs within several hours after cessation of drinking in an alcohol-dependent person who has been drinking for several days or longer. In an older person with previous withdrawal problems, this may often occur after only three or four days of heavy drinking. The principal features are a coarse tremor of the hands, tongue, or eyelids and associated symptoms such as nausea and vomiting; malaise; autonomic hyperactivity with rapid pulse, sweating, or increased blood pressure; anxiety; depression or irritability; or postural hypotension. Sleep is often fitful, with disturbing dreams that sometimes merge into illusions or poorly formed hallucinations. The withdrawal symptoms are usually over in five to seven days, but a number of elderly alcohol abusers have been noted to take two to three weeks to recuperate from a serious drinking bout.

Some may go on to more severe problems, such as alcohol withdrawal delirium, which used to be called delirium tremens or the D.T.'s. This usually begins on the second or third day after cessation of drinking, but it can occur as late as the tenth day in older alcoholics. It may be heralded by a grand mal seizure, or it may be characterized by vivid, delirious hallucinations of a visual or sensory modality and by confusion. If treated promptly and properly, it will have run its course in two or three days; untreated, it may have a mortality of up to 15 percent.

Some may develop varied auditory hallucinations, usually within 48 hours of withdrawal. They tend to be unpleasant and disturbing and are often of voices discussing the patient; they occur in an otherwise clear sensorium, however. Most of these symptoms are over within a week, but some may persist for weeks or months. They may even develop into a chronic form, especially if there have been repeated bouts of this disorder.

In some people an alcohol amnesia disorder develops after an episode of Wernicke's encephalopathy, which involves confusion, staggering gait, eye-movement problems, or other neurologic signs. The disorder is related to vitamin deficiencies, especially of thiamine, and is manifested by memory deficits. It is also known as Korsakoff's disease, and it usually persists indefinitely.

After prolonged alcohol abuse, the individual may develop varying degrees of dementia that may be profound and permanent. Gaitz and Baer noted that of their elderly alcohol abusers who were admitted, 29 of 44 (66 percent) had evidence of organic mental syndrome (OMS).[26] Those with OMS tended to be males and to be much younger than unaffected patients (65 years for those with OMS; 73 years for those who had no OMS).

It is important to keep in mind that various withdrawal problems may arise unexpectedly in secretly alcohol-dependent people who are admitted to the hospital for acute medical or surgical problems. A sudden change in behavior or onset of withdrawal-type symptoms two or three days after admission, by which time patients have been acutely deprived of their alcohol source, should prompt rapid consultation and investigation, and often treatment for withdrawal states.

Assessment and Diagnosis

If the patient has a history of alcohol abuse, the health professional will be more likely to suspect and detect an alcohol-associated disorder. As many elderly people and their families tend to hide drug-related problems, a number of cases will be overlooked until unexpected withdrawal reactions or peculiar physical problems arouse suspicion or even create gross awareness of an underlying alcohol abuse problem. Some elderly people have the notion that drinking beer or wine instead of "hard stuff" will prevent them from getting alcohol-related problems. In the acute phase, a blood alcohol level may be helpful, but this will be of little value in most cases with the elderly.

A good general physical examination will pick up various signs, such as tremors, alcohol on the breath, an enlarged liver, or red palms, that are suggestive of an alcohol-related problem. Useful biochemical tests include those that check blood sugar, liver function, electrolytes, serum magnesium level (which is often low in chronic alcohol abuse), serum proteins, and folic acid levels. An electrocardiogram might show cardiomyopathy. The electroencephalogram may provide an indication of diffuse brain damage or evidence of a subdural hematoma (blood clot on the brain); such is certainly a good possibility in older persons, who are more susceptible to falls because of the alcohol use but less inclined to remember having fallen. They also have more fragile blood vessels than younger people.

The National Council on Alcoholism has developed criteria for early recognition of alcoholism.[27] Many of these have already been covered, but other things to look for include morning shakes, which may indicate a withdrawal reaction even after the brief abstinence that occurs during sleep. The person will often drink an "eye-opener" shortly after arising. Tolerance to alcohol may be expected in someone who consumes large quantities of alcohol without becoming noticeably intoxicated. Blackouts in which the person seemed to be functioning normally but cannot remember, or only vaguely remembers, what he or she did are highly indicative of alcohol dependence. A person who drinks in spite of strong medical, social, or psychological contraindications should certainly be considered a potential alcohol abuser. A useful six-point scale of the degree of alcohol abuse based on such characteristics was developed by Zimberg.[28]

The complex interaction of alcohol with other drugs used by the elderly makes their problems both more severe and less clear. Alcohol interacts with more than 150 commonly prescribed drugs, as described by Hartford and Samorajski.[29] This subject is covered in more detail later. Acute alcohol intake impairs breakdown by the liver of many drugs, such as chloral hydrate and barbiturates, and so potentiates the effects of these and other drugs. Chronic alcohol use, on the other hand, increases the metabolism of other drugs, necessitating higher dosages. Some drugs used by older persons, such as the tricyclic antidepressants and the major and minor tranquilizers, may increase the response to alcohol markedly, so older people should be cautioned not to use these drugs and alcohol simultaneously.

Epidemiology

There have been several reports on epidemiological issues related to alcohol abuse in the elderly. While the results of different studies are somewhat disparate, some of them will be cited to help explain the problem. About two-thirds of the people with alcohol use disorders began drinking heavily earlier in life, and about one-third are late-life-onset drinkers. A number of reports are summarized by Petersen and Whittington.[30] The younger-onset drinkers tend to drink more. Alcohol-related disorders have a tendency to peak in the 35- to 50-year-old age group, but a second peak occurs among people 65 to 74 years of age. Alcohol abuse tends to be a male-dominated practice, with about two out of three involved being males. Generally, the earlier the onset of significant drinking, the more likely it is to have associated physical problems and the less likely to have a good treatment outcome. Fewer of the late-onset males fit the criteria for personality disorders or report the use of illicit drugs than those who have early-onset alcohol problems.[31] Drinking patterns in the two groups tend to differ, with the late-onset drinkers more likely to drink daily but drinking less (four drinks) per occasion. The late-onset alcoholic is more likely to enter treatment voluntarily and to stay there. Most people with late-life-onset alcohol problems are white. A study by Meyers and his group in Boston did not find clear evidence of late-life-onset drinking problems, and found no significant relationship between problem drinking in old age and marital status, household composition, or employment status.[32] They did find that those with alcohol-related problems (ARP) were less satisfied with their lives in general and in specific life areas. A small but interesting study was done by Dunham, who found six life patterns of drinking that showed rising and falling alcohol use over the life span.[33] In his group he found that 68 percent were lifelong abstainers, and these were more likely to be female, married, Latin, and Catholic. Four of the drinking patterns were problematic for the elderly: the "rise-and-sustained" pattern of a heavy drinker, who continues heavy drinking into old age; the pattern of a "light-and-late-riser," whose light drinking rose to moderate levels in old age; the "late starting" pattern, with onset of drinking late in life; and the "highly variable" pattern, with episodic heavy drinking. He did believe that certain types of people characteristically fell into different patterns with various types of problems and needs for treatment, but the study needs replication.

Treatment

Treatment of the elderly person with an alcohol problem has a potentially large number of variables, so precise instructions cannot be given. Early intervention is an ideal, but the health professional often has little opportunity for this, since—as Mendelson and Mello point out—even the disease conceptualization of alcohol abuse involves a complex interaction between the person, the pharmacologic properties of alcohol, and the general social and environmental context of the individual.[34] Thus, the patient may not be available until the situation has progressed enough either to reveal the problem or force the issue. As with younger patients, the family must accept the problem and the patient must be confronted with it, as the customary patient denial is often fostered by the family's acceptance of that denial.[35] Treatment generally falls into four overlapping but sequential phases, as suggested by Blume: the identification/intervention phase, the detoxification phase, the rehabilitative phase, and the long-term follow-up.[36] As Pattison indicates, alcohol problems are varied and complex, so treatment programs must be reasonable and selective.[37] For the elderly, hospitalization or other institutionalized care (such as in a detoxification center) should be considered for anything more complicated than simple intoxication, as many elderly alcohol abusers are malnourished and have multiple medical problems.

The cornerstone of treatment of alcohol withdrawal syndromes is the use of a drug with depressant properties similar to those of alcohol—followed by the gradual withdrawal of the drug—along with good medical, nursing, and nutritional care. The drug usually prescribed for this is chlordiazepoxide (Librium), because of its relatively long half-life and it's cross tolerance with alcohol.[38] A useful set of guidelines is given by Mayfield.[39] First, if there are obvious signs of alcohol intoxication but no emergency otherwise, wait for the signs of intoxication to clear before beginning other drugs. If there is no history of previous withdrawal problems such as the shakes or D.T.'s, and no present signs, one may observe closely and begin medication at the first such signs. If withdrawal signs are not present but are expected or have occurred previously, begin chlordiazepoxide at 25 mg. every 6 hours. If no signs appear over three days, the medication can be tapered and stopped. If signs do appear, the medication should be increased to 50 mg. every 6 hours for one to two days, then tapered over two to four days. Should withdrawal signs continue, give 50 mg. of chlordiazepoxide every 6 hours, and continue or increase the dosage until the patient has been stabilized for 24 to 36 hours, at which time the drug can be tapered over four days. Should an alcohol withdrawal delirium occur, a rather hazardous condition exists, since this may be associated with seizures, hyperthermia, and cardiac irregularities, as described by Simon.[40] This state can be managed by giving 50 to 200 mg. chlordiazepoxide every 6 hours as needed to achieve sedation to allow sleep but still permit the patient to be awakened. The dosage should be maintained until the delirium has cleared, then gradually be reduced over five to seven days. Valium and other benzodiazepines can be used for withdrawal in comparable doses as well, but close monitoring is essential in the elderly. The patient's fluid and electrolyte situation must be watched carefully. The serum magnesium should be checked as well, since it is often low in alcoholic states and may need supplementation. Vitamin supplements are important, especially the B complex group. It is well to check the patient's folic acid level, as it, too, is often low in those with chronic alcohol problems and may need special supplementation. General malnutrition is common in elderly people with alcohol problems, and the services of a dietitian are often helpful.

Mood disorders are common in alcohol abuse; most are depressive but some are manic. Lithium carbonate has been used when mania is present, but the toxic dose range is uncomfortably close to the therapeutic range in the elderly.[41] Some have advocated progressive tapering of the alcohol level for withdrawal, but Becker feels this to be both psychologically and metabolically undesirable.[42] Paraldehyde has been used for many years, but more adverse reactions have occurred with that than with the benzodiazepine derivatives. Disulfiram (Antabuse) has no place in treatment of the acute withdrawal phase and is generally not necessary (and probably not desirable) in the chronic treatment of alcohol abuse in the elderly, since the effects of adverse reactions may be very severe.

Course of Illness

The rehabilitative phase, of course, plays a substantial part in whether the individual will move to recovery or lapse back into the use of alcohol or some other drug. As Pattison points out, there are no distinct categories of alcohol abusers; rather, degrees of alcohol use are complexly interwoven with other psychosocial variables.[43] A variety of treatment systems exist, and the therapist needs to know which of these are available and which would best suit the needs of each patient. Facilities offer a system of treatment programs that can involve such things as a detoxification center, an information center, a mental hospital, a halfway house, the legal system, the vocational rehabilitation system, psychiatric and medical outpatient clinics, and such groups as Alcoholics Anonymous. Generally, it is important to have family members involved in counseling programs as well, or in such groups as Al-Anon. Patients' goals in such programs are to augment their motivation for change, to understand themselves better, to gain an understanding of the disease, and to develop new ways of handling problems. Zimberg noted that environmental manipulation, medical services, day hospital care, home visiting, and social interactions were most effective in eliminating alcohol abuse among elderly patients.[44] A very low dose of antidepressant, such as 25 mg. of doxepin at bedtime, has frequently been used on a long-term basis to help stabilize the dysphoria and anxiety that are often present and also to serve as a bridge between therapist and patient. A medication may symbolize a relationship between the two, as well as providing a rationale for not drinking and for returning for follow-up treatment. It is important not to give the patient the impression that regular use of some drug is needed to get along, and thus run the risk of the abuse of some other drug.

Course of Alcoholism

It is difficult to generalize about the course of alcohol abuse in the elderly since there are so many variables involved. The presence of physical disease can cause increased pathology from the adverse effects of alcohol in any organ system. As cited by Schuckit and Pastor, those who develop an alcoholic life style prior to age 40 have a very high premature death rate, tending to die 10 to 15 years before their expected life span is over.[45] Older alcoholic men show an elevated rate of medical problems, complicated by the fact that many also smoke.[46] As already mentioned, among older alcoholics who were admitted to a hospital, Gaitz and Baer noted an incidence of about 66 percent with organic mental syndrome (OMS).[47] These individuals tended to be younger than those with OMS without a history of alcohol abuse, and they died at a significantly younger age. This is probably related to the observations of Blusewicz and his group that alcohol abuse causes damage related to sensorimotor functions, auditory and visual perception, short-term memory, and abstract reasoning; thus, "premature aging" is evident.[48] About one-third of older alcoholics presenting for treatment live alone; about 85 percent are white males, according to Schuckit and Pastor.[49] The incidence of suicide in elderly alcohol abusers is not clear, but certainly they are at high risk for self-destruction of some type. Among those who survive into their seventies, a number will be able to stop their drinking or reduce it.

Sedative or Hypnotic Abuse

The term *sedative* is an old one used for drugs that calm anxiety and decrease wakefulness, while a *hypnotic* produces drowsiness or induces a sleep-like state.[50] It was in 1903 that the first barbiturate was introduced, and various derivatives dominated the sedative and hypnotic market until the introduction in 1961 of the first "minor" tranquilizer, chlordiazepoxide (Librium). There are a variety of hypnotics, but most of the older ones are barbiturates, such as pentobarbital (Nembutal) or secobarbital (Seconal). More recently a variety of hypnotic drugs have appeared, such as glutethimide (Doriden), methyprylon (Noludar), and methaqualone (Quaalude). All of these drugs are potentially habit-forming, and so could be or have been abused as street drugs. The literature, which is very limited, shows that the illegal abuse of these substances in the elderly is very rare. A study by Peppers and Stover showed that among the elderly involved in a statewide program for detecting substance abuse, 96 percent were affected by alcohol while only about 1.3 percent were involved in illegal drug use, with 0.2 percent having barbiturate abuse as a primary problem; 0.3 percent, abuse of other sedatives; and 0.4 percent, marijuana-hashish abuse.[51] Many of these substances are illegally abused so infrequently by older patients because they are legally misused so frequently. This problem is discussed later in the section on prescribed drug misuse.

Opioid Abuse

Of the older illicit substance abusers identified in the Peppers and Stover studies, only 0.3 percent had heroin or other opiate abuse as the primary problem. As Cohen points out, there are basically three types of older opioid abusers: surviving street addicts, medical addicts, and what he calls the "Southern-type" addicts.[52] Previously it was thought that the outcome for an older addict was either death or outgrowing the habit. Many surviving opioid addicts continue in their drug-taking habits, as noted by Capel and his group.[53, 54] Generally they assume a very low profile, however, by switching to cheaper narcotics than heroin and by alternating them with codeine cough syrup, paregoric, alcohol, or barbiturates as necessary. A small but increasing number of these people are enrolling in methadone maintenance clinics. There are some ethnic groups with relatively high numbers of elderly opiate addicts, such as the Chinese population in some large cities, as described by Deely and her group.[55] The reasons given by these elderly addicts for their initiation of drug use were peer pressure, curiosity, and availability. These are still major factors among young substance abusers. We can expect a rapidly increasing number of elderly addicts as the present groups grow older; Pascarelli and Fischer predict a potential twentyfold increase over two decades.[56]

The "Southern-type" addict belongs to a group of elderly people who got involved with narcotics long ago, when opiates were much more available than they are today in patent medicines, cough syrups, and paregoric. These persons—generally middle- and upper-class women from small towns—have been maintained by receiving ongoing prescriptions from sympathetic doctors. This practice was predominantly a Southern rural phenomenon. It is, of course, dying out through attrition and changed regulations on drugs.

Another small but distinct group of older opiate addicts are physicians and other medical personnel who have had easy access to these drugs over a period of years.

Misuse of Legal Drugs by the Elderly

The other major area of concern in geriatric substance use disorders is the misuse of legally prescribed drugs. By definition of the federal Strategy Council on Drug Abuse, drug *misuse* is the inappropriate use of drugs intended for therapeutic purposes, whereas drug *abuse* is the nontherapeutic use of any psychoactive substance such that it adversely affects some aspect of the user's life.[57] Pascarelli points out that misuse of drugs can mean not only overuse but also underuse, erratic use, or use in unnecessary or contraindicated circumstances.[58] The three principal areas of misuse of legal drugs are (1) the misuse of prescribed drugs, (2) the misuse of over-the-counter drugs, and (3) iatrogenic or physician-related problems. These are examined in detail.

Incidence

The frequency of drug misuse has, of course, a considerable correlation with the frequency of drug use, especially in the elderly. Studies are scant, however, and often hard to compare with each other. One study of a community population by Chien, Townsend, and Ross-Townsend showed that only 8 percent of this population were medication free; the mean number of drugs taken per interviewee was 3.8.[59] Of this group, 83 percent were taking at least 2 drugs and 15 percent were on between 7 and 15 different drugs. Of psychotropic drugs being taken, 22.3 percent were antianxiety agents, 12 percent were hypnotics, 4.1 percent were antipsychotics, and 2.5 percent were antidepressants. Of great significance was the fact that 33.1 percent of those on drugs were taking one or more medications they could not identify. Of the identified medications, 60 percent were prescribed and 40 percent were over-the-counter (OTC) preparations. Of the OTC group, 26 percent were self-prescribed, 11 percent had been suggested by a doctor, and 3 percent were suggested by a friend or relative. A study by Guttman of community elderly in Washington, D.C., in 1977 showed that 17.4 percent were known to be taking psychotropic medication and 55 percent were on OTC drugs.[60] Studies at Duke University have shown that among the elderly of Durham County, North Carolina, 28 percent of those in the community were on psychoactive preparations, while 65 percent of those living in extended care facilities or institutions were taking such substances. A study of community elderly in Michigan reported by Solomon and Weiner showed that none were "drug free," with 71 percent using prescription drugs, 54 percent using OTC preparations, and 20 percent using home remedies.[61] One-third of those interviewed indicated that they saved their old unused medicines, feeling they might need them again.

Of course, the prevalence of multiple drugs and psychoactive compounds does not necesarily mean that misuse is taking place. The study by Chien and associates also looked at the incidence of symptoms and illness.[62] Only 2.5 percent of their sample reported no illness, and the mean number of illnesses were in four body systems. When they correlated drug use with disease or symptoms, they found that irrational usage (misuse) due to misunderstanding the indications for use of the drugs occurred in only 14 percent overall.

In his study of the Washington group, Guttmann looked at many variables and reached a number of important conclusions.[63] He found that almost all (98.7 percent) of the users of psychoactive drugs got their drugs from physicians, that 50.7 percent felt they could not perform their regular daily activities without the drug, that they were knowledgeable about what the psychotropic drugs were supposed to do, and that most (76 percent) consulted their physician before taking other drugs as well. This group of psychoactive drug users had a significantly higher rate of combining multiple drugs, including alcohol, than the users of all other drugs in general. Males tended to use more alcohol than OTC drugs, and women had the opposite pattern.

The OARS study of the institutionalized elderly (introduced in Chapter 2) showed that 71 percent of them were impaired from a mental health standpoint in contrast to 13 percent of the community group, obviously indicating the need for a much higher level of psychoactive drug use.[64]

The frequency of adverse drug reactions is a rough measure of drug misuse, and some studies give an indication of that. Drug-induced illness may be the major contributing cause of hospitalization in from 5 to 30 percent of all those over age 65, compared to only 2 to 8 percent in the general population, as noted by Williamson and Chopin.[65] Inside a hospital, the likelihood of experiencing an adverse drug reaction is a direct function of age. Hurwitz showed that only 3 percent of those between ages 20 and 29 may have adverse reactions, while 10.7 percent of those between 60 and 69 and 21.3 percent of those between 70 and 79 may have problems.[66] Of the elderly living at home, up to 25 percent may complain of side effects of drugs, according to Eberhardt and Robinson.[67]

Pharmacology and Physiology

It must be emphasized that adverse reactions do not necessarily mean drug misuse, since hardly any physician, pharmacist, or patient would want a bad reaction to occur. A number of physiological factors common in older persons predispose them to drug-related difficulties, and they are well detailed by Friesen.[68] Age-related changes that occur in organ systems of the body, such as the kidneys and liver of the digestive system, make it much more difficult for older people to metabolize and excrete various drugs. Changes also occur in the rate and extent of absorption, in the distribution of the drug in plasma and fat, and in the responsiveness of target tissues. The effects in the body of various diseases, or of the drugs to treat them, create wide and often unpredictable variations in drug response.[69] The nutritional status of the elderly, which is more likely to be inadequate in the ill, has a considerable effect on drug effects and the person's response.[70] Our ability to detect and understand these complex conditions is still very limited, so the response of any particular older individual to a drug is still often unpredictable.

Misuse of Prescription Drugs

The clinical effects of misuse vary widely depending on the drug, the pathology, and the person.

The obvious problem is overuse, which may result in the previously described problems of substance-induced, acute or chronic organic mental disorder or in disorders of abuse or dependence. The addiction potential varies with the drug used and with the frequency and mode of use. Narcotics have a generally high addiction potential, but this well-known property, combined with the fact that many elderly people are relatively intolerant of them, reduces the habituation problem somewhat. Narcotics certainly may cause sedation, confusion, nausea, hallucinations, and nightmares. Probably the most commonly misused drug of this group is propoxyphene (Darvon), which has been cited as the agent in about 10 percent of acute toxic drug reactions in older people.[71] Propoxyphene presents a special problem in that it is one of the most frequently prescribed analgesics for the elderly, and a mild dependency state can develop.[72] There is question, moreover, about whether it has any analgesic superiority over aspirin.[73] Most acute drug reactions in older people are caused by overuse of prescribed drugs. The most commonly misused ones are diazepam (Valium), secobarbital (Seconal), amobarbital (Tuinal), phenobarbital, and propoxyphene. Barbiturates are generally poorly tolerated in the elderly, with oversedation, confusion, and dependence occurring easily. Although barbiturates should rarely be used with older patients, these drugs are still widely prescribed for this group.

Some, such as Pascarelli, felt that antidepressant drugs are potential drugs of abuse, especially amitriptyline (Elavil), which may cause euphoria and then mild withdrawal symptoms on abrupt cessation.[74]

Probably a greater problem than overuse is misuse related to noncompliance. There is a rapidly growing literature on this problem, the importance of which is suggested by the "1975 United States National Institute on Drug Abuse" study, which indicated that between 25 and 60 percent of elderly patients make errors in self-administration of prescribed medications.[75] One report indicated that 30 percent had stopped medication earlier than directed, 20 percent had not filled the prescription, and 14 percent had varied the prescription dose. The frequency of noncompliance is directly related to age, as found by Brand and his associates, who noted rates of 26 percent for those in their forties, 46 percent in their seventies, and 62 percent for patients in their eighties.[76] They found positive correlations between noncompliance and low income, single status, lack of education, and taking several prescriptions. Another study by Schwartz and her group indicated that the errors were in omission (47 percent), inaccurate information (20 percent), erratic self-medication (17 percent), incorrect dose (10 percent), and incorrect timing (4 percent).[77] An interesting study done in Finland found that misuse of prescription drugs reached a rate of about 50 percent and was related to the number and nature of drugs, with underuse and self-adjustment being the major problems.[78] Those drugs most likely to be underused were those used mainly for symptomatic relief rather than cure, those with side effects, those the patient felt were no longer needed, and those that were most expensive. Prescription drugs related to sleep, appetite, and mood were most likely to be overused.

A number of factors conducive to the misuse of drugs by elderly people were identified by Gollub.[79] These were drug overdoses either through error or emotional disturbance, misuse resulting from organic mental disorder, use of multiple prescriptions without the doctor's knowledge, overuse of prescriptions by improper use of automatic or telephone refills, exchange of drugs with others, and use of outdated drugs. In another study, Cooper and his group found that intentional nonadherence to a drug program was more likely to occur when the patient used two or more physicians and pharmacies.[80]

Misuse of Over-the-Counter (OTC) Drugs

Self-medication is supposed to be only for the treatment of minor and self-limiting ailments, but following the advertisements for these multitudinous drugs could make self-medication a national obsession. As Moore indicates, any drug can be abused, whatever its pharmacologic properties.[81] There are four groups of OTC drugs, however, that have been associated with psychoactive properties: sedatives, cold and cough products, analgesics, and appetite suppressants.

Many elderly have, or complain of, sleep disorders, and OTC hypnotics are used by about 23 percent of those using drugs to treat this problem. Until 1979, these preparations contained scopolamine and sometimes bromides, both of which were notorious for producing nervous system toxicity among the elderly. Now they all contain antihistamines, which have a sedative side effect. While these are much safer, they still have significant anticholinergic effects and may produce confusion if they are overused or added to other anticholinergic drugs the individual might be taking. Additional side effects of weakness, heaviness, or paradoxical insomnia may develop.

Most cold and cough preparations contain several ingredients, including an antihistamine, a decongestant, a cough suppressant, and alcohol (often up to 25 percent of content). While these preparations do not usually create trouble, the older person taking them may have problems either with sedation or overstimulation. The preparations certainly potentiate other psychoactive drugs the patient may be using.

Analgesics generally contain salicylates or acetaminophen, often in combination with caffeine. In high doses, salicylates may produce both an acute and chronic toxicity resembling alcohol inebriation. Some elderly people develop an allergy or intolerance to aspirin.

While most elderly do not share the preoccupation with weight that fascinates the young, those who do have the appetite suppressants available. The OTC preparations generally contain the stimulant phenylpropanolamine and caffeine. Use of such preparations may produce irritability, insomnia, apprehension, and even psychosis.

Iatrogenic Problems

The problem of drug misuse includes the health professionals in various ways. Four factors were identified by Gollub: inaccurate diagnosis; inaccuracies in drug treatment; polypharmacy, leading to drug interactions; and overmedication or arbitrary medication.[82]

A fundamental principle of medicine is to establish as accurate a diagnosis as possible to serve as the basis for the therapeutic plan. The elderly are by far the most difficult group to diagnose accurately, both because they have multiple problems with atypical presentations and also because most physicians have not been trained in geriatrics. Both geriatric medicine and psychiatry are almost new fields in American medicine, but some knowledge of both these areas is important since almost two-thirds of elderly medical patients have psychiatric illness and vice versa.[83] Failing to diagnose problems correctly may result in inadequate drug treatment or placement in the wrong facility, both of which tend to create poor results for the patient and increased stress on the staff. A team approach, such as that in the OARS program, helps to achieve a more accurate total assessment because of the multiple inputs involved, as well as the wide range of therapeutic possibilities provided.

Inaccuracies in drug treatment may be related to incorrect diagnosis, but may also be a result of failing to take into account the age-related alterations in an individual's response to medications. The body's capacity to maintain biochemical homeostasis is reduced with age, leading to more frequent side effects and toxicity. Neither specific doses nor simple guidelines for treatment of the elderly have been established for most drugs, but a number of books and publications are coming out now.[84] A listing of the usual geriatric doses of many psychoactive drugs appears in Appendix B of this volume.

The use of multiple drugs among the elderly is widespread, and it creates a major area for misadventure and misuse. Studies have previously been cited indicating the relatively high frequency of polypharmacy in the elderly, as well as the frequency of side effects and interactions. A drug interaction is not the same as a contraindicated combination where there is a known problem or risk. As Blaschke points out, multiple drug therapy is often necessary in the elderly, and sicker patients often require more drugs anyway.[85] As the number of drugs increases, a sharp increase occurs in the possible combinations of two drugs that might interact. For instance, if a patient is receiving 7 drugs concurrently, there are 21 different possible interactions; and if a patient is receiving 10 drugs there are 45 different possible combinations. Not all interactions are toxic; some result in a loss of efficacy instead. When using a rational combination of drugs, physicians must be aware of the potential drug interactions. They must adjust doses accordingly and must maintain a high level of vigilance during treatment in order to deal with problems so that older patients will receive the best care possible. Interestingly, Prien and his group found that the proportion of hospitalized psychiatric patients receiving two or more psychoactive agents decreased from 26 percent for those aged 60 to 65 years to 12 percent of those over age 75.[86] Substantially more women than men received multiple psychoactive agents.

Overmedication has been a significant problem for the elderly, especially those who have been institutionalized. A study reported by Prentice in 1970 showed that of the 10 drugs most prescribed in nursing homes, 9 were psychoactive agents.[87] The issue of using medicine, perhaps unnecessarily, to control patients has, of course, been raised. Certainly there have been abuses, but it must be remembered that most of the patients in nursing homes do have major psychiatric problems, as our studies among the institutionalized elderly here have shown. A study by Zawadski of psychotropic drug use among the institutionalized and noninstitutionalized aged showed, however, that the amount spent on prescription drugs for an institutionalized older person was more than twice as much as for the noninstitutionalized.[88] Most of this increased cost went for psychoactive drugs; the institutionalized aged had 17 times more expenditures on psychotropic drugs than the noninstitutionalized, including an impaired group in a community day-care program.

Caffeine

While low on the list of dangers to the elderly as a drug of abuse, caffeine may nevertheless create some problems. It is a central nervous system stimulant that is widely used in drinks and OTC medications. A dose of 200 mg. (the equivalent of two cups of coffee) will produce definite cortical arousal, which may produce insomnia. In susceptible people, it may produce irritability and anxiety, and many elderly become increasingly sensitive to it. Chien and associates report that nearly a third of the people studied drank four to six cups of coffee a day.[89] Checking and advising on caffeine intake may help the therapist reduce an older person's tension and anxiety considerably without the use of any psychoactive drugs.

FACTORS IN ETIOLOGY AND TREATMENT

It should be evident that substance abuse in the elderly is a very complex issue, both to understand and to treat. In an interesting study in Durham, North Carolina, Back and Sullivan looked at the relationship between self-image, medicine, and drug use.[90] They found that drug use among women was significantly correlated with three factors: insecurity, sick role, and, curiously, the fear of medicines. The relationship in men was much less clear, but still they concluded that some people are psychologically predisposed to the heavy use of drugs and some, conversely, to the avoidance of drugs. This predisposition may affect the extent of drug use or misuse, perhaps regardless of the level of health or other obvious influences. A study by Hochhauser led him to believe that substance abuse is related to learned helplessness, including a sense of the loss of control, which is essential to successful coping.[91] He speculated that drugs, notably alcohol, may restore a sense of personal control or power and thus reduce anxiety and distress while giving a predictable pleasurable effect. Thus, the extent to which the elderly believe that they can predict and/or control environmental events will have important effects on their levels of substance use, misuse, and abuse.

Treatment is complex, dealing both with immediate problems of intoxication or withdrawal from drugs and also with developing long-range plans to reduce the ignorance and stresses that surround and perpetuate the problem. Help is needed both for the care givers—to improve their knowledge of the proper use of therapeutic substances—and for the patients—to help them utilize medications in a safe, proper, and healthful way.

CASE STUDY—A COMPLICATED CASE OF ALCOHOLISM IN AN OLDER MAN

Present Illness

Dr. B. is a 70-year-old, white, retired obstetrician who was referred to the OARS-GET Clinic by his psychiatrist from a medium-sized city in an adjoining state for long-term follow-up care. He had recently been hospitalized in that city because of a recurrent depression that had required a course of electroconvulsive therapy (ECT). He had become increasingly despondent prior to that admission and was very restless, with a poor sleep pattern. Several antidepressants had been prescribed for him without much positive effect, and he complained of increasing difficulty in concentrating and of loss of his ability to function. Increasingly he had become suicidal, and he finally handed his wife a large bottle of barbiturates that he had hidden away. He was fearful that he would indeed commit suicide, either by overdosing or by hanging himself, so he turned to his wife, who then got him in touch with his psychiatrist again.

He first sought psychiatric help eight years before, when he had become suicidally depressed. He required hospitalization at that time. Fourteen years ago, while intoxicated, he had an automobile accident in which his left arm was injured; a woman in the car he struck was rather seriously injured. Following that, he curtailed his practice moderately. Then 10 years ago he decided to retire from practice after a mild heart attack. He had some tension and angina on exertion and began to drink some sherry two or three times a day to help him relax. His wife reported that he progressively became more socially withdrawn and would sit in his study for long periods of time, slowly going through old books and medical journals. About four months prior to his first admission, his wife had a hysterectomy for a precancerous lesion. While she had a good recovery, his already faltering sexual performance failed completely, and he referred to himself as "washed out."

At that time he was hospitalized for about three and a half months, during which three different antidepressants were tried and he underwent psychotherapy. A gradual but fairly good improvement occurred, and he was followed by his psychiatrist for about two years on an outpatient basis on decreasing medication. He and his wife again became more socially active with a small group of old friends, and his wife said that he began "being his old self" again, meaning that he was rather outgoing, talkative, and argumentative. Then he began to try to write an article on the philosophy of obstetrics, an idea he had been talking about periodically for a number of years, but this work progressed very slowly.

About two years before the most recent admission, he began to get despondent and withdrawn again. This state progressed over three months to the point of his being suicidal. Again he was hospitalized, and a course of nine ECT treatments were given; results were good for approximately one year, until his present episode.

His wife, Mrs. B., who is retired from teaching music at a small college in the city in which they live, was becoming increasingly upset and depressed over the situation, and his psychiatrist felt that she should get some type of therapy for herself. As both of them are well known locally, the B.'s expressed a wish to get therapy in another city. For that reason, as well as to get another opinion on Dr. B., they were referred to us.

Psychiatric History

The patient considered himself rather normal from an emotional standpoint until his depression eight years ago, although he admitted that he usually likes a "good argument," which he also likes to win. In addition, he admitted to occasional use of amphetamines during busy times in his medical practice, and he had self-medicated on codeine after his automobile accident for about three months. He had become concerned about the codeine and had managed to taper off his use of it. One younger brother had had a recurrent alcohol problem and died from liver complications about five years ago. His father was generally a very energetic individual, but the patient remembered that on several occasions his father as moody for several weeks at a time. The wife recalled that the patient had been somewhat depressed at ages 35 and 38, but it had cleared spontaneously without his seeking treatment.

Medical History

Until the injury in the auto accident 14 years ago, Dr. B. had been in generally good health, but now he has residual stiffness and arthritis in the left arm. Following his heart attack, he made a rather good recovery in three months but has continued to have occasional angina pains on exertion, which he treats with sublinguinal nitroglycerine. Four years ago, it was found that he had early glaucoma in both eyes, as well as cataracts, which have gradually grown. He cannot drive at night because of the glare, but he has not wanted to do anything yet about the cataracts. For control of the glaucoma, he was put on pilocarpine eyedrops four times daily. He complains greatly of his eyes blurring, and he does very little reading as a consequence. When he was hospitalized two years ago, it was noted that he had frequent premature ventricular contractions (PVCs) and occasional runs of rapid ventricular heartbeat, and he was put on quinidine four times daily, with considerable improvement.

Social and Family History

The patient is the second of five children. One sister is three years older; another sister is younger. Of two younger brothers, one died five years previously. His mother, to whom he had felt very close, died of a complication of childbirth when he was 9 years old. His father was a very well known and popular general practitioner who not only had a large practice but also had been involved in politics and real estate. He was a very busy and strict person whom the patient respected but found difficult to love. There was a common expectation both by the people of the city and by his family that the patient would go into practice with his father and eventually would take over his practice. Indeed, he did work with him and had a very thriving practice, but his father died suddenly of a heart attack when the patient was 45. The father had remarried a "good woman" who treated the patient rather well, but the patient always tended to resent her and called her by her first name.

The patient's wife is four years younger than he and has a master's degree in music. They have three children: a son who is a lawyer and two married daughters, one of whom has been treated for alcoholism. None of the children live in the same town, but the patient and his wife feel that the relationships are fairly good. Both consider their marriage to be basically good.

Examination

Mental Status

When first seen, the patient had been out of the hospital for about two weeks, and thus was about three weeks from ECT. He is a large, slightly obese, white male who looks about his stated age. He was pleasant and cooperative but had an air of slight confusion and perplexity, and his speech was slow. In spite of that, he was oriented to the date, time, place, and circumstance and knew that he had had ECT, although he thought he had had just four instead of nine treatments. He could give little detail about his illness, and he was not up on current events, stating that he did not watch television and has difficulty concentrating. He described his mood as slightly depressed and "73 percent of normal." His major complaint was restlessness, and he worried that his wife was probably suffering because of his illness. There was no paranoid or delusional thinking, and his insight seemed fairly good. In some formal memory testing he got eight figures forward and five in reverse.

Functional Status

During administration of the OARS Multidimensional Functional Assessment Questionnaire, the patient was generally cooperative but tried to laugh some things off in a feeble way. He made one error on the preliminary questionnaire. On the Social Resources (SR) he was rated 2, as his wife could take care of him indefinitely; but his other family and friends had tended to drift away during his recurrent depressions. Economically he was rated 1, as he had ample income from inheritance and his own investments during his practice. On the Mental Health (MH) scale he was rated 4, or moderately impaired, because of the persistence of some depression and a mild organic mental syndrome. Physically he was rated 4, because of the existence of several problems that needed ongoing medical treatment and that interfered with his functioning. The rating on the Activities of Daily Living (ADL) scale was 3; it was close to 4 because he was not doing some things he could do; his wife was doing them for him because of his dependent attitude.

Assessment and Discussion

About three weeks after the initial contact, the case was presented to the intake conference, at which time Dr. B. was interviewed alone and then with his wife. At that time he was somewhat defensive and showed mild hostility, probably because of being in the position of patient rather than physician. He spoke with some bitterness about the things that had happened to him and brought up analogies of unfinished work and business. The examining psychiatrist felt these analogies referred not only to having had to retire early because of illness but also to possible unresolved feelings of inadequacy in light of the standards and achievements of his father. Dr. B complained of great difficulty in remembering things, but almost casually excused some of his past behavior because of his inability to remember.

When Dr. and Mrs. B. were interviewed together, it was noted that they both were very tense and rather guarded. She tended both to speak up if he hesitated and to defend him. On direct questioning, she indicated that he was occasionally rather overenergetic and overactive, and at times moody, and that he tended to drink more on these occasions. They indicated that they had a "glass or two" of sherry in the late afternoon together. They did indicate a wish for any type of treatment that might help prevent the recurring depression. She also recalled that he had been having some memory and concentration problems for several years and that these seemed variable.

The attending geropsychiatrist commented afterward that this patient presented a complicated problem consisting of a recurring affective illness, a long-standing personality problem, and somewhat more memory deficit than one would expect to see six weeks after ECT. There is a past history of some abuse of amphetamines, codeine, and alcohol, although he had apparently managed to get these under control himself. As a physician, he is part of a group at very high risk for substance abuse; the abuse rate of the profession is about 30 times that of the general population. Common potential problems are work strain, marital difficulties, physical pain, omnipotence, and easy availability of drugs. Reflection about his history of mood swings over much of his adult life, as well as his rather poor history of response to the usual tricyclic antidepressants, yielded the feeling that he may actually have manic-depressive disease that has become more obvious and more depressive in recent years. Therefore, it was recommended that a trial of lithium therapy be undertaken. The exact nature of the organic mental syndrome could not be determined this soon after ECT, but—in light of his known arteriosclerotic vascular problem—the impairment might be the result of cerebral vascular disease. More likely, it might be from drug intoxication, since he had been on quinidine, pilocarpine, and several antidepressants and tranquilizers, any one of which might produce confusion. Another possibility, in light of his recurrent severe depressions, is that he might be manifesting a pseudodementia.

The social worker who had seen the patient, as well as his wife, for the initial evaluation was struck by the fact that this highly trained and well-known man had become so isolated. He had tended to be a "workaholic" until his illnesses handicapped him, and he had developed little in the way of recreational activities or skills. His wife described him as "sitting like a vegetable" when he was depressed, with little desire to see either his friends or his children. Recently his wife has been his main social contact.

The psychologist indicated that baseline psychologic tests would be helpful to determine the extent and progress of the organic mental syndrome. It was too close to the ECT for such tests to be of much value, however, and they should be done in three to six months.

Therapeutic Plan

The recommendation of the intake conference was that Dr. B. should be seen by one of the geropsychiatrists every other week for individual therapy, and that the wife should be seen by the social worker every other week. They should also be seen together by both therapists to help support each of them and to better understand and treat the conflicts that had arisen between them. The wife was moderately depressed, and it was felt that psychotherapy should be the primary choice for her. Dr. B., on the other hand, should be put on lithium carbonate to see if recurrences of the depression could be stopped. This would be done on an outpatient basis, with frequent checks of the serum lithium level, since older people get lithium toxicity easily at lower levels than younger people and the levels are often somewhat erratic.

The physical therapist recommended a course of physical therapy to try to decrease the pain and stiffness in the patient's left arm, as well as a general, mild progressive exercise program.

Dr. B.'s lack of interests and hobbies and his loss of social contacts are continuing problems for the patient and his wife, and the social worker indicated that efforts would be made to involve him in more social and volunteer activities and to help him renew contacts with his old acquaintances.

Intervention and Follow-up

Both Dr. and Mrs. B. were quite faithful about attending the scheduled appointments, and they were given support for Dr. B.'s slow recovery. His mood gradually improved. He began to attend a Senior Citizens' Day program, and they both joined a health spa where they occasionally did water exercise. The patient's lithium level stabilized, and he had few side effects other than an intermittent fine tremor. Gradually, his ability to concentrate and remember improved considerably, and he began to read again. Psychologic testing at six months showed mild, diffuse organic mental syndrome. The frequency of the visits was decreased to once monthly.

The cataracts began to grow worse, however, and after about a year he was having trouble reading and had to give up driving, which was a great blow to him. Gradually he became more and more depressed again, and the antidepressant doxepin was added at a very low dose, along with Hydergine, which has some antidepressant effect and a very low incidence of toxicity. Slowly he began to withdraw again and to get more and more confused, with hesitancy and occasional slurring of his speech. The frequency of visits was increased. He began to show some staggering in his gait, and both of them admitted to drinking a "couple" of glasses of wine together daily. He was counseled to reduce his drinking, but he denied drinking "too much." Within two weeks his situation had obviously deteriorated further; he had become quiet and lethargic and had fallen twice. He had developed marked aphasia, and as he groped for words, he had several catastrophic-type reactions with marked flushing and brief confusion. His wife admitted that he had been drinking a fifth of a gallon of sherry daily for several weeks and that she had joined him in this. When seen, he was unsteady and disoriented to time and recent events. He was disheveled and had a shaggy beard growth. He was admitted to the hospital for evaluation and withdrawal. It was noted that he complained of depression and that his liver was slightly enlarged and tender. He was tremulous; this worsened within the first 24 hours after admission, so a Librium withdrawal was undertaken. An electroencephalogram (EEG) showed diffuse cortical slowing, and a computerized tomographic (CT) brain scan showed some cortical atrophy with ventricular enlargement that the neurologist felt was compatible either with an Alzheimer's-type dementia or, more likely, an alcohol-related degeneration. Over a four-week period he improved moderately and was discharged. The patient and his wife were confronted with the neurologic deterioration. This seemed to reach them, and they both decided to give up their long-standing pattern of daily wine consumption. He stabilized physically, but remained confused and depressed after discharge. Within four months, he actually became depressed to the point of suicidal preoccupation in spite of the antidepressants lithium, Hydergine, and doxepin; he was readmitted. It was felt that the amount of medication necessary to relieve his depression was also sufficient to confuse him further. Therefore, after some debate, he underwent another course of ECT, with good results. Within about six weeks he cleared up fairly well and was put back on the lithium.

Subsequently, he has had gradual improvement in intellectual function, socialization, and mood. Dr. B. and his wife have been followed for two more years, and both of them remain totally off alcohol. He had his cataracts extracted about eight months after his last hospitalization and did well with that. Subsequently, he has resumed reading, and they have become socially active again. Both were surprised when he became potent again about 12 months after stopping the alcohol.

Commentary

This case represents a complicated problem of sequential prescribed and self-prescribed polydrug abuse in an individual with major affective disorder of a circular type. People like Dr. B often self-medicate with alcohol to help their depression when they are low and to slow the mania when they are excited. His profession has a high substance abuse rate, which is probably related to work stress and the availability of drugs, as well as to personality factors. He and his wife had been used to drinking almost daily much of their lives, and it was hard for them to accept the fact that alcohol had become increasingly toxic because of his increased sensitivity with age, his brain damage, and interactions with other drugs. The brain changes indicated significant damage over many years, but it is important to note that he gradually improved to a surprising extent over a year's time after stopping the alcohol. Even the professionals sometimes forget that alcohol is a potent drug, especially in the elderly.

NOTES

1. American Psychiatric Association, *Diagnostic and Statistical Manual of Mental Disorders 3rd ed. (DSM III)*, (Washington, D.C.: American Psychiatric Association, 1980), pp. 163-179.

2. Charles Winick, "Maturity Out of Addiction," *Bulletin on Narcotics* 14 (1962): 1-7.

3. John A. O'Donnell, *Narcotic Addicts in Kentucky* (Washington, D.C.: Public Health Service, 1969), Pub. no. 1881.

4. William C. Capel and G.T. Stewart, "The Management of Drug Abuse in Aging Populations: New Orleans Findings," *Journal of Drug Issues* 1 (1971): 114-121.

5. E.F. Pascarelli, "Drug Abuse and the Elderly," *Substance Abuse, Clinical Problems, and Perspectives*, eds. J.H. Lowinson and P. Ruiz (Baltimore: Williams & Wilkins, 1981), pp. 752-757.

6. A. Helps, "Friends in Counsel," in *The Home Book of Quotations*, 10th ed., ed. B. Stevenson (New York: Dodd, Mead, 1967).

7. G.L. Maddox, "Drugs, Physicians, and Patients," in *Drugs and the Elderly*, eds. D.M. Petersen, F.J. Whittington, and B.P. Payne (Springfield, Ill.: Charles C Thomas, 1979), pp. 5-13.

8. Ibid., pp. 5-13.

9. APA, *Diagnostic and Statistical Manual*, pp. 163-179.

10. Larry G. Peppers and Ronald G. Stover, "The Elderly Abuser: A Challenge for the Future," *Journal of Drug Issues* 9 (1977): 73-83.

11. Emil F. Pascarelli, "An Update on Drug Dependence in the Elderly," *Journal of Drug Issues* 9 (1979): 47-54.

12. M.A. Schuckit, "Geriatric Alcoholism and Drug Abuse," *Gerontologist* 17 (1977): 168-174.

13. David M. Petersen, F.J. Whittington, and E.T. Beer, "Drug Use and Misuse among the Elderly," *Journal of Drug Issues* 9 (1979): 5-26.

14. C. Eisdorfer and M.M. Basen, "Drug Misuse by the Elderly," in *Handbook on Drug Abuse,* eds. R.I. Dupont, A. Goldstein, and J. O'Donnell (Washington, D.C.: National Institute on Drug Abuse, U.S. Department of Health, Education, and Welfare and Office of Drug Abuse Policy, 1979), pp. 271-276.

15. D.G. Peck, "Alcohol Abuse and the Elderly: Social Control and Conformity," *Journal of Drug Issues* 9, no. 1 (1979): 63-71

16. B.L. Mishara and R. Kastenbaum, *Alcohol and Old Age* (New York: Grune & Stratton, 1980).

17. C. P. Chien, E.J. Townsend, and A.A. Ross-Townsend, "Substance Use and Abuse among the Community Elderly: The Medical Aspect," *Addictive Diseases* 3, no. 3 (1978): 357-372.

18. P.J. Forni, "Alcohol and the Elderly," in *Drugs and the Elderly,* ed. R.C. Kayne (Ethel Percy Andrus Gerontology Center, University of Southern California, 1978), pp. 75-83.

19. M.A. Schuckit, E.R. Morrissey, and M.R. O'Leary, "Alcohol Problems in Elderly Men and Women," *Addictive Diseases* 3, no. 3 (1978): 405-416.

20. A. Simon, L.J. Epstein, and L. Reynolds, "Alcoholism in the Geriatric Mentally Ill," *Geriatrics* 23 (1968): 125-131.

21. C.M. Gaitz and P.E. Baer, "Characteristics of Elderly Patients with Alcoholism," *Archives of General Psychiatry* 24 (1971): 372-378.

22. Donna S. Woolf, "CNS Depressants: Alcohol," in *Substance Abuse: Pharmacologic, Developmental and Clinical Perspectives,* eds. G. Bennett, C. Vourakis, and D.S. Woolf (New York: John Wiley & Sons, 1983), pp. 17-38.

23. APA, *Diagnostic and Statistical Manual,* pp. 101-162.

24. M.A. Schuckit and P.A. Pastor, Jr., "The Elderly as a Unique Population: Alcoholism," *Alcoholism* 2 (1978): 31-38.

25. M.J. Eckardt, "Consequences of Alcohol and Other Drug Use in the Aged," in *The Biology of Aging,* eds. J.A. Behnke, C.E. Finch, and G.B. Moment (New York: Plenum Press, 1978), pp. 191-204.

26. Gaitz and Baer, "Characteristics of Elderly Patients," pp. 372-378.

27. Criteria Committee, National Council on Alcoholism, "Criteria for the Diagnosis of Alcoholism," *American Journal of Psychiatry* 129 (1972): 127-135.

28. S. Zimberg, "Diagnosis and Treatment of the Elderly Alcoholic," *Alcoholism* 2 (1978): 27-29.

29. James T. Hartford and T. Samorajski, "Alcoholism in the Geriatric Population," *Journal of the American Geriatrics Society* 30, no. 1 (1982): 18-24.

30. D.M. Petersen and F.J. Whittington, "Drug Use among the Elderly: A Review," *Journal of Psychedelic Drugs* 9, no. 1 (1977): 25-37.

31. M.M. Glatt, "Experiences with Elderly Alcoholics in England," *Alcoholism: Clinical and Experimental Research* 2, no. 1 (1978): 23-26.

32. Allan R. Meyers et al., "Social and Psychologic Correlates of Problem Drinking in Old Age," *Journal of the American Geriatrics Society* 30, no. 7 (1982): 452-456.

33. Roger G. Dunham, "Aging and Changing Patterns of Alcohol Use," *Journal of Psychoactive Drugs* 13, no. 2 (1981): 143-151.

34. Jack H. Mendelson and Nancy K. Mello, "Diagnostic Criteria for Alcoholism and Alcohol Abuse," in *The Diagnosis and Treatment of Alcoholism*, eds. J.H. Mendelson and N.K. Mello (New York: McGraw-Hill, 1979), pp. 1-18.

35. Ruth Maxwell, *The Booze Battle* (New York: Praeger Publishers, 1976).

36. Shelia B. Blume, "Alcoholism," in *Current Therapy*, ed. H.F. Conn (Philadelphia: W.B. Saunders, 1982), pp. 921-925.

37. E.M. Pattison, "The Selection of Treatment Modalities for the Alcoholic Patient," in *The Diagnosis and Treatment of Alcoholism*, eds. J.H. Mendelson and N.K. Mello (New York: McGraw-Hill, 1979), pp. 125-229.

38. E.W. Busse and D.G. Blazer, "Disorders Related to Biological Functioning," in *Handbook of Geriatric Psychiatry*, eds. E.W. Busse and D.G. Blazer (New York: Van Nostrand Reinhold, 1980), pp. 390-414.

39. D.G. Mayfield, "Alcohol Problems in Aging Patients," in *Drug Issues in Geropsychiatry*, eds. W.E. Fann and G.L. Maddox (Baltimore: Williams & Wilkins, 1974), pp. 35-40.

40. Alexander Simon, "The Neuroses, Personality Disorders, Alcoholism, Drug Use and Misuse, and Crime in the Aged," in *Handbook of Mental Health and Aging*, eds. J.E. Birren and R.B. Sloane (Englewood Cliffs, N.J.: Prentice-Hall, 1980), pp. 653-670.

41. Bijan Etemad, "Alcoholism and Aging," *Current Psychiatric Therapies* 19 (1980): 111-114.

42. C.E. Becker, "Pharmacotherapy in the Treatment of Alcoholism," in *The Diagnosis and Treatment of Alcoholism*, eds. J.H. Mendelson and N.K. Mello (New York: McGraw-Hill, 1979), pp. 283-303.

43. E.M. Pattison, R. Coe, and H.O. Doerr, "Population Variation among Alcoholism Treatment Facilities," *International Journal of Addiction* 8 (1973): 199-229.

44. Zimberg, "Diagnosis and Treatment of the Elderly Alcoholic," pp. 27-29.

45. Schuckit and Pastor, "The Elderly as a Unique Population," pp. 31-38.

46. M.A. Schuckit and P.O. Miller, "Alcoholism in Elderly Men: A Survey of a General Medical Ward," *Annals of the New York Academy of Sciences* 273 (1976): 558-571.

47. Gaitz and Baer, "Characteristics of Elderly Patients," pp. 372-378.

48. M.J. Blusewicz et al. "Neuropsychological Correlates of Chronic Alcoholism and Aging," *Journal of Nervous and Mental Disease* 165, no. 5 (1977): 348-355.

49. Schuckit and Pastor, "The Elderly as a Unique Population," pp. 31-38.

50. D.S. Woolf, "CNS Depressants: Other Sedatives-Hypnotics," in *Substance Abuse: Pharmacologic, Developmental, and Clinical Perspectives*, eds. G. Bennett, C. Vourakis, and D.S. Woolf (New York: John Wiley & Sons, 1983), pp. 39-51.

51. Peppers and Stover, "The Elderly Abuser," pp. 73-83.

52. S. Cohen, *The Substance Abuse Problems* (New York: Haworth Press, 1981), pp. 329-335.

53. W.C. Capel et al., "The Aging Narcotic Addict: An Increasing Problem for the Next Decades," *Journal of Gerontology* 27 (1972): 102-106.

54. W.C. Capel and L.G. Peppers, "The Aging Addict: A Longitudinal Study of Known Abusers," *Addictive Diseases* 3, no. 3 (1978): 389-403.

55. P.J. Deely et al. "The Special Problems and Treatment of a Group of Elderly Chinese Opiate Addicts in New York City," *British Journal of Addiction* 74 (1979): 403-409.

56. E.F. Pascarelli and W. Fischer, "Drug Dependence in the Elderly," *International Journal on Aging and Human Development* 5 (1974): 347-357.

57. Strategy Council on Drug Abuse, *Federal Strategy for Drug Abuse and Drug Traffic Prevention* (Washington, D.C.: Strategy Council on Drug Abuse, 1979).

58. E.F. Pascarelli, "Drug Abuse and the Elderly," in *Substance Abuse, Clinical Problems, and Perspectives,* eds. J.H. Lowinson and P. Ruiz (Baltimore: Williams & Wilkins, 1981), pp. 752-757.

59. Chien, Townsend, and Ross-Townsend, "Substance Use and Abuse among the Community Elderly," pp. 357-372.

60. D. Guttmann, "Patterns of Legal Drug Use by Older Americans," *Addictive Diseases* 3, no. 3 (1978): 337-356.

61. J.R. Solomon and A.S. Weiner, "Drug Misuse in the Elderly," in *Pharmacologic Aspects of Aging,* eds. L.A. Pagliaro and A.M. Pagliaro (St. Louis: C.V. Mosby, 1983), pp. 34-44.

62. Chien, Townsend, and Ross-Townsend, "Substance Use and Abuse among the Community Elderly," pp. 357-372.

63. Guttmann, "Patterns of Legal Drug Use by Older Americans," pp. 337-356.

64. A.D. Whanger and P. Lewis, "Survey of Institutionalized Elderly," in *Multidimensional Functional Assessment. The OARS Methodology,* ed. E. Pfeiffer (Durham, N.C.: Center for the Study of Aging and Human Development, 1975), pp. 71-77.

65. J. Williamson and J.M. Chopin, "Adverse Reactions to Prescribed Drugs in the Elderly: A Multicenter Investigation," *Age and Aging* 9 (1980): 73.

66. N. Hurwitz, "Predisposing Factors in Adverse Reactions to Drugs," *British Medical Journal* 1 (1969): 536-538.

67. R.C. Eberhardt and L.A. Robinson, "Clinical Pharmacy Involvement in a Geriatric Health Clinic at a High-rise Apartment Center," *Journal of the American Geriatrics Society* 27 (1979): 514.

68. A.J.D. Friesen, "Adverse Drug Reactions in the Geriatric Client," in *Pharmacologic Aspects of Aging,* eds. L.A. Pagliaro and A.M. Pagliaro (St. Louis: C.V. Mosby, 1983), pp. 257-293.

69. J.I. Walker and H.K.H. Brodie, "Neuropharmacology of Aging," in *Handbook of Geriatric Psychiatry,* eds. E.W. Busse and D.G. Blazer (New York: Van Nostrand Reinhold, 1980), pp. 102-124.

70. A.D. Whanger, "Nutrition, Diet, and Exercise," in *Handbook of Geriatric Psychiatry,* eds. E.W. Busse and D.G. Blazer (New York: Van Nostrand Reinhold, 1980), pp. 473-497.

71. D.M. Petersen and C.W. Thomas, "Acute Drug Reactions among the Elderly," *Journal of Gerontology* 30, no. 5 (1975): 552-556.

72. Pascarelli, "Drug Abuse and the Elderly," pp. 752-757.

73. W.D. Poe and D.A. Holloway, *Drugs and the Aged* (New York: McGraw-Hill, 1980), p. 108.

74. Pascarelli, "Drug Abuse and the Elderly," pp. 752-757.

75. Solomon and Weiner, "Drug Misuse in the Elderly," pp. 34-44.

76. F.N. Brand, R.T. Smith, and P.A. Brand, "Effect of Economic Barriers to Medical Care on Patient's Noncompliance," *Public Health Report* 92 (1977): 72-78.

77. D. Schwartz et al. "Medication Errors Made by Elderly Chronically Ill Patients," *American Journal of Public Health* 52 (1962): 2018-2029.

78. E. Memminki and J. Heikkila, "Elderly People's Compliance with Prescriptions, and Quality of Medication," *Journal of Social Medicine* 3 (1975): 87-92.

79. J. Gollub, "Psychoactive Drug Misuse among the Elderly: A Review of Prevention and Treatment Programs," in *Drugs and the Elderly,* ed. R.C. Kayne (Ethel Percy Andrus Gerontology Center, University of Southern California, 1978), pp. 84-102.

80. James K. Cooper, David W. Love, and Paul R. Raffoul, "Intentional Prescription Nonadherence (Noncompliance) by the Elderly," *Journal of the American Geriatrics Society* 30, no. 5 (1982): 329-333.

81. D.F. Moore, "Over-the-Counter Drugs," in *Substance Abuse: Pharmacologic, Developmental, and Clinical Perspectives,* eds. G. Bennett, C. Vourakis, and D.W. Woolf (New York: John Wiley and Sons, 1983), pp. 102-109.

82. Gollub, "Psychoactive Drug Misuse among the Elderly," pp. 84-102.

83. D.B. Larson, A.D. Whanger, and E.W. Busse, "Geriatrics," in *The Therapists Handbook,* 2nd ed., ed. B.B. Wolman (New York: Van Nostrand Reinhold, 1983), pp. 343-388.

84. L.A. Pagliaro and A.M. Pagliaro, *Pharmacologic Aspects of Aging* (St. Louis: C.V. Mosby Company, 1983).

85. T.F. Blaschke, "Potential Drug Interactions in Aging Patients," in *Age and the Pharmacology of Psychoactive Drugs,* eds. A. Raskin, D.S. Robinson, and J. Levine (New York: Elsevier, 1981), pp. 93-103.

86. R.F. Prien, C.J. Klett, and E.M. Caffey, "Polypharmacy in the Psychiatric Treatment of Elderly Hospitalized Patients: A Survey of 12 Veterans Administration Hospitals," *Diseases of the Nervous System* 37 (1976): 333-336.

87. R. Prentice, "Patterns of Psychoactive Drug Use among the Elderly," in *The Aging Process and Psychoactive Drug Use,* National Institute on Drug Abuse, Services Research Monograph Series, pub. no. 79-813 (Washington, D.C.: U.S. Department of Health, Education and Welfare, 1979), pp. 17-41.

88. R.T. Zawadski, E.B. Glazer, and E. Lurie, "Psychotropic Drug Use among Institutionalized and Noninstitutionalized Medical Aged in California," *Journal of Gerontology* 33, no. 6 (1978): 825-834.

89. Chien, Townsend, and Ross-Townsend, "Substance Use and Abuse among the Community Elderly," pp. 357-372.

90. K.W. Back and D.A. Sullivan, "Self-Image, Medicine, and Drug Use," *Addictive Diseases* 3, no. 3 (1978): 373-382.

91. M. Hochhauser, "Learned Helplessness and Substance Abuse in the Elderly," *Journal of Psychoactive Drugs* 13, no. 2 (1981): 127-133.

Chapter 10

Personality, Marital, Family, Psychosexual, and Sleep Disorders

David B. Larson, Susan S. Larson, and Alan D. Whanger

This chapter's intent is to satisfy two goals. The first is to discuss subjects not dealt with in the rest of the book. These include two character disorders (passive-aggressive personality and hysterical personality), marital problems, family problems, psychosexual problems, and sleep disorders. The first four topics are discussed and a representative case example presented. The latter two are very briefly addressed. The two character disorders presented have been chosen because of the frequency and the severity that they can bring into the treatment setting. The second aim is to present a combined systems approach to dealing with character disorders and marital and family problems. An especially effective mode of dealing with problems of the aged is by treating not only the individual but also the involved system, such as the marriage and the family.[1-4]

CHARACTER DISORDERS

Passive-Aggressive Personality Disorder

An excellent description of the passive-aggressive personality as seen in the elderly has been given by Verwoerdt.[5] He describes how the passive aspects of the personality are used as the mode for expressing anger. The anger is often dealt with by "being hurt" by another and then holding onto the old "hurts," seeking retribution with these memories. A second passive aspect of passive-agressive personality involves dependence. These persons are infrequently conscious of their dependency needs, getting into relationships where unspoken demands are placed on another to fulfill their unexpressed dependency wishes.

Verwoerdt points out that the passive-aggressive person often latches onto others who are also passive or dependent, creating the potential for an

189

eventually stressful relationship. Problems occur when the passive-aggressive person no longer has enough ego strength to maintain a presentation of independence. The individual first fights losing face, but often cannot continue "the fight," giving way to a regressive-dependent state.

According to *The Diagnostic and Statistical Manual for Mental Disorders (DSM-III)*, the criteria for passive-aggressive personality disorder are based on both the individual's current and long-term functioning.[6] These criteria include the following:

1. Noncompliant with the responsibilities expected of them (especially in their jobs or social lives).
2. Indirect types of uncooperativeness (with several examples listed):
   a. intentional inefficiency
   b. "forgetfulness"
   c. stubbornness
3. As a result of the above, there is a history of problems with their jobs or social lives.
4. A persistence of the passive-aggressive behavior even when other interactive behaviors might be more effective.

According to the *DSM-III*, other complications of the passive-aggressive personality disorder are: (1) major depressive disorder, (2) dysthymic personality disorder, and (3) alcohol dependence. In agreement with Verwoerdt, *DSM-III* sees the passive-aggressive individual as dependent, lacking in self-confidence, and pessimistic about the future.[7] Last, it is important to note that those who have passive-aggressive cores have little realization that it is their own behavior that is largely responsible for their difficulties.[8] The passive-aggressive personality is a distinct clinical entity, according to the *DSM-III*. It will be found in the geriatric population.

Another way to consider the concept of passive-aggression is as a coping strategy for handling stress. George Vaillant does this in his writings. He defines passive-aggression as a behavior where "aggression toward others [is] expressed indirectly and ineffectively through passivity or [else it is] directed against the self."[9] Vaillant, instead of viewing passive-aggression as a unique clinical syndrome, sees it as one of five immature defenses, or coping strategies. One immature defense is often clustered with other immature defenses. Vaillant found that the males in his 30-year follow-up study demonstrating immature defenses had a much greater potential for a bad marriage or a divorce than they had for a satisfactory marital experience. Additionally, those with immature defenses more frequently had problems with alcoholism and depression than those with more mature defenses.[10]

In summary, passive-aggression has been considered both (1) a unique clinical syndrome and (2) an immature coping strategy. Either can be seen among the elderly and will be associated with the individual's trying to cope effectively with unrecognized dependence and hostility.

For passive-aggressiveness to express itself, a "significant other," or someone else, is needed with whom the passive-aggressive person can interact passive-aggressively. Consequently, it is often most hopeful to intervene in this "passive-aggressive" system. This system, for the passive-aggressive elderly, frequently includes their spouse and their children—both by birth and by marriage. Thus, the therapist should at least consider including the spouse and the rest of the family of the elderly passive-aggressive patient in order to interrupt the passive-aggressive system effectively.

Case Example

Mrs. C. was a 71-year-old widow whose husband had died 12 years previously. She lived in a small city of 100,000, with her daughter and son, respectively, living 5 miles and 40 miles away from her. Since the time of her husband's death, she had become increasingly passive-aggressive with them. Both children agreed that their mother had been passive-aggressive with her husband, their father. After his death, she had shifted her focus of interest from him to them.

Her passive-aggression was demonstrated in her difficulty in handling anger and dependence. She had become increasingly dependent on both her children for personal contact, calling them on the phone constantly. The daughter had reached the point where she answered very few telephone calls and frequently left the phone off the hook, not knowing how to deal with her mother's dynamics. If she answered the telephone and listened to her mother, then she would be supporting her mother's unspoken dependency needs and the mother would increase the frequency of her calls. If she answered the telephone and told her mother that she could not talk, then her mother would be "hurt" for several days or weeks. Either way, the daughter was "the loser" and the mother was "the winner" in this passive-aggressive system. The referral was eventually made because the patient had started to entangle a local internist with her telephoning dynamics. He rapidly and wisely referred her to a geropsychiatry clinic.

The patient did fulfill the *DSM-III* criteria for passive-aggressive personality. Historically, she had demonstrated criteria 1 and 3. Similarly, she had expressed resistance through (1) stubbornness, (2) intentional inefficiency, and (3) "forgetfulness" (see criterion 2).

On the therapist's initial contact with Mrs. C., he set firm limits about the number of times she could call the therapist per week, since she had called the internist more and more often. Thereafter, the problems seemed to worsen with her children. This was understandable, for the therapist had created a shift in the system. To assist the children the therapist encouraged both to set fair but firm limits concerning the number of telephone calls Mrs. C. could make per week.

The adult offspring were not able to follow the therapist's direction. Thus, he called the mother, daughter, and son together to have a "family" session. In that session he played a mediator role, setting limits for the number of telephone calls Mrs. C. could make, the amount of time that she could talk, and how the son and daughter could respond if she went beyond her limits.

In individual therapy, the therapist worked with Mrs. C. first by starting to fulfill her dependency needs through social activities—in particular, her church and a local day-care center. Mrs. C. also started to work in therapy on her dependency and hostility issues. She started to see the therapist as her son who had died at age 7 after a tonsillectomy. She openly talked of her anger toward "that doctor" and spoke of her hopes for "that son" who had died and had not achieved what she had wished for him. For Mrs. C., the doctor-son-therapist became someone with whom she could more openly discuss her anger and dependency impulses.

Meanwhile, as the latter process intensified, there was a movement by the daughter back into the passive-aggressive relationship with her mother. The therapist intervened by reminding the daughter to continue with the previously set and bilaterally agreed-upon limits. He set further limits, telling the daughter that if the situation continued, it might be important for her to obtain therapy herself. The daughter was then able to extract herself from the passive-aggressive system.

In summary, the case involved individual approaches with: (1) limit setting, (2) forming a therapeutic alliance (with Mrs. C.), and (3) developing a transferencelike relationship (Mrs. C. with the therapist-son-doctor). Additionally, the system was included, involving the two offspring. The main system intervention was to help the children to set fair limits with their mother over her telephone calling and, later, to help them continue with the original contract concerning limits.

The Hysterical Personality

The hysterical personality disorder as characterized by Verwoerdt is one in which the individual acts in an emotionally unpredictable and dramatic fashion.[11] Verwoerdt sees the dramatic aspect of the personality as an attention-seeking mechanism. Celani agrees, stating that the hysteric is one who "communicates frailty and helplessness" to structure the social setting in order to gain attention.[12] The hysterical syndrome is one that, according to Celani, reinforces the individual's taking on various roles, including those of

(1) illness, (2) frailty, (3) passivity, and (4) seductiveness. In the aging hysteric, as Verwoerdt points out, it "becomes more difficult or inappropriate to employ the instrument of genital sex" for fulfilling dependency needs.[13] In other words, with increasing age, it becomes more difficult for the hysteric to be seductive. On the other hand, the aging hysteric can certainly continue to use and even enlarge the roles of being ill, frail, and passive.

In *DSM-III*, the hysterical personality is called the histrionic personality disorder. There are two major criteria:

1. Behavior that is demonstrated by at least three of the following:
   a. Exaggerated responses to minor events
   b. Strong desire for exciting activity
   c. Tendency to draw attention to the self
   d. Exaggerated emotional expression
   e. "Temper tantrums"
2. Problems in interacting interpersonally, indicated by demonstrating at least two of the following:
   a. Demands much from others
   b. Is inconsiderate of others
   c. Is seen by others as superficial
   d. Seeks reassurance and frequently is dependent on others
   e. Tends to manipulate others with suicidal threats or gestures[14]

The major impairment with histrionic disorder is that interpersonal relationships are usually difficult and ungratifying to the individual. There are multiple complications that can result from this disorder (refer to *DSM-III*). Associated features are as follows:

1. Achieves little intellectually although the person frequently is "creative and imaginative."
2. Is easily influenced by others and by various fads, and they can "adopt convictions strongly and readily."
3. Frequently complain of problems with their health.[15]

Goodwin and Guze point out that far more females than males in the general adult population would be diagnosed as being histrionic personalities.[16] With aging, one would assume that this male/female ratio would remain the same or even increase, since, in general, women live longer than men.

In the following case example, as in the previous section on passive-aggression, therapeutics consist of an individual and systems approach.

Case Example

Mrs. N. was a divorced 77-year-old woman who initially presented to a geropsychiatric clinic after she was moved from a Florida retirement condominium community to her daughter's home. Mrs. N.'s problems had started some five years ago, after mandatory retirement at the age of 72. She had had a very enjoyable career in a major medical center, training radiology technicians. She particularly enjoyed and reminisced about the attention and respect the doctors who knew her had for her.

She had not been so successful in bringing up her four daughters. She and her husband had divorced, and she was left to raise the children alone. At the time of the referral, two of her daughters had little interest in seeing her and openly discouraged her from visiting them and their families. The other two children seemed rapidly to be approaching a similar viewpoint.

The daughter involved in the case said that Mrs. N. had been anticipating retirement for years but that when it happened, she was not ready emotionally. Mrs. N. had not been able to make any friends in the last five years. Additionally, she had not become involved in social groups, such as church, clubs, voluntary hospital organizations, and so forth.

Over the last few months, the situation had become worse, since Mrs. N. had become suspicious that her third daughter's husband had "eaten up" much of her financial cushion. She had become very angry at this daughter and her husband. She conveyed to her referring daughter that "all was lost"—in essence, a dramatic sense of hopelessness, fragility, and weakness. The daughter traveled 1,000 miles to rescue her mother from the perils that now beset her.

Once the daughter had completed the rescue from Florida, things were fine—for several days. Soon, though, Mrs. N. demonstrated many symptoms that would confirm her histrionic dynamics. To illustrate:

- She became very upset over small events.
- Frequently, when she became upset, she would have an outburst of anger.
- She constantly was drawing attention to herself. She became upset when her daughter gave attention to others (such as the adolescent sons in the family).
- On the surface, she was usually very polite and courteous. She had difficulty, though, forming any close relationship where she could not keep control.
- She was inconsiderate of others and their problems.
- She was extremely demanding of her daughter, expecting her to be readily available.

- Mrs. N. frequently apologized to seek reassurance from her daughter. In addition, she maintained her dependency by not obtaining a new driver's license, although she had no physical problems and, on psychological testing, still had an IQ near 115.
- Last, and this is what finally precipitated Mrs. N.'s referral to the clinic, she had begun to threaten to kill herself if things did not improve. The daughter tried to improve Mrs. N.'s environment, but this was to no avail.

Finally, a very frustrated, worn-out, and angry daughter called the clinic for assistance.

In treatment, Mrs. N. was found to be a dependent, emotionally dramatic, and emotionally shallow individual. She did overreact to small events when she did not get what she wanted. In essence, Mrs. N. had a hysterical personality disorder whose dynamics had worsened after she retired. This exacerbation occurred, for she lost attention and recognition from some very significant people when she retired from her job.

The tack taken in therapy was first to work with Mrs. N. to gain a small amount of her trust and to form at least a partial therapeutic alliance. From there, a mother–daughter dyadic approach was taken. Both were included to (1) clarify their fears of each other and (2) decrease the mother's hysterical and, thus far, successful manipulation of her daughter. By the third of the five mother–daughter sessions, the daughter was far less responsive to being manipulated when her mother became dramatically angry, depressed, or anxious. With an unconscious realization of this, Mrs. N.'s displayed "helplessness" worsened. In individual therapy, the therapist pointed out the interactive aspects of Mrs. N.'s "weakness." She saw the connection and wept, realizing that she could effectively keep her children near her only through similar manipulative means.

In the last two mother–daughter sessions, there was much more of a sense of relief and working together. Mrs. N. made a decision to leave Florida permanently, and to be more openly dependent on her daughter. The daughter made a decision to try to become "closer to Mom," and yet to say "no" to Mrs. N. when necessary.

The therapy used individual and systems techniques; both types were needed. Mrs. N. needed to be seen individually to develop at least a partial therapeutic alliance with her attending doctor. Then the mother–daughter sessions were used to help the daughter respond less and less to Mrs. N.'s hysterical manipulations. Last, the therapist utilized Mrs. N.'s conscious and unconscious realizations in individual therapy about the mother–daughter sessions to help her consciously recognize (1) her dependency needs and (2) her need for others, in addition to her family, to fulfill these dependency needs.

MARITAL PROBLEMS

Some research has evaluated marital satisfaction among the aged. Zarit and Peterson point out that a variety of losses can affect elderly couples and can lead to a decline in marital satisfaction. These include: (1) loss of a job because of retirement, (2) loss of spouse or friends through death, and (3) loss of capabilities (of spouse or self) through physical, emotional, or cognitive debilitation.[17,18]

In a 20-year follow-up of marriages Pineo found that marital satisfaction did decline as the spouses approached their fifties and sixties.[19] Important changes that seemed to relate to lowered satisfaction in these marriages were (1) a decrease in sharing activities outside the home and (2) a decrease in intimate interactions. Rollins and Feldman found that lowered marital satisfaction was associated with husbands in retirement.[20]

The findings already briefly discussed might indicate that getting old and being married are a risky combination. Other studies have found that not to be the case. Comparing elderly married, widowed, and divorced people, Gubrium found that the widowed and divorced had a far greater chance of experiencing desolation in their everyday lives than did the elderly married.[21] Lowenthal and Haven demonstrated that those elderly couples with an intimate and stable marriage relationship had good morale and continued together in social participation.[22] Understandably, the authors viewed intimacy in elderly couples as a buffer against the role and personal losses of aging. Similarly, Roberts completed a very interesting study of couples who were married more than 50 years.[23] These couples experienced great satisfaction in their individual lives and in their marriage. These were not "perfect" marriages, but they had the aspects of commitment, companionship, and caring that seem to be crucial in the effectiveness of these long-standing marriages.

In summary, there does seem to be a potential for marital satisfaction to decrease with aging. The factors that counter this are maintaining (1) stability, (2) intimacy, and (3) social participation in the marriage. Last, an unsatisfying marriage, among the elderly, seems less desolate than being divorced or widowed.

How does one help marriages that are ailing? Bloch's summary of a review by Gurman and Kniskern illustrates that one should proceed with some form of marital therapy.[24] In their review, marital therapy was better than individual therapy 70 percent of the time when problems were predominantly of a marital type; results were statistically significant. On the other hand, individual therapy was better than marital therapy about 15 percent of the time. No statistical difference emerged between individual and marital therapy in 10 percent.

There is a scarcity of papers about marital therapy with the elderly, but some of the few are discussed. LaWall discusses a creative marital approach in which the therapist becomes a type of cotherapist with the spouse to assist with:[25]

- information gathering
- reality testing
- reality orientation
- monitoring treatment response

This approach does not relate as much to problems of marital conflict as it does to assessing the elderly with more individual physical, emotional, or senile problems.

Turning to marital conflict therapy, Lynch and Waxenberg, in a case presentation, emphasize "maximizing the positive [and] mutually satisfying aspects of the [spouses'] lives, while at the same time, helping them to express previously unvoiced dissatisfactions."[26] Zarit similarly agrees, emphasizing goals that increase marital satisfaction as critical for elderly couples with conflict.[27] These therapeutic directions are consistent with research findings, showing an increased risk for lowered marital dissatisfaction.

For a more thorough and excellent systems approach to treating elderly couples and their families, the reader is referred to *Counseling Elders and Their Families,* by Herr and Weakland, whose authors state that a realistic goal for the elderly is "revising the situation," instead of "reforming the person."[28] In their second chapter, they discuss what to avoid; in their third chapter, what to pursue.

In treating the elderly marriage, however, one should also be aware of individual and family therapeutic needs. The following case should illustrate.

Case Example

Mr. and Mrs. R. came to the clinic, having had marital problems for half of their 40-year marriage. Both were now 65 years old. Mrs. R. was already in individual therapy for recurrent problems with depression. With a recent worsening in her condition, her therapist, recognizing continuing problems in the marriage, referred them both for marital therapy.

The marital problems differed according to the husband's and the wife's analyses. The wife's list included: (1) his spending more time with repairing the house than being with her; (2) giving her little personal attention and support; and (3) giving "in to her" instead of attempting to resolve their marital conflicts. His list was composed of the following: (1) her constantly making social demands of him and (2) always wanting to have her way and being angry when she did not get it.

In addition, there was one problem on which they both agreed: Their second daughter who was now 32 years old. She was a "problem" because: (1) she previously had to get married; (2) she had a 10-year-old son she could not care for; (3) thus, mother constantly had to care for and discipline the boy; (4) she had not finished college; and (5) now, she still was not married. Both also agreed that over the last few years, neither had experienced much satisfaction in the marriage.

The therapist started by emphasizing the problems that they agreed on— the daughter and the low marital satisfaction. Second, he had to ally himself more with the husband, at times, due to the husband's fears that the therapist would join forces with the wife, and that they both would make unfair demands of him and "always want their way."

The therapist supported their contrasting therapeutic goals. He clarified that the husband was more task oriented in his goals, while the wife was more emotionally oriented. He affirmed both positions as acceptable to him as a therapist.

Therapeutic work continued, and within four or five sessions, the husband was spending more time with his wife socially and she was spending more time with him in accomplishing his home repairs. As they both started to enjoy their marriage more, problems with the daughter became worse. From a systems perspective, this was not unexpected, for as part of the system shifted (toward improvement), another part of the system shifted (toward debilitation) to restore the system's equilibrium.

The therapist pointed out that both had become more frustrated over their daughter—they both agreed. Thus, the therapist recommended including their daughter in family work. The mother stated, "She'll never come." To prevent the mother from sabotaging the daughter's participation, the therapist called the daughter. She readily came, expressing surprise that (1) "my parents would ever get marital therapy" and (2) "my Dad would ever willingly get into therapy."

In family therapy, the daughter started out somewhat similarly to Mr. R., fearing that the therapist might ally himself with her mother and agree with her unfair expectations and demands. Finding this not to be the case, she expressed her differences with her mother and found that she was surprisingly (albeit reluctantly) supported by her father. The problem centered on the daughter's ability to be responsible. The mother felt that she still was not capable of being responsible. On the other hand, the daughter and the father felt that the mother needed to give up trying to be responsible for the daughter. In other words, it was time for the mother to stop making the type of demands upon her daughter that she would make of an uncontrollable 8-year-old.

Toward the end of the family therapy sessions, the daughter was supported in responding less and less to her mother's demands. It was important then to move the husband to a closer emotional alignment with his wife. If such a move had not occurred, the mother would have had no one but the daughter and grandson to relate to emotionally and might eventually have recreated the previous problematic relationships.

The daughter felt that she would also need to help to (1) refrain from continuing to respond to her mother as she had previously and (2) learn to take on the responsibility of her son. The therapist agreed and helped her find an individual therapist.

In summary, the foregoing marital therapy case led to both family and individual therapies. In the 12 marital therapy sessions, the husband and wife learned, in short, that they could agree to disagree. As the marriage improved, the daughter's status worsened. The daughter was then brought into the system, and five family therapy sessions were held, interrupting the continuing emotional struggle between daughter and mother. Consequently, the mother turned to her husband for a far more constructive emotional interaction, while the daughter sought to build her own life and her relationship with her son by finding an individual therapist.

FAMILY PROBLEMS

In this section, difficulties the elderly might have with their families are reviewed. Related research findings are then presented along with family therapy interventions and a case example.

Larson et al. and Zarit list stresses for the aged that might cause them psychiatric symptomatology.[29,30] These include (1) decreased finances, (2) decreased social involvement, and (3) increased problems with their now adult children. This section centers on the last—increased problems the elderly might experience with their adult children.

Shanas believes that most of the elderly's families provide a great deal of emotional and financial support for their elderly parents.[31] Isaacs found that "neglect by relatives played a negligible part in the need for admission" to a geriatric unit in Glasgow.[32] Thus, there are many, if not most, geriatric families who care for their own, whether meeting their emotional, financial, or physical needs.

Much research related to the elderly and their families has evaluated the older person's morale within the family unit. Lawton has operationalized the concept of morale and sees it composed of a variety of items, such as (1) attitude toward one's own aging, (2) degree of loneliness, and (3) anxiety.[33]

Other less critical items are one's social availability, positive affect, and self-rated help. Thus, morale is certainly not a single factor but a compilation of factors. Two studies evaluating morale in the elderly are worth discussing. Seelbach and Sauer found that the less dependent aging individuals were on their adult children, the greater was their morale.[34] Mancini found that when elderly people felt they could understand their adult children emotionally, their morale was better.[35] Both findings demonstrate the importance for the aging person to feel that he or she has mastered the art of relating to adult children. Such mastery is associated with a high degree of morale.

Problems with Grown-up Offspring

What about those who do not feel in such control with their adult children—whether due to increasing dependence on them, inability to understand them, or other factors not yet studied? Gurman and Kniskern have demonstrated very well that with problems predominantly involving the family, one should proceed with some type of family therapy.[36] They have documented their review of research comparing family therapy to both individual therapy and control groups. Their findings are impressive in light of research outcome findings about other types of therapy.[37]

Dealing with a family therapeutically is more complex than interacting with one person. Thus, a therapist or clinician often first needs to be convinced that involving the family might have more therapeutic gains than working with a single individual. Reifler and Eisdorfer demonstrated relatively low broken-appointment and missed-appointment rates in a clinic for impaired elderly where the family was included in the individual elderly patient's care.[38] They felt that their services created a more effective treatment setting both for the individual and the family.

So how does one interact with a geriatric patient's family? Kuypers and Trute recommend four tasks to the family participant therapist:[39]

1. participating in the work as a therapist with a "balanced sense of optimism"
2. helping the family to know and agree to the present task
3. identifying and communicating to the family their strengths
4. helping the family to experience success early in the family work (and also identifying that success)

These tasks are not just for family members in family therapy. Having a "balanced sense of optimism" is an attitudinal task for the therapist as well, and one that these authors believe is crucial. The next task, "helping the family . . . to agree to the present task," is one of establishing some agreed-upon goals for family therapy. The other two tasks emphasize recognizing family strengths and family therapeutic successes. Both tasks, once performed, will make possible a furthering of the "sense of optimism" for the family, drawing members closer to the end of therapy.

Taking a more practical approach, Blazer discusses interventions he considers important for therapists interacting with families of geriatric patients.[40] He describes helping the family in:

1. recognizing the older person's capabilities
2. identifying behavior that is acceptable and unacceptable
3. providing specific training that may help them to be more effective caretakers
4. encouraging them to take breaks from the continuous (or near continuous) care that may be required for their elderly relative
5. finding available community resources
6. affirming they might have understandable negative feelings or frustrations in assisting in the care of their impaired elderly relative

Having considered the "how-to's" and "what-to-do's" in approaching the family, let us discuss some of the types of family therapy for the elderly.

Karpf recognizes family therapy as one of the five basic modalities for treating psychological disorders in late life.[41] The others are psychoanalytic, supportive, group, and behavioral. The authors propose two different types of family therapy for the elderly. There are (1) family therapy for more recent problems and (2) family therapy for longer term problems.

Grauer et al. believe that it often is possible to resolve family conflict if the patient gives a history of:

• gratifying relationships with parents and siblings
• a satisfying marriage
• a reasonably good work record
• adapting to the retirement[42]

If a history of most of the preceding is present, Grauer et al. believe that there are "welfare emotions" that will augment resolution of the family conflict. Larson et al. agree with the Grauer group, believing that there frequently is a "family adjustment reaction."[43] This results from the family's being unable to cope with one of their own experiencing difficulty with aging. These families might look extremely stressed but with a few therapy sessions, they can be reequilibrating back to their more normal, nonstressed state. Thus, there are families who have been able to cope with various stresses of family development but have had difficulties with aging. A short family therapy crisis intervention type of treatment is recommended for these groups.

On the other hand, some families have experienced stress for much of their lives together. Again, Herr and Weakland advise that it is important therapeutically to "revise the situation" and not to revise the person(s).[44] There are a number of forms of family therapy that might benefit these families.

An intergenerational therapy has been described by Framo in which elderly parents are frequently involved to assist in the marital therapy of one of their adult children.[45] Spark uses a similar approach, stating "The therapeutic process enables a new phase of identification to begin between the generations and may replace the old, deprived or distorted aspects of their relationship."[46] Framo and Spark recommend a family therapy that starts with the adult children and works up in generations. On the other hand, Quinn and Keller describe a family therapy approach in which the elderly come for help with their adult children.[47] This might not be so surprising, considering the previously noted findings of Mancini.[48] Thus, there are family therapies for longer term problems starting with the adult children and working up to the aging parent, and forms that start with the aging parent and work down to the adult children.

In summary, there are three ways that families—including aging parents and their grown-up children—may cope with the stresses of aging. First, they might cope with it successfully, as most seem able to do. Second, they might experience stress but—with a long-term history of successful family functioning—be able to make use of a more crisis-oriented intervention. Third, they might experience stress and—having had a longer family history of unsuccessful functioning—need not only to resolve the crisis but also to attempt to change the "deprived and distorted"parts of the intergenerational relationship to make it emotionally richer and more honest.

The case illustrates the second category.

Case Example

Mrs. S. was a 79-year-old woman who came to a geropsychiatry clinic because of her family's recent and continuing frustrations with her.

She and Mr. S. had 40 years of a very satisfactory marriage. He was now 83, and although he had some hearing and cardiovascular limitations, he was still doing rather well physically and was able to drive the tractor around the small family farm. The S.'s had four children, all living within a four-hour drive of the parents' home. The children felt that both parents had diligently worked and cared for them in their formative years. They felt that Mrs. S. had been especially committed to their receiving the love and caring they needed as children.

Eight months prior to the first visit at the geropsychiatry clinic, Mrs. S. had fallen and strained her left knee. She had an almost constant mild to moderate pain level resulting from the fall. One daughter's opinion was that it was not only the "pain that bothered Mom" but also her "not being able to do as much as she had previously" and a confrontation that "she's really getting old." Several of the other children agreed.

Mrs. S. wanted relief. Thus, in that eight-month period, she had seen at least 12 doctors, including neurosurgeons, orthopedic specialists, and general practitioners. All had said that (1) she did have pain, (2) they could not provide total relief, and (3) they would recommend exercise and/or analgesics for partial relief.

Mrs. S. was dissatisfied with the evaluations she received although they continued to be similar in content. She thus ended up at our clinic for evaluation "number 13." The family was stressed by her (1) constant complaining about her knee pain and (2) frequent pleadings to be taken to another doctor, clinic, or medical center for evaluation. It was at the children's urgings that this visit was to a psychiatric clinic. After finding out that psychiatry could not give total relief for knee pain, Mrs. S. wanted to go on to number 14. The therapist asked if she would complete the present session and have one more session to which—in addition to herself and her daughter—her husband, one son, and two other daughters would come. She agreed, insisting that "it wouldn't do any good."

The therapist finished the session by talking to and forming a therapeutic alliance with the daughter. He discovered that the children tried to "help" their mother with her pain complaints by (1) reminding her what the doctors had said, (2) insisting that her pain was not as bad as she thought, and (3) finally getting angry with her. None of these interventions had been very effective. In asking the daughter why the children continued to take their mother to medical evaluations, she responded that they "felt that it was the least that they could do, considering all the good years that mom had given us."

The daughter went on to describe a family that, through the years, had functioned well. With their mother's recent deterioration, the children had made efforts to help, but frequently these efforts were made out of guilt, were unsuccessful, and ended in anger. The children wanted to help, yet they realized that their help thus far had been ineffective and had made them even more frustrated than if they had not tried at all.

The therapist recommended a second session at which the daughter would be responsible for making sure that the rest of the children and the husband were present. The second session was to be a month later and the family and therapist would decide then how to start to handle the family's present problem—their mother. One month later in the family session, with all present, all agreed that efforts to help Mrs. S. with her pain had thus far been unsuccessful and no one now knew what to do.

The therapist told the mother that she had a right to complain about her pain, for no one had found relief for her. From there, the therapist told the children that no longer would they have to listen to excessive complaints from their mother. When they had enough of her complaining, they were to remind her politely what the doctor had said, tell her they could not listen anymore, and leave the room. As for taking her to further medical evaluations, the therapist emphasized that Mrs. S. could see as many medical doctors as she chose, but now she might have to go alone to see them. No longer did her children have to respond affirmatively to her requests to be taken. She could still ask them to take her, but the therapist gave them permission to say no to these requests.

In a one-year follow-up, the therapist found that Mrs. S.'s pain complaints continued, although their intensity was less. She had gone to see two doctors on her own and seemed more receptive to their telling her that there was little that could be done for "complete relief" of her pain. The family realized that when they did what the therapist directed them to do, the situation improved. They still went back to their old family dynamics at times, trying to "get her to stop" complaining. Such efforts were as ineffective as they ever had been. The therapist encouraged them to come back for a third session if they felt it might help. The daughter said that they would do so if the family status again started to worsen. Because of the distance involved, the family did not return to the clinic. The therapist did call one of the daughters every two to three months to check on the status, which remained stable.

In summary, this therapy included the family, for the family's efforts at bringing "complete relief" to the mother's complaining did little to resolve her wish for "complete relief" of her pain. The family members stopped their ineffective responses by, in essence, saying they disagreed. They politely left when the complaining became excessive and no longer took her (covertly supporting her hope) to see any more doctors. This is an example of a family adjustment reaction due to aging within the family. The therapist revised the situation, not the person.

PSYCHOSEXUAL DISORDERS

The importance of sex to the elderly is not yet a well-researched subject. In this brief section the authors discuss (1) how sexual problems affect elderly people's marriages and (2) how aging changes some of the stages of sex.

Results from the Duke University longitudinal study on aging revealed that there was much variation among study participants' sexual activity and interests.[49] In other words, there seemed to be a wide range of what might be considered "normal" for the elderly. Concerning sexual difficulties, Murphy and his group found in a community sample that 20 percent of the couples 60 and over admitted to having sex-related problems in their marriages.[50]

Turning to how these sex-related problems might influence the marriage, Murphy demonstrated a strong association between elderly marriages with sex-related problems and elderly marriages with marital problems.[51] Pineo demonstrated that disenchantment in the later years of marriage was partially due to a lessened frequency of sexual intercourse.[52] An interesting finding by Lowenthal and Haven was that the elderly who are still experiencing satisfactory sexual relationships deal with losses in their later years, such as death or retirement, more successfully than those who are not sexually satisfied.[53]

In summary, these research findings reveal that (1) most of the elderly people who are still married experience satisfactory sex; (2) those elderly not enjoying their sexual relationships often are not satisfied with their marital relationships; and (3) those who are still enjoying their sexual relationships seem to cope more successfully with some of the stresses of aging.

How Aging Affects the Stages of Sex

Scheingold and Wagner, extracting from Masters and Johnson, point out that aging alters the excitement, plateau, orgasmic, and resolution phases of sexual activity for both males and females.[54] Many of the alterations potentially make the sexual experience less intense for both sexes. Problems for the man may be increased by the greater length of time needed and difficulty encountered in reaching an erection, and by the decreased intensity of the orgasm itself.

On the other hand, difficulties for the woman may result from (1) changes in how long it takes for vaginal lubrication to appear, (2) the reduced size of the orgasmic plateau, and (3) the shorter orgasmic phase. For a more thorough discussion of normal physical changes in aging and how they affect sexuality, the reader is referred to Scheingold and Wagner or to *Sex After Sixty*, by Butler and Lewis.[55,56] The latter also has an excellent summary of how various emotional problems, physical problems, and drugs may affect sex for the elderly.

Case Presentation

The B.'s had had an enjoyable 35-year marriage. In the last 5 years, though, they had become increasingly dissatisfied. The factors that led to their marital problems included (1) both retiring from jobs they had enjoyed, (2) his gradually worsening diabetes, (3) both experiencing biological depressions necessitating antidepressant medication, (4) the moving away of their son, and (5) the death of Mrs. B.'s father who was a close friend to both of them.

When they first saw the therapist, they felt that their individual depressions were much improved. They saw their marriage as substandard for them and their sexual lives as poor, for they had not had satisfactory sex for two years.

They described the basis for their marital problems as Mr. B.'s inactivity and lack of responsibility, coupled with Mrs. B.'s overactivity and excessive responsibility for the various tasks of the home. Mrs. B. saw herself as "worn out," while Mr. B. perceived himself as burdensome—someone who "got in the way" of Mrs. B.

Sexually, Mr. B. could no longer maintain an erection. He was embarrassed by his problem, and Mrs. B. knew he was. Thus, she was reluctant to "push" him to have sex or to get help with his problem. In addition, Mrs. B. was frequently worn out at the end of the day because of her multiple "responsibilities." Thus, she frequently had little interest in sex herself. Mr. B., although physically less tired, knew that she felt worn out; therefore, he was reluctant to "push" her to have sex with him.

A similar type of problem existed in both the marriage and the sexual lives of these two people. This problem could best be conceptualized as a stalemate. The stalemate consisted of both parties being so afraid to change the status quo that they would rapidly concede that the other spouse's position, although frustrating, was unalterable without making the situation even worse. Thus, although the wife was frustrated with Mr. B.'s sexual and marital difficulties, she really never expected anything more of him; similarly with Mr. B. concerning Mrs. B.

Since the marital and sexual problems were of a similar nature, the therapist made a choice initially to improve the marital system and then later to assist with the sexual dissatisfaction. The B.'s agreed to this approach.

During the first four marital sessions, the therapist clarified that for Mr. B., although he had given up his responsibilities to make life easier for his wife, he had, in essence, made her life far more stress filled. Mrs. B. enthusiastically supported this stance. For Mrs. B., the therapist clarified that although she had taken on more and more responsibilities to make life simpler for her diabetic husband, she had in actuality infantilized him. He now had few if any responsibilities. Her approach had not made life simpler; it had made life far more complex and difficult for him. Mr. B. strongly supported this clarification.

Because the marriage had been a successful one through the years, the B.'s were able to give up their efforts at "helping" and return to their old and far more successful marital patterns. As the marriage improved, the B.'s wanted to improve their sex life. The therapist directed them to not "have any sex at all" on a certain upcoming night. He also directed Mr. B. to direct Mrs. B. in sexually stimulating him. They agreed to attempting the intervention and were pleasantly surprised when Mr. B. not only had an erection but also an orgasm. On a two-month follow-up, the B.'s were continuing to have enjoyable sex.

In this case, there were both sexual and marital problems. The therapist chose to deal with the marital problems first, because the B.'s seemed less anxious over immediate success than they did for the sexual difficulties. Since the sex and marital problems were of a similar nature, the couple's experiencing success with the marriage facilitated success with their sexual difficulties. The therapist further assured their success by (1) encouraging Mr. B. to be in control and (2) telling them not to have sex. The latter instruction was to keep their success from being based on a successful orgasm; paradoxically, it was based on having no orgasm. The B.'s responded very well both to the paradox and to Mr. B.'s new-found control.

SLEEP DISORDERS

There are various sleep functions that decrease or increase with progressing age.[57] These include:

- decrease in the total amount of sleep time
- decrease in sleep efficiency (taking more time in bed to effect the same amount of net sleep)
- increase in the total amount of time it takes to fall asleep
- increase in the number of times one wakes up during the night
- increase in insomnia

For the clinician, it is important to note that, according to Spiegel, some 20 percent of persons older than 50 have problems sleeping through the night; while 20 to 30 percent of those between the ages of 45 and 70 and approximately 40 percent of those over 70 experience difficulty falling asleep at night.[58] Spiegel also notes that when the elderly individual brings a sleep complaint to a clinician's attention, it is frequently demonstrable through polygraphic sleep studies, and that elderly men with sleep problems tend to have an underlying psychological problem.[59] The latter is not the case for women.

Butler and Lewis emphasize that "what may seem like a need for less sleep" among the elderly "may be the result of illness, anxiety [or] depression."[60] They also point out that older people may need more sleep because of illness or degenerative disease. They see the additional sleep in these cases essentially "a vital restorative." On the other hand, a potential danger results if elderly people need excessive sleep because of too much medication.

Treating Sleep Problems in Elderly Patients

For the treatment of sleep problems among the elderly, Butler and Lewis recommend first trying nondrug treatments.[61] These include any selection of the "just before going to bed" items listed here:

1. having a back massage
2. taking a warm bath
3. drinking a glass of warm milk
4. taking a small amount of beer or wine
5. reading a book
6. not having any stimulants (e.g., coffee, Coke)
7. not watching TV programs that might get one excited

For a further description of medications that might be used for sleep problems in the elderly, the reader is referred to Verwoerdt's *Clinical Geropsychiatry*.[62] Drs. Whanger and Verwoerdt recommend chloral hydrate as the best present hypnotic since it leaves little hangover, has a low risk of habituation, and does not suppress REM sleep very significantly. They recommend one of the shorter-acting benzodiazepines (e.g., temazepam, oxazepam, or lorazepam) as their second choice.

Case Example

Mrs. O. was a 63-year-old woman who had had increasing sleep difficulties for the last four months. She had tried: (1) stopping her bedtime coffee, and drinking some warm milk instead, (2) having her husband give her a back massage just before going to sleep, and (3) reading a dull, boring book. None of these efforts had worked, and she now was finding herself increasingly tired and irritable. The clinician looked for any other symptoms consistent with her being depressed or highly anxious but found none.

The clinician discussed with her using a sleep medication, chloral hydrate. She was willing to "try anything" at this time. They discussed the side effects of the drug, especially reviewing the potential for gastric irritation. He encouraged her not to take it nightly unless she felt that she had to in order to sleep. Mrs. O. found that she needed it nightly for the first five days, and then needed it less and less over the next two months. She then stopped taking the medication.

In reviewing the case with her clinician, Mrs. O. said she felt that just having the medication made it easier for her to go to sleep. She knew that if she was unsuccessful, the chloral hydrate was there. She also came to realize that her insomnia was due to "my uncertainty about my heart." She had a slightly abnormal electrocardiogram (EKG) that at first did not bother her. In time, though, she came to worry about her heart, its regularity, any chest pain, and so forth. She finally went to have her EKG rechecked. When it was retaken and found to be normal, she was relieved. She said, "Ever since I realized my heart was fine, I've had no problems with sleep whatsoever." Thus, the medication was useful, both to help her get the sleep she needed when she couldn't get to sleep on her own, and to take some of the worry out of whether or not she would be able to get to sleep.

NOTES

1. John J. Herr and John H. Weakland, *Counselling Elders and Their Families* (New York: Springer Publishing, 1979).

2. D.B. Larson and D.G. Blazer, "Family Therapy with the Elderly," in *A Family Approach to Health Care in the Elderly*, eds. D.G. Blazer and I. Siegler (Menlo Park, Calif.: Addison-Wesley, 1983), pp. 95-111.

3. A.C. Robin Skynner, *Systems of Family and Marital Psychotherapy* (New York: Brunner/Mazel, 1976).

4. Dan G. Blazer, "Working with the Elderly Patient's Family," *Geriatrics* 33 (1978): 117-123.

5. A. Verwoerdt, "Anxiety, Dissociative and Personality Disorders in the Elderly," in *Handbook of Geriatric Psychiatry*, eds. Ewald W. Busse and Dan G. Blazer (New York: Van Nostrand Reinhold, 1980), pp. 368-380.

6. *The Diagnostic and Statistical Manual for Mental Disorders*, 3rd ed. (Washington, D.C.: American Psychiatric Association, 1980), pp. 328-330.

7. APA, *Diagnostic and Statistical Manual*, p. 328.

8. Ibid., p. 328.

9. George E. Vaillant, *Adaptation to Life* (Boston: Little, Brown, 1977), p. 384.

10. Ibid., pp. 322-326.

11. Adrian Verwoerdt, *Clinical Geropsychiatry*, 1st ed. (Baltimore: Williams & Wilkins, 1976), p. 92.

12. David Celani, "An Interpersonal Approach to Hysteria," *American Journal of Psychiatry* 133 (1976): 1414-1418.

13. Adrian Verwoerdt, *Clinical Geropsychiatry*, 1st ed. (Baltimore: Williams & Wilkins, 1976), p. 93.

14. *The Diagnostic and Statistical Manual for Mental Disorders*, 3rd ed. (Washington, D.C.: American Psychiatric Association, 1980), pp. 313-315.

15. APA, *Diagnostic and Statistical Manual*, p. 314.

16. Donald W. Goodwin and Samuel B. Guze, *Psychiatric Diagnosis*, 2nd ed. (New York: Oxford University Press, 1979), p. 74.

17. Steven H. Zarit, *Aging and Mental Disorders: Psychological Approaches to Treatment* (New York: The Free Press, 1980), pp. 338-343.

18. James A. Peterson, "Marital and Family Therapy Involving the Aged," *The Gerontologist*, 13 (1973): 27-31.

19. Peter C. Pineo, "Disenchantment in the Later Years of Marriage," *Marriage and Family Living* 23 (1961): 3-11.

20. Boyd C. Rollins and Harold Feldman, "Marital Satisfaction over the Life Cycle," *Journal of Marriage and the Family* 32 (1970): 20-28.

21. Jaber F. Gubrium, "Marital Desolation and the Evaluation of Everyday Life in Old Age," *Journal of Marriage and the Family* 36 (1974): 107-113.

22. Marjorie Fisk Lowenthal and Clayton Haven, "Interaction and Adaptation: Intimacy as a Critical Variable," *American Sociological Review* 33 (1968): 20-30.

23. William L. Roberts, "Significant Elements in the Relationship of Long-Married Couples," *International Journal of Aging and Human Development* 10 (1979-80): 265-271.

24. D.A. Bloch, "Family Therapy," in *The Family: Evaluation and Treatment*, eds. Charles K. Hofling and Jerry M. Lewis (New York: Brunner/Mazel, 1980), pp. 225-239.

25. John LaWall, "Conjoint Therapy of Psychiatric Problems in the Elderly," *Journal of the American Geriatric Society* 29 (1981): 89-91.

26. Gerald Lynch and Barbara Waxenberg, "Marital Therapy with the Aging: A Case Study," *Psychotherapy: Theory, Research and Practice* 8 (1971): 59-63.

27. Steven H. Zarit, *Aging and Mental Disorders: Psychological Approaches to Treatment* (New York: The Free Press, 1980), pp. 343-349.

28. Herr and Weakland, *Counselling Elders and Their Families*, pp. 6-7.

29. Larson and Blazer, "Family Therapy with the Elderly."

30. Zarit, *Aging and Mental Disorders*, pp. 77-105.

31. Ethel Shanas, "Social Myth as Hypothesis: The Case of the Family Relations of Old People," *The Gerontologist* 19 (1979): 3-9.

32. Bernard Isaacs, "Geriatric Patients: Do Their Families Care?" *British Medical Journal* 4 (1971): 282-286.

33. M. Powell Lawton, "The Philadelphia Geriatric Center Morale Scale: A Revision," *Journal of Gerontology* 30 (1975): 85-89.

34. Wayne C. Seelbach and William J. Sauer, "Filial Responsibility Expectations and Morale among Aged Parents," *The Gerontologist* 17 (1977): 492-499.

35. Jay A. Mancini, "Family Relationships and Morale among People 65 years of Age and Older," *American Journal of Orthopsychiatry* 49 (1979): 292-300.

36. Alan S. Gurman and David P. Kniskern, eds., *Handbook of Family Therapy* (New York: Brunner/Mazel, 1981), pp. 742-752.

37. Nathan B. Epstein and Louis A. Vlok, "Research on the Results of Psychotherapy: A Summary of Evidence," *American Journal of Psychiatry* 138 (1981): 1027-1035.

38. Burton V. Reifler and Carl Eisdorfer, "A Clinic for the Impaired Elderly and Their Families," *American Journal of Psychiatry* 137 (1980): 1399-1403.

39. Joseph A. Kuypers and Barry Trute, "The Older Family as the Locus of Crisis Intervention," *The Family Coordinator* 27 (1978): 405-411.

40. Blazer, "Working with the Elderly Patient's Family," pp. 117-123.

41. Ronald J. Karpf, "Modalities of Psychotherapy with the Elderly," *Journal of the American Geriatrics Society* 28 (1980): 367-371.

42. H. Grauer, D. Betts, and F. Birnbom, "Welfare Ⴚmotions and Family Therapy in Geriatrics," *Journal of the American Geriatrics Society* 21 (1973): 21-24.

43. Larson and Blazer, "Family Therapy with the Elderly."

44. Herr and Weakland, *Counselling Elders and Their Families*, pp. 6-7.

45. James L. Framo, "Family of Origin as a Therapeutic Resource for Adults in Marital and Family Therapy," *Family Process* 15 (1976): 193-210.

46. Geraldine M. Spark, "Grandparents and Intergenerational Family Therapy," *Family Process* 13 (1974): 225-239.

47. William H. Quinn and James F. Keller, "A Family Therapy Model for Preserving Independence in Older Persons: Utilization of the Family of Procreation," *The American Journal of Family Therapy* 9 (1981): 79-84.

48. Mancini, "Family Relationships and Morale," pp. 292-300.

49. Adrian Verwoerdt, Eric Pfeiffer, and Hsioh-Shan Wang, "Changes in Sexual Activity and Interest of Aging Men and Women," *Journal of Geriatric Psychiatry* 2 (1969): 163-180.

50. Gerald J. Murphy, Walter W. Hudson, and Paul P. L. Cheung, "Marital and Sexual Discord among Older Couples," *Social Work Research and Abstracts* (1980): 11-16.

51. Ibid., pp. 11-16.

52. Pineo, "Disenchantment in the Later Years of Marriage," pp. 3-11.

53. Lowenthal and Haven, "Interaction and Adaptation," pp. 20-30.

54. Lee D. Scheingold and Nathaniel N. Wagner, *Sound Sex and the Aging Heart* (New York: Human Sciences Press, 1974), pp. 36-38.

55. Ibid.

56. Robert N. Butler and Myrna I. Lewis, *Sex After Sixty*, (New York: Harper and Row, 1976).

57. Rene Sepigel, *Sleep and Sleeplessness in Advanced Age* (New York: SP Medical and Scientific Books, 1981), pp. 213-226.

58. Ibid., pp. 1-8.

59. Spiegel, *Sleep and Sleeplessness in Advanced Age*.

60. Robert N. Butler and Myrna I. Lewis, *Aging and Mental Health* (St. Louis: C. V. Mosby, 1977), p. 303.

61. Ibid.

62. Adrian Verwoerdt, *Clinical Geropsychiatry*, 2nd ed. (Baltimore: Williams & Wilkins, 1981), pp. 193-195.

Part III

Thinking Systematically about Improving Therapeutic Interventions

Chapters 11 and 12 mark a transition in perspective from a clinical to an epidemiological orientation. Yet the reader will note that the application of epidemiological methods to clinical practice helps to ensure that inherent bias on the part of the clinician regarding diagnosis and intervention procedures does not limit the advances of the health care delivery system. Clinical epidemiology not only involves the classic task of the epidemiologist—to count the frequency and distribution of disease in a given population—but also the development of methods for studying the workings and effectiveness of clinical practice. In other words, empiricism is reduced and the processes of making decisions about clinical management of the older adult is placed on a more rational basis.

Chapter 11

The Use of Epidemiologic Survey Data in Planning for Geriatric Mental Health Services

Dan G. Blazer and George L. Maddox

INTRODUCTION

Most mental health centers face the challenge of planning new, effective, and efficient services for older adults. The extension of the Community Mental Health Center Acts in 1975 specifically mandated services for persons 65 years of age and older.[1] This mandate was a response to an increased awareness of the high prevalence of mental disorders among the elderly and the high number of people aged 65 and older being admitted to and residing in mental hospitals.[2-5] Furthermore, many individuals are admitted to long-term care facilities (i.e., nursing homes) with significant mental health impairment (which, in fact, may be a significant reason for the admission).[6-8] In European countries a number of comprehensive mental health programs have been developed for the elderly that can serve as models for development in this country.[9-11] Yet a review of existing community mental health centers in the United States reveals that few have developed or initiated specific programs for the elderly.[12,13] This challenge will undoubtedly be looked upon by many as an additional burden on centers with overextended personnel and continued budgetary restraints. Yet the mandate may serve as a nidus for the development of planning strategies that have a greater probability of success than those used in the past. An epidemiologic approach can serve as a basis for planning mental health services in the community by highlighting objectives of the services, predicting the type and numbers and personnel, and therefore predicting the cost of services.

Epidemiology is the study of the distribution of health and disease in populations and of the factors that influence this distribution. Lillienfeld has stated that one goal of epidemiology is "the provision of the basis for the development and evaluation of . . . health services."[14] Epidemiologic data have traditionally been used to compute the rates of illness, so Lillienfeld has, to some degree, stepped outside these traditional boundaries. In describing the uses of epidemiology, Morris speaks of an "epidemiology for administrators" in which "community diagnosis" provides the basic information for comprehensive planning of services.[15] In this community analysis he also correctly identifies the distinction between need and demand. Medical, psychological, and social needs are defined by society and its professionals when it is believed that something can and should be done about them, yet many individual and social factors influence the translation of need for services into demand for services. Demand, obviously, is a more accurate predictor than need of service utilization. Epidemiologic data, therefore, should assess not only the need of services but also the demand for services in a defined population if it is to be effective in mental health service planning.

The classic psychiatric epidemiologic surveys of the late 1950s concentrated on either specific psychiatric designs (e.g., New Haven, Lundby, and Ireland) or mental impairment (e.g., the Stirling County Study and the Mid-Manhattan Study).[16–20] The latter surveys revealed the prevalence of mental impairment in the community as high and the risk of developing mental impairment as large for certain groups. In addition, the heavy burden of treatment was concentrated in inpatient psychiatric facilities. Therefore, the Joint Commission on Mental Illness and Health recommended that "emotionally disturbed patients should have skilled attention and helpful counselling available to them in their community."[21] Yet the community mental health centers (CMHCs) that were meant to address the commission's recommendations have not been the success that had been hoped. Consumers began to attack the system (e.g., the Nader Report on the NIMH: *The Madness Establishment*).[22] In 1971 and 1974 the Government Accounting Office sent detailed reports to Congress that criticized the CMHCs.[23] Among issues singled out for criticism were (1) the need for planning related to the area to be served (i.e., community diagnosis), (2) the need for planning related to services provided, and (3) the need for coordination of center activities. A fourth area, which could have been added, was the need for assessing the translation of need into demand.

The Department of Psychiatry and the Center for the Study of Aging at Duke University Medical Center worked with the Durham County Community Mental Health Center during the past six years to develop a program of geriatric mental health services. Epidemiologic data collected within the county served as a basis for the development of this program. The prevalence of functional impairment in the community and the perceived needs of community-based elderly were assessed. A conceptual framework for planning is described and then applied to the Durham County experience in this chapter. Be aware that planning and development are ongoing processes, however. The geriatric mental health program operating today continues to change as it is influenced by newly identified needs, demands, financial constraints, and so forth. The experience cannot be universally applied, but serves as a model of systematic program planning and development.

PROGRAM PLANNING

A Conceptual Framework

Ideally, the planning of a new community-based program for the management of older persons with mental health impairment requires the following steps (modified from Wing):[24]

1. Identify the catchment area and individuals with the behaviors of interest (i.e., the target population):
   a. Define the catchment area.
   b. Define the behaviors of interest (i.e., diseases, symptoms, and/or disabilities).
   c. Assess the number, percentage, and distribution of individuals with the behaviors of interest within the catchment area.
2. Define and determine potential services that might prevent or delay the natural course of individuals suffering from the diseases, symptoms, and disabilities of interest.
3. Identify the perceived need of services by the target population.
4. Identify the present utilization of service.
5. Identify factors that interfere with or augment the use of services by the target population (i.e., those social and individual factors, in addition to need, that determine service utilization, such as the capability of the service providers, clients' access to and satisfaction with services, and so forth).
6. Determine the types and amounts of personnel required to provide the specified services (i.e., staffing pattern).
7. Evaluate the accuracy of the planning efforts in predicting the types of services required, the utilization of new services, and the staffing pattern necessary for effective service delivery.

The planning team progressed through each of these steps in translating epidemiologic data into the development of a new geriatric mental health service. A brief review of this process follows. Details of the epidemiologic survey are presented elsewhere, including major findings and validity and reliability studies.[25,26]

PLANNING THE OARS-GET CLINIC

Identify the Catchment Area and Individuals with the Behaviors of Interest

Durham County, North Carolina, is the *catchment area* for the Durham Community Mental Health Center and was the catchment area for this study. No specific program was available for the treatment of older adults seven years ago. The Community Mental Health Center and the Center for the Study of Aging agreed that a clinic for the treatment and management of the elderly mentally impaired would be established at Duke University Medical Center (i.e., the Older Americans Resources and Services Geriatric Evaluation and Treatment Clinic, or OARS-GET Clinic). This clinic would serve as a satellite of the CMHC to care specifically for the elderly. The development of this clinic was associated with an epidemiologic survey of elderly people in Durham County, as described next.

Subjects

A stratified 1 in 10 sample of Durham County residents 65 years and older ($n= 997$) was drawn for an epidemiologic survey in early 1972 (see Table 11-1). Eighty-five percent of these people agreed to be interviewed in their homes. Institutionalized individuals (e.g., those living in a nursing home) were included in a separate sample, not reported here.[27]

The investigators chose functional impairment in mental health as the indicator of need for mental health services within the community. Those demonstrating functional impairment in mental health thus became the target population. This selection coincides with the stated goals of the original community mental health centers:

1. To reduce the incidence, prevalence and degree of *disability* associated with mental illness.
2. To keep mentally ill patients living and *functioning* in their own communities where they have the support of their families and friends.[28]

Limitations in the concepts of mental health and illness have led many psychiatric epidemiologists to use operational measurements of morbidity and measured impairment.[29,30] Impairment, or limitation in function, is an easier concept to define and measure than the presence or absence of specific psychiatric illnesses.[31] An AMA committee has, in fact, stated that "the aim of the psychiatric evaluation is to delineate the loss of function resulting from mental illness."[32] With an increasing emphasis on case identification in

Table 11-1 Percentage Distribution of the Demographic
Characteristics in the OARS-Durham Survey
(*n*=997)

Demographic Characteristics	%
Age	
65–74	68
75+	32
Sex	
Male	37
Female	63
Race	
White	66
Black	34

Source: OARS, *Multidimensional Functional Assessment: The OARS Methodology* (Durham, N.C.: Duke University Center for the Study of Aging and Human Development, 1978) p. 76. Used with permission.

psychiatric epidemiology, however, many believe that functional impairment is not synonymous with psychiatric disability.[33] A useful compromise is represented in *DSM III*, where operational definitions of both psychiatric disorders and levels of function are combined into a multiaxial approach to diagnosis.[34]

The use of mental health functioning is more valuable when it can be combined with functioning in other areas. For example, an impairment in social functioning may significantly determine which is best: community or institutional care for a mentally impaired elderly person. The cross-sectional survey focused on *individual functional assessment* in five areas (social resources, economic resources, mental health, physical health, and activities of daily living [ADL]). The questionnaire systematically obtained subjective and objective information regarding the subjects' functioning in such a way that data in each of the five areas could be compressed or summarized into a single summary functional rating of impaired or not impaired. A combination of questions assessing perceived mental health, life satisfaction, and the "Mini-Mult" (a short form of the MMPI) were used to derive the rating of mental health function.[35] The operational definition of mental health impairment is shown in Table 11-2.

The survey revealed the following distribution of functional impairments in the catchment area. Thirteen percent of the sample were suffering from an

Table 11-2 Mental Health Rating Scale

1. Outstanding psychological health. Intellectually alert, vigorous, and active, with personality resources adequate to function well in most environments.

2. No gross psychological impairments observed, no psychiatric symptoms. Intellectual resources, emotional and behavioral controls, and social competence are adequate.

3. Mildly symptomatic or mildly psychologically impaired. May function poorly in some areas of life but can cope adequately with most everyday situations.

4. Moderately symptomatic or psychologically impaired. Has difficulty coping in one major or several smaller areas of daily life or reacts adversely to minor stresses. May function well in some areas but shows definite signs of psychological distress or intellectual impairment in other areas.

5. Severely psychologically impaired. Psychological distress or intellectual impairment either so severe or so constant as to interfere reqularly with routine interpersonal and intrapersonal interactions.

6. Grossly psychotic or severely demented to the point of requiring either intermittent or constant supervision because of aberrant or potentially harmful behavior.

Source: OARS, *Multidimensional Functional Assessment: The OARS Methodology* (Durham, N.C.: Duke University Center for the Study of Aging and Human Development, 1978), p. 192. Used with permission.

---

impairment in mental health at the time of the survey (i.e., approximately 1,300 people aged 65 and older were suffering from mental health impairment in Durham County) (see Table 11-3). Further studies indicated that approximately 7 percent of the community residents had definite cognitive impairment; 2.3 percent had symptoms of a major depressive disorder, as defined by *DSM-III*; and 14 percent perceived their physical health as poor when it was actually good.[36-38] Correlation of mental health impairment with impairment in other functional areas was as follows: social resources (r = .42), economic resources (r = .42), physical health (r = .55), and daily activities (r = .61). It is apparent from these findings that the level of mental health impairment among the elderly in Durham County is significant but not overwhelming, yet the mentally impaired are quite likely to be suffering impairment in other areas of functioning.

Table 11-3 Functional Status by Dimension for Community and Clinic Populations

Dimension	Mean Rating	% Impaired
Community Population (n=997)		
Social resources	2.0	9
Economic resources	2.6	14
Mental health	2.3	13
Physical health	2.8	26
ADL	2.4	22
Clinic Population (n=98)		
Social resources	3.2	41
Economic resources	3.1	45
Mental health	4.2	81
Physical health	3.5	49
ADL	3.7	61

Source: OARS, *Multidimensional Functional Assessment: The OARS Methodology* (Durham, N.C.: Duke University Center for the Study of Aging and Human Development, 1978), p. 78. Used with permission.

Define and Determine Potential Services That Might Prevent or Delay the Natural Course of Individuals Suffering from the Diseases, Symptoms, and Disabilities of Interest

These findings suggested that any new program must be prepared for patients with multiple problems. Psychotherapy, counseling, and the use of psychotropic drugs are classic services considered in establishing a program for the mentally impaired. These individuals, however, also require services directed at improving function in other areas—namely, medical evaluation and treatment, social interaction, nursing care, physical therapy, and so on. A new program may be able to provide some of these services, but would be more efficient if it made use of the potential of existing service providers (e.g., the Visiting Nurse Association). Arranging such services with other providers requires multidimensional assessment and coordination of service delivery by the new program. Unfortunately, the definition of a service frequently cannot be separated from a definition of the service provider. The OARS questionnaire focused on a series of generic services.[39] Twenty-four services were defined in such a way as to be independent of service providers (see Table 11-4). The operational definition of mental health services is outlined in Table 11-5. Certain services, such as transportation, could be provided by an agency or by family members and friends. Given the multiple impairments encountered by the elderly, any new program must be aware of, and involved in, the prescription of a variety of services, without neglecting appropriate mental health services (e.g., implementing insight-oriented psychotherapy versus supportive therapy).

Identify the Perceived Need of Services by the Target Population

Need for services must be distinguished from demand for services, and the OARS survey assessed the perceived need by the elderly for the same set of generic services mentioned earlier. Upon systematic questioning, 10 percent of the subjects perceived a need for some type of counseling. Thirty-one percent of those with mental health impairment perceived the need for a

Table 11-4 Twenty-Four Generic Services

Basic Maintenance Services

1. Transportation
22. Food, groceries

23. Living quarters (housing)

Supportive Services

9. Personal care services
14. Continuous supervision

15. Checking services
18. Meal preparation

17. Homemaker-household services
19. Administrative, legal, and protective services

Remedial Services

2. Social/recreational services
3. Employment services
4. Sheltered employment
5. Educational services, employment related
6. Remedial training
7. Mental health services
8. Psychotropic drugs
10. Nursing care

11. Medical services

12. Supportive devices and prostheses

13. Physical therapy
16. Relocation and placement services

20. Systematic multidimensional evaluation

21. Financial assistance
24. Coordination, information, and referral services

Source: OARS, *Multidimensional Functional Assessment: The OARS Methodology* (Durham, N.C.: Duke University Center for the Study of Aging and Human Development, 1978) p. 200. Used with permission.

Table 11-5 Example of a Generic Service Definition

Mental Health Services

Purpose: To identify and evaluate mental impairments that relate to both intra- and interpersonal relationships, including individual, marital, familial, and environmentally related problems; to provide counseling and/or therapy in order to aid the individual to resolve these problems or to cope with them.
Activity: Mental health evaluation, diagnosis, and treatment.
Relevant personnel: Psychiatrist, social worker, psychologist, nurse; educational, rehabilitation, and pastoral counselors.
Unit of measure: Sessions.
Examples: Psychotherapy (individual or group), counseling, crisis intervention, evaluation of need for psychiatric hospitalization.

Source: OARS, *Multidimensional Functional Assessment: The OARS Methodology* (Durham, N.C.: Duke University Center for the Study of Aging and Human Development, 1978), p. 203. Used with permission.

trained counselor, whereas 8 percent of the nonimpaired perceived a need for such counseling. Seventeen percent perceived a need for "nerve medication." Other services perceived necessary by over 15 percent of the subjects included transportation (27 percent), medical treatment (24 percent), coordination of services (21 percent), housekeeping (17 percent), and social interaction (15 percent).

Identify the Present Use of Services

Need for services was quite different than actual use of services. Survey data revealed that only 10 subjects (1 percent) were receiving some type of counseling or psychotherapy from any source. Twenty percent of the subjects were receiving a tranquilizer or nerve medicine (almost all being prescribed by their primary care physician). The very low utilization rate of mental health services (excluding medications) is similar to trends seen nationally. Statistics from the State of North Carolina indicate that less than 1 percent of persons aged 65 and older make use of community mental health center facilities annually.[40] Yet even this figure probably includes individuals in long-term care facilities. A very small percentage (less than 8 percent) of the community-based elderly with functional impairment of their mental health were receiving mental health services at the time of the survey.

Identify Factors That Interfere with or Augment the Use of Services by the Target Population

There is no accurate method for predicting the level of utilization of a new program, yet certain factors can be identified that affect that use. First, less than one-third of the mentally impaired elderly perceived a need for trained counseling (and this was counseling defined in its broadest sense). The team assumed that those with adequate economic resources would seek private care. Only 40 percent of the mentally impaired had impairment of economic resources as well. Therefore an estimate was made that an active new case load of approximately 12 percent of those in need might be generated by the development of a new program, once the program was fully operative.

The survey indicated that certain approaches should increase the likelihood of success with intervention in this population. For example, those with impaired mental health tended to live in three-generation families or with other relatives if they did not live with a spouse (when compared with the nonimpaired) (see Table 11-6). An impaired elder is likely to precipitate a crisis in the home.[41] The high correlation of mental health impairment with impairment in physical health and daily activities also increases the probability that a crisis in mental health will seriously jeopardize the older person's ability to continue living independently. Even if the older adult does not live with the family, a family crisis may ensue about future living arrangements of the elder. Therefore, the clinic should provide family therapy and family counseling (i.e., a family approach to the mentally impaired elder).[42] The family approach in turn may increase potential use of the clinic, for family members, especially middle-aged offspring, might themselves seek help in working with the impaired elder.

Determine the Types and Amounts of Personnel Required To Provide the Specified Services

Determining the services that were included in planning the OARS GET Clinic and predicting the possible case load enabled the planning team to define the essential staff for a mental health clinic serving a catchment area of about 10,000 persons 65 years of age and over. This staff included a psychiatrist-director (75 percent), a social worker (100 percent), a physician with experience in internal medicine and geriatrics (10 percent), a registered nurse with experience in gerontological nursing (20 percent), and a secretary-receptionist-record librarian (100 percent). Given this multidisciplinary staff, the clinic is multidimensional in its assessment and intervention, team oriented, and integrated with existing service providers (i.e., primary care

Table 11-6 Living Arrangements of Community and Clinic Populations by Marital Status (as Percentage of Each Marital Status)

Population	Alone	Spouse	Spouse and Kin	Kin Only	Non-Kin	N(%)
Community Population						
Married	1	77	20	1	1	440
Single, widowed,						(44)
or Divorced	49	–	–	43	8	557
						(56)
Total %	28	35	9	24	5	
N	276	345	88	243	45	997
						(100)
Clinic Population						
Married	5	76	19	–	–	37
Single, widowed,						(45)
or divorced	41	–	–	46	13	46
						(55)
Total %	25	35	8	25	7	
N	21	28	7	21	6	83
						(100)

Source: OARS, *Multidimensional Functional Assessment: The OARS Methodology* (Durham, N.C.: Duke University Center for the Study of Aging and Human Development, 1978), p. 77. Used with permission.

physicians, social services, senior citizens' groups, and so on), with an emphasis on consultation and education to existing service providers.

Evaluate the Accuracy of the Planning Efforts in Predicting the Types of Services Required, the Utilization of the New Services, and the Staffing Pattern Necessary for Effective Service Delivery

Intervention and outcome evaluative studies are presently under way in the OARS GET Clinic, and results are not yet available. However, information is available on the first 98 patients evaluated in the clinic. These data can be compared with data from the community survey used in planning the clinic.

The accuracy of predictions of the numbers and characteristics of patients using the clinic can therefore be determined.

The clinic was established essentially with the staff and the potential for service provision already described. After four years of operation, the active patients averaged 150 and the clinic averages 150 patients per month. This is almost exactly the predicted number (12 percent of 1,300 = 156). The number of patients seen and the number of active patients have been growing steadily during the past two years, paralleling the growth of the elderly population in Durham County, North Carolina. Predictions of the type of patient the clinic would encounter have proved less accurate. As expected, a high percentage (81 percent) had significant impairment in mental health and demonstrated increased impairment in other areas of functioning as well (see Table 11-2). Multiple impairments are the rule rather than the exception in the clinic. For example, 61 percent of the patients had an impairment in self-care capacity (ADL). Yet the proportion of economically impaired elders in the clinic population is only 45 percent.

Regardless of the nature of the presenting complaint in a geriatric mental health facility, problems in maintaining independent living are likely to be significant. The clinician must intervene to prevent institutionalization as well as to treat the primary illness. Though 15 of the original 98 patients were referred from an institution, the remaining 83 came from the community, indicating that a primary goal of the clinic—namely, to treat community-based elders—was realized. More than 80 percent of the patients seen in the clinic at present continue to come from the community. Only 25 lived alone, and family members accompanied their impaired elders to the clinic on the first visit in most cases.

Table 11-7 shows the services most frequently prescribed by clinicians for the first 98 patients seen in the OARS GET Clinic. The three mental health services (individual therapy or counseling, psychotropic drugs, and family therapy or counseling) are prescribed in over 60 percent of the cases. In addition, coordination of services is the second most frequently prescribed service. This was expected since the average number of different services prescribed for each patient was six. Medical and nursing services were frequently prescribed, emphasizing the clinic's need to maintain an orientation toward both mental and physical health. Finally, a number of services related to social and economic functioning were prescribed, the most frequent being services that increase social interaction. The clinic's staffing pattern has been instrumental in delivering the services already described, both in the disciplines represented and in the full-time equivalents of each discipline. The psychiatrist-director has coordinated patient care, provided long- and short-term psychotherapy, and prescribed psychotropic medication. Coordination of service delivery and work with the family, in addition to psychotherapy

Table 11-7 Services Most Frequently Prescribed by Clinicians in the OARS GET Clinic (*n*=98)

Counseling-psychotherapy-individual	77%
Coordination of services	63%
Psychotropic drugs	61%
Counseling-therapy-family	60%
Medical treatment	46%
Social interaction	44%
Relocation and placement	27%
Financial services	23%
Food services	18%
Transportation	15%
Nursing services	13%

Source: OARS, *Multidimensional Functional Assessment: The OARS Methodology* (Durham, N.C.: Duke University Center for the Study of Aging and Human Development, 1978), p. 85. Used with permission.

and counseling, have been important contributions of the social worker. The presence of a nurse and an internist in the clinic (and on the treatment team) has been invaluable in managing the difficult problems of mental impairment associated with physical illness (especially when the physical illness is being treated by a physician outside the clinic).

CONCLUSION

The experience gained in developing the OARS GET Clinic at Duke University Medical Center has demonstrated the value of epidemiologic services data in planning for services. Specifically, the planning team accurately predicted the numbers and characteristics of patients likely to use the clinic as well as the staffing pattern necessary to deliver those services deemed most appropriate in the intervention process. Evaluating the impact of services is the next step in effective program planning and evaluation.

NOTES

1. *Community Mental Health Center Amendments of 1975* ,Title III, Public Law 94-63 (Washington, D.C.: National Council of Community Mental Health Centers, 1975).

2. D. Blazer, "The OARS Durham Surveys: Descriptions and Applications," in *Multidimensional Functional Assessment: The OARS Methodology*, 2nd ed. (Durham, N.C.: Center for the Study of Aging and Human Development, 1978), pp. 75-88.

3. D.W.K. Kay, P. Beamish, and M. Roth, "Old Age Mental Disorders in Newcastle-upon-Tyne: A Study of Prevalence," *British Journal of Psychiatry* 110 (1964): 146, 668.

4. E. Essen-Moller et al., "Individual Traits and Morbidity in a Swedish Rural Population," *Acta Psychiatrica et Neurologica Scandinavica* Supplement 100 (1956): 5-160.

5. K.R.W. Redick, M. Kramer, and C.A. Taube, "Epidemiology of Mental Illness and Utilization of Psychiatric Facilities among Older Persons," in *Mental Illness in Later Life*, eds. E.W. Busse and E. Pfeiffer (Washington, D.C.: American Psychiatric Association, 1973).

6. Blazer, "The OARS Durham Surveys," pp. 78-88.

7. R.B. Teeter et al., "Psychiatric Disturbances of Aged Patients in Skilled Nursing Facilities," *American Journal of Psychiatry* 133 (1976): 1430.

8. B.A. Stotsky, *The Nursing Home and the Aged Psychiatric Patient* (New York: Appleton-Century-Crofts, 1970).

9. P. Sainsbury and J. Alarcon, "Evaluating a Service in Sussex," in *Roots of Evaluation: The Epidemiological Basis for Planning Services*, eds. J.K. Wing and H. Hafner (New York: Oxford University Press, 1973), pp. 239-256.

10. J. Wertheimer et al., "Evaluating a Service in Lausanne," in *Roots of Evaluation: The Epidemiological Basis for Planning Services*, eds. J.K. Wing and H. Hafner (New York: Oxford University Press, 1973), pp. 257-268.

11. R.M. Glasscote, J.E. Guderman, and D.G. Miles, *Creative Mental Health Services for the Elderly* (Washington, D.C.: American Psychiatric Association, 1977).

12. B.S. Gurian and M.H. Cantor, "Mental Health and Community Support Systems for the Elderly," in *Aging: The Process and the People*, eds. G. Usdin and C.K. Hofling (New York: Brunner/Mazel, 1978).

13. Mary Adams, Coordinator of Geriatric Services, Division of Mental Health, Department of Human Resources, State of North Carolina, 1978: personal communication.

14. A.M. Lillienfeld, *Foundations of Epidemiology* (New York: Oxford University Press, 1976).

15. J.N. Morris, *Uses of Epidemiology* (London: Churchill Livingstone, 1975).

16. A.B. Hollingshed and F.C. Redlich, *Social Class and Mental Illness. A Community Study* (New York: Wiley, 1958).

17. Essen-Moller et al., "Individual Traits and Morbidity in the Swedish Rural Population," pp. 5-160.

18. T. Helgason, "Epidemiology of Mental Disorders in Ireland," *Acta Psychiatrica et Neurologica Scandinavica* Supplement 173 (1964): 11-258.

19. D.C. Leighton et al., *The Character of Danger* (New York: Basic Books, 1963).

20. T.S. Langner and S.T. Michael, *Life Stress and Mental Health* (New York: Free Press, 1963).

21. Joint Commission on Mental Illness and Health, *Action for Mental Health*, Final Report (New York: Basic Books, 1961).

22. F.D. Chu and S. Trotter, *The Madness Establishment* (New York: Grossman, 1974).

23. D.F. Musto, "Whatever Happened to Community Mental Health?" *Psychiatric Annals* 7 (1977): 508.

24. J.K. Wing, "Patients with Psychiatric Disorders," in *Community Mental Health*, eds. R.H. Williams and L.D. Ozarin (San Francisco: Jossey-Bass, 1968), pp. 237-260.

25. OARS, *Multidimensional Functional Assessment: The OARS Methodology* (Durham, N.C.: Duke University Center for the Study of Aging and Human Development, 1978).

26. G.L. Maddox, "Intervention and Outcomes: Notes on Designing and Implementing an Experiment in Health Care," *International Journal of Epidemiology* 1 (1972): 339-345.

27. OARS, *Multidimensional Functional Assessment.*

28. *Community Mental Health Centers Act of 1963,* Federal Register 29:5951 (Washington D.C.: 1964).

29. Leighton et al., *The Character of Danger.*

30. Langner and Michael, *Life Stress and Mental Health.*

31. J.J. Schwab and M.E. Schwab, *Sociocultural Roots of Mental Illness: An Epidemiologic Survey* (New York: Plenum, 1978).

32. Committee on the Rating of Mental and Physical Impairment, "Mental Illness," *Journal of the American Medical Association* 198 (1966): 1284.

33. M.M. Weissman and G.L. Klerman, "Epidemiology of Mental Disorders: Emerging Trends," *Archives of General Psychiatry* 35 (1978): 705-712.

34. *Diagnostic and Statistical Manual of Mental Disorders,* 3rd ed. (Washington, D.C.: American Psychiatric Association, 1980), pp. 23-32.

35. J.C. Kincannon, "Prediction of the Standard MMPI Scale Scores from 71 Items: The Mini-Mult," *Journal of Consulting and Clinical Psychology* 32 (1968): 319.

36. E. Pfeiffer, "A Short, Portable Mental Status Questionnaire for the Assessment of Organic Brain Deficit in Elderly Patients," *Journal of the American Geriatrics Society* 23 (1975): 433.

37. D.G. Blazer and C. Williams, "Epidemiology of Late Life Dysphoria and Depression," *American Journal of Psychiatry* 137, no. 4 (April 1980): 439-444.

38. D.G. Blazer and J. Houpt, "Perception of Poor Health in the Healthy Older Adult," *Journal of the American Geriatrics Society* 27, no. 7 (1979): 33.

39. OARS, *Multidimensional Functional Assessment.*

40. Adams, personal communication.

41. B.G. Danis, *Stress in Individuals Caring for Ill Elderly Relatives,* paper presented at the annual meeting of the Gerontological Society, Dallas, Texas, November 1978.

42. D.G. Blazer, "Working with the Elderly Patient's Family," *Geriatrics* 33 (1978): 117.

Chapter 12

The Living Textbook of Geriatric Care

Gerda G. Fillenbaum and Dan G. Blazer

INTRODUCTION

The importance of medical records as a means of providing organized information about a client, protecting the care giver (particularly in the event of malpractice claims), and serving diverse research and educational goals has long been established. But, as Kincaid points out, these are but "subsets of the overall goal of assuring quality in health care."[1] In order to attain this goal, there has been increasing recognition that it is necessary to gather appropriate information in a standardized manner, and to maintain an ongoing record so that—particularly where chronic diseases are concerned—it is possible to trace their progress accurately, and determine the impact of intervention.

The advent of modern computers has made it possible not only to store substantial quantities of information but, importantly, to access that information rapidly and in diverse ways, and to analyze it using sophisticated statistical techniques for which hand operation is barely feasible. While computers have long been used for office management purposes (e.g., billing, scheduling appointments), they are also being used increasingly for patient monitoring and to develop data banks concentrating on particular chronic diseases. Two quite different examples of monitoring in the acute care field are a computer-assisted approach in assessing metabolic requirements of critically ill patients and in checking whether outpatients with certain symptoms were administered the treatment of preference within a specific time interval.[2,3] Where chronic diseases are concerned, several have particularly well developed data banks. To cite one national and one local example: rheumatism is served nationally through the ARAMIS data bank, and substantial ongoing data on heart disease are gathered locally through the Duke University Cardiovascular Information System.[4,5] A comprehensive and readable survey of computer-based systems and applications, focusing on those funded by the National Center for Health Service Research (NCHSR) between 1968 and 1978, is provided by *Computer Applications in Health Care.*[6]

Most computer-based medical applications have focused on single diseases or disease clusters. Consequently, these systems are not entirely applicable to use with the older person, for the ailing elderly typically suffer from more than one illness; their illnesses are more likely to be chronic, and their problems tend to be multiple. Under such circumstances, treatment depends on accurate evaluation of the whole person; utilization of a broad array of services, any one of which may have multiple impacts; and careful monitoring of progress. The elderly present the clinician with all the problems inherent in simultaneously monitoring multiple chronic diseases and problem areas, and in assessing the impact of a range of services.

The Living Textbook of Geriatric Care, a computer-based client information system, is specifically designed to handle such computer issues. Unlike most other client-based information systems, The Living Textbook has been designed not only to gather relevant data but also to permit examination of information within a particular conceptual and analytic framework—the OARS model.[7] This model requires that information permitting assessment of the whole person and of the services that person uses be gathered, and suggests a strategy for examining the data. The Living Textbook is flexible. It does not demand that the strategy be used, but permits alternative ways of examining data. The model does facilitate the gathering of information relevant to the care and treatment of the elderly and so, as shown, provides information that is useful at a number of levels, ranging from individual client application and clinician training, to evaluation of clinic performance and resource allocations.

The Living Textbook has been in use in the OARS Geriatric Evaluation and Treatment Clinic at Duke Hospital, Duke University, Duke University Medical Center, Durham, North Carolina. Work started on this system in 1978. If a system is indeed valuable, users will undoubtedly place additional demands on it and further programming will be necessary. It has already had a significant impact on clinic operation and client evaluation, however.

The OARS model was specifically developed as a means of assessing the impact of services on functional state.[8] This model has three elements:

1. a procedure for assessing individual functional status, permitting the development of a functional classification system (i.e., a system in which individuals having equivalent functional statuses are classed together, and in which a limited number of such classes account for an entire population)

2. disaggregation of services into their generic components disregarding site or provider, and reaggregation of services (into service packages) according to individual use
3. a transition matrix that permits assessment of the impact of specific service packages on individuals arrayed according to functional status

The first two elements are operationalized by the OARS Multidimensional Functional Assessment Questionnaire (OARS MFAQ).[9] This two-part questionnaire permits assessment of functional status (part A) and assessment of service utilization (part B). Personal functional status is assessed in five areas: social, economic, mental health, physical health, and self-care capacity. For each area, detailed, clinically relevant information is summarized to provide a rating on a 6-point scale (where a level of functioning rating of 1 represents excellent, 2 equals good, and 3, 4, 5, and 6 represent mild, moderate, severe, and total impairment, respectively), which results in a client profile. Information on service receipt, by provider, is obtained for each of 24 generically defined services, a nonoverlapping, broadly encompassing set. The services the client receives, as indicated on part B, represent a service package.

The five 6-point scales permit the development of a functional classification system. All possible combinations of these five 6-point scales result in 7,776 profiles of classes. Since this number is too large for practical use, each scale is, typically, dichotomized simply to indicate whether functioning is adequate (ratings of 1 to 3) or inadequate (ratings of 4 to 6). All possible combinations of the five dichotomized scales yield 32 classes, and these are illustrated in Table 12-1, Column 1. When the OARS MFAQ is administered to members of a particular group, it is possible to determine how that group is distributed among these 32 classes. (Individual responses to individual items on the questionnaire may also be examined and are available in The Living Textbook; but that is not relevant to the present argument.) For instance, in Table 12-1 Column 2 shows the distribution of 37 selected OARS GET clinic clients. Even from this small sample, certain matters are obvious. Only 15 of the 32 states are represented; and of these 15 states, some are more heavily represented than others. The state with the highest representation is the one that indicates that functioning is adequate in all five areas (recall that, by definition, adequate functioning includes minor impairments). This indicates that while the majority of new clients are distinctly impaired in one or more areas, a substantial minority have borderline impairments.

Six months after entry to the OARS GET clinic, these 37 clients were reevaluated. Table 12-1, Column 3, shows the status of the group at this time. Eleven of the 15 states represented initially are still represented, and only 1 new one has been added. This suggests that in this specialized clinic setting,

Table 12-1 Client Distribution by Functional State, Initial Status, and Reevaluation Status (N=37)

Column 1 SEMPA*	Column 2 Initial		Column 3 Six months later	
	#	%	#	%
00000	10	27.0	15	40.5
0000X				
000X0	3	8.1	1	2.7
00X00	3	8.1	4	10.8
0X000	1	2.7	2	5.4
X0000			1	2.7
000XX				
00X0X	2	5.4	2	5.4
00XX0	3	8.1	0	0
0X00X				
0X0X0				
0XX00				
X000X				
X00X0				
X0X00	3	8.1	1	2.7
XX000				
00XXX	1	2.7	3	8.1
0XX0X	1	2.7	2	5.4
0XXX0	2	5.4	1	2.7
0X0XX				
X00XX				
X0X0X	3	8.1	3	8.1
X0XX0				
XX00X				
XX0X0				
XXX00				
0XXXX	1	2.7	0	0
X0XXX	1	2.7	0	0
XX0XX				
XXX0X	1	2.7	0	0
XXXX0				
XXXXX	2	5.4	2	5.4

*S = Social
E = Economic
M = Mental Health
P = Physical Health
A = Activities of Daily Living

O = Adequate functioning
X = Inadequate functioning

certain combinations of impairment are more likely to be found than others; clinicians need to learn how to handle certain combinations, but not necessarily all of them. Further, it is evident that there has been improvement in the status of these clients during their first six months of treatment. While three clients were initially found to be impaired in four of the five areas, six months later none are so broadly impaired; at the other extreme, 15 clients are now functioning adequately—a 50 percent increase over that found initially.

The importance of reevaluation information goes beyond showing what has happened to a particular group. Such data can be used to draw up a transition matrix—that is, a table that shows for each initial class what proportion of members of that class remain in it and what proportion moves to each of the other classes. An illustration of such a transition matrix, based on information from these 37 clients, is given in Table 12-2. While this sample is small, it is useful for illustrative purposes. Each row of the table represents a different initial functional state; it shows what proportion of those initially in that state remain there (these figures are underlined) and what proportion moves to each of the other states. Consider, for instance, the second row (000X0). Of the clients in this state, .33 (33 percent) remain in it, but .67 (67 percent) move to 00000 (functioning adequately in all areas). The table has been so arranged that the number of dimensions impaired increases as one moves across the table, while the underlined cells on the diagonal indicate those functional states that are the same on both occasions. Consequently, movement to the left of the diagonal tends to indicate improvement in functioning, while movement to the right tends to indicate deterioration. These statements are not absolutes, since we have ordered only by number of dimensions impaired, and have not ordered within these categories. Such ordering (of the separate states) is not a simple matter, and tends to reflect social preferences that clinician and client may have to determine jointly.

It is not sufficient to know how treatment affects clients. To be able to replicate a desired change, it is necessary to know what services were used. Such information is available from part B of the OARS MFAQ. It is possible to use The Living Textbook to isolate those clients moving to a preferred state, to determine what services they received, and to compare these services with those received by clients who were initially similar but who did not make a comparable improvement. Information on service cost has not yet been added to The Living Textbook. The addition of cost information would provide a further basis for selecting among service packages that have comparable impact.

A particular advantage of the OARS approach is that it makes it possible to capitalize on naturally occurring events, an important attribute since

Table 12-2 Transition Matrix: Initial Functional State of Selected Clients by Functional State Six Months Later

Initial SEMPA*	Six months later												N	%
	00000	000X0	00X00	0X000	X0000	00X0X	X0X00	00XXX	0XX0X	0XXX0	X0X0X	XXXXX		
00000	.80		.20										10	27.0
000X0	.67	.33											3	8.1
00X00			.67	.33									3	8.1
0X000					1.00								1	2.7
X0X0X						.50	.50						2	5.4
00X0X	.67					.33							3	8.1
00XX0	.67			.33									3	8.1
X0X00	1.00												1	2.7
00XXX								1.00					1	2.7
0XX0X									1.00				2	5.4
0XXX0								.50		.50			3	8.1
X0X0X											.67	.33	1	2.7
0XXXX								1.00					1	2.7
X0XXX								1.00					1	2.7
XXX0X											.67		1	2.7
XXXXX								.50				.50	2	5.4
N	15	1	4	2	1	2	1	3	2	1	3	2	37	
%	40.5	2.7	10.8	5.4	2.7	5.4	2.7	8.1	5.4	2.7	8.1	5.4		

*See footnote to Table 12-1.
Underlined figures indicate proportion remaining in their initial functional state.

random allocation of clients to specific services or the deliberate withholding of service is rarely feasible. The procedure also permits examination of the impact of a broader array of service packages than would typically be the case if a classical experimental design was being used.

As is probably obvious from the illustration used, the information made available through The Living Textbook's application of the OARS model has relevance at a number of levels. These levels include the individual assessment (as a guide in deciding what services to recommend to a client having a particular functional status); clinic or treatment site assessment (assessing the performance of a particular site—e.g., a clinic); and decisions regarding service provision (e.g., what services should be provided, and the manner in which different services should be combined). We consider each of these in turn as they can be operationalized through The Living Textbook.

The Individual Clinical Level

Good clinic practice requires that each new client be evaluated so that appropriate services can be recommended. There is evidence that, as people grow older, functional status in one area becomes more closely tied to functional status in another, so if one area becomes impaired, other areas of functioning are also more likely to be affected.[10, 11]

Consequently, where the elderly in particular are concerned, evaluation should not be restricted to an examination of a particular presenting problem, but should encompass the major areas of functioning. This, in turn, implies that the services recommended must take into account not only the presenting problem, but also other problems that are present. Thus both evaluation and service recommendation must bear in mind the whole person. Good clinic practice also requires that functional status be monitored so that the impact of services can be evaluated. Since the diagnosis of a chronic illness does not typically change over time, the measure of the impact of a service must reflect the goal of the service, such as improved function. In order to evaluate accurately the impact of services, reevaluation should be comparable to the initial evaluation. Only in this way is it possible to determine the broad-range impact of a particular package of services.

Desirable though it may be, client reassessment, comparable in intensity and extensity to an initial assessment, rarely occurs. The reasons for this are diverse: reassessment is seen as expensive in time and money; clients might object; reassessment of a terminated client seems inappropriate; clinicians "know" how their clients feel, what their concerns are, and how those concerns change; reassessment is an intrusion, and so on. However, without the monitoring of services and timely reassessment, objective information on the services a client has received and on the current status of the client is not available, and it is not possible to assess the impact of clinician-based interventions. Thus, the first demand placed by The Living Textbook is for good clinical data that will permit evaluation of the outcome of treatment. It is essential to recognize that until such time as service impact is fully understood, it is clinically important to gather such data so that client treatment can continue to be responsive to client state. Thus The Living Textbook capitalizes on, and in many circumstances may even impose, good clinical practice—by requiring that each client be assessed, followed, and reassessed in an appropriate manner.

When such information is available on a group of clients, other assets of this computerized system become evident. Let us assume that on entry to the clinic, each client receives an overall assessment and a services recommendation, that the services received by clients who remain with the clinic are recorded, and that the status of clients is reassessed at regular, clinically appropriate intervals (in the OARS GET Clinic such reassessments are scheduled six months after the initial assessment, and annually thereafter). Such information permits application of the OARS model. That is, a transition matrix can be constructed that shows client change in functional class. Since service use data are available, it is possible to link change in functional status to services used. This provides a clinician with very important information: by matching the functional status of the client to be served with that of clients whose functional status was initially the same, but who have received services and been evaluated, the clinician can (a) determine what happens to such clients over a specific time interval, (b) determine what services were related to a particular outcome, and (c) thus be provided with some guidance in trying to decide what services will best benefit the client. Actual receipt of those services will depend on a number of factors, including the clinician's decision regarding the advisability of the services in question for the particular client, the client's agreement to those services, their availability, and the development of new services.

Continual aggregation of such longitudinal information provides system users with a substantial base of experience on which to draw. Hitherto, an individual clinician could only accumulate a limited amount of such information and could do so slowly. While clinicians typically shared their experiences, this still provided less systematically gathered information on fewer clients than a system such as The Living Textbook can provide. The less experienced the clinician, the greater the value of The Living Textbook— both to the clinician and to the client who must be served—for The Living Textbook provides the clinician with an extensive experience base. It should be noted that this system does not make clinical judgments; it does not tell the clinician what to do. Rather, it offers information so that a better informed decision can be reached.

Clinic Practice

The relevance of The Living Textbook goes beyond the immediate client application just described. Both the initial client evaluation and the reevaluation provide information important to clinic administrators. The initial information indicates what type of clientele is attracted to the clinic (e.g., as in Table 12-1, Column 2). This information is crucial in determining whether a clinic is servicing those it is mandated to serve, and in deciding whether it is necessary to take steps either to attract the desired clientele, or to change clinic philosophy regarding who should be served. The reevaluation data, when compared with initial evaluation data, permit objective assessment of clinic performance (e.g., comparison of Columns 2 and 3 of Table 12-1). Once a performance baseline has been established, deviations from the baseline may be used to indicate the impact of diverse, clinically relevant intervening events, such as a change in the professional mix of clinicians or in the services available. The transition matrix also has relevance for the clinic administrator—providing, for instance, information indicating which types of clients are most likely to improve and which are not, which types of clients demand more services and which, fewer.

Resource Allocation

Information is gathered here on both functional status of clients and change in that status, and on service use. As indicated earlier, a particular concern of this system is to permit comparison of the impact of alternative services. It is possible to determine what services are actually used, what type of person uses them, and what impact they have. Knowing the types of persons to be served, it is then possible to assess what type of service, in what volume, and in combination with which other services, must be provided if certain preferred levels of functioning are to be reached. Knowing what impact different services have, and given the bounding constraints (typically of personnel and of money), the resource allocator may now make decisions on a more rational basis.

Operationalization of The Living Textbook

The Living Textbook has been operational within the OARS Geriatric Evaluation and Treatment Clinic at Duke Hospital. The information being entered into the computer base includes, and goes beyond, that required by the OARS model.

The first contact with a new client is generally by telephone, when either the client or someone concerned about the client calls, makes inquiries and sets the date for the initial visit. On the initial visit the OARS MFAQ is administered by a clinician or a technician. The client and, where appropriate, members of the family are seen in clinical interview. Additional information on the client may also be obtained from other care givers. Once sufficient information has been obtained, information on the client is presented at a multidisciplinary staff conference and a decision is reached regarding a recommended service plan. The plan is carried out and the services provided to the extent feasible. Each client contact, change in service, and change in client problem is recorded and entered. Reevaluation that parallels the initial evaluation is scheduled for six months following the initial evaluation, and annually thereafter. The following information is therefore entered into the system.

Initial evaluation

- office management information---e.g., address, telephone number, contact person, insurance data
- OARS MFAQ: Part A—Assessment of functional status
            Part B—Assessment of service use and need
- Assessment and service plan summary data, including information on living arrangements, presenting problems, current functional status, services currently used with recommendation for continuation, cessation and new services (by intensity, duration, and provider), medical and psychiatric diagnoses, realistic desired functional outcome

Ongoing information

- Each client visit is recorded; any changes in diagnosis, problems, and services are noted and entered

Reevaluation information

- Readministration of the OARS MFAQ
- Reassessment of service plan

Thus the information being gathered and entered into the system permits full utilization of the OARS model. Information is not restricted to the OARS model, however. The additional details can be used to facilitate office management procedures, provide more extensive clinical information (e.g., diagnoses, presenting problems, service use in more specific detail), and provide clinicians with a realistic client goal for which to aim.

Outline of The Living Textbook Computerized Record System

Figure 12-1 is a schematic representation of the computer design for The Living Textbook. Once the system has been accessed, the user may choose one of three alternative routes, two of which themselves offer alternative procedures. The main routes are called DATAIN, MANAGER, and RETURN. DATAIN offers six options. Four of these permit entry of specific client data: INTAKE, designed for entry of administrative details; ASSESSMENT, to enter information on the assessment and service plan summary, one of the primary clinic forms; OARS MFAQ, designed for OARS questionnaire data; and RETURN VISIT, which permits information recorded on the return visit form to be entered. Of the two remaining options, one is the EDIT option, through which entry errors may be corrected; the other is designed for information on family support and is not currently operational. MANAGER is intended for management procedures. It has five options; the three that are operational are: REEVALUATIONS, which provides a list of clients eligible for six-month and annual evaluations; RETURN SUMMARY, which provides return visit information on single clients who come in unexpectedly; and SEE, which allows users to view all online data for a specified client. The other two options, which are not presently operational, will permit the development of additional programs. Finally, the third major route is called RETURN. It has only one purpose—to provide batches of return visit summaries, such as summaries for all clients scheduled to come to the clinic in a particular week.

Once accessed, the system is easy to handle, since all the user need do is type in the answers to questions that appear on a screen and that will lead the

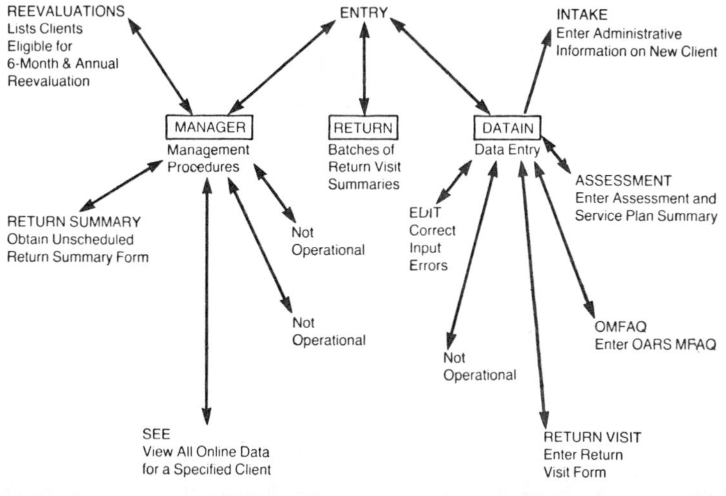

Figure 12-1 Outline of the OARS Computerized Client Record System: The Living Textbook of Geriatric Care

user to those parts of the system he or she wishes to access. First the user indicates which of the three main routes he or she wishes to use. Where options are available, one can then be selected, and the user is led through that option. At logical intervals the user is asked whether work on that option is completed. When it is completed, the user then has three choices: moving to another option on the same main route, returning to the entry point and selecting one of the other main routes, or exiting the system.

The major operational programs tend to be of a managerial type, but space has been allocated for additional programs that will have primarily clinical relevance. Such programs will include those that will permit online (i.e., immediate call-up) examination of the different aspects of the OARS model— for example, comparing a specific client with other similar clients in order to determine better what services to recommend, or reviewing all new clients coming within a particular period of time and comparing them with clients entering at some other time. Such comparisons can be obtained now, but only with the aid of a computer programmer. There is no difficulty in getting this information, but it is not received as expeditiously as it will be once appropriate programming has been linked into the current system.

The Living Textbook of Geriatric Care is an ambitious undertaking. It is intended to be of clinical relevance, but instead of simply being a databank, it has been specifically developed to utilize the OARS model fully. As a result, it can provide direction regarding the type of information that should be gathered and recommends a specific approach for examining that information. It not only provides historical accountability for client care but also facilitates good clinic practice. When fully operational, it can not only be a unique data base on the elderly but will also be a teaching instrument, helping new clinicians, in particular, benefit from the experience of others; it will provide information that is important to assessing the functioning of a clinic, and relevant to resource allocators in determining service provision.

NOTES

1. William H. Kincaid, "The International Health Record Year," in *New Challenges for Vital and Health Records*, Proceedings of the 18th National Meeting of the Public Health Conference on Records and Statistics, DHHS pub. no. (PHS) 81-1214 (Washington, D.C.: Department of Health and Human Services, 1980).

2. John H. Siegel et al., "Computer Based Consultation in 'CARE' of the Critically Ill Patient," *Surgery* 80 (1976): 353-364.

3. G.O. Barnett, *Computer-Stored Ambulatory Record (COSTAR)*, Public Health Service, Health Resources Administration, National Center for Health Services Research, NCHSR Research Digest Series, DHEW pub. no. (HRA) 76-3145 (Washington, D.C.: U.S. Department of Health, Education and Welfare, 1976).

4. Dennis J. McShane et al., "TOD: A Software System for the ARAMIS Data Bank," *Computer* (1979): 34-40.

5. R.A. Rosati and J. McNeer, "A New Information System for Medical Practice," *Archives of Internal Medicine* 135 (1975): 1017-1024.

6. *Computer Application in Health Care*, National Center for Health Services Research, Research Report Series, DHHS pub. no. (PHS) 80-3751; formerly (PHS) 79-3251 (Washington, D.C.: Department of Health and Human Services, 1980).

7. Duke OARS *Multidimensional Functional Assessment: The OARS Methodology, a Manual*, 2nd ed. (Durham, N.C.: Center for the Study of Aging and Human Development, Duke University, 1978).

8. G.G. Fillenbaum et al., "Assessment of Individual Functional Status in a Program Evaluation and Resource Allocation Model," in Duke OARS *Multidimensional Functional Assessment: The OARS Methodology, a Manual*, 2nd ed. (Durham, N.C.: Center for the Study of Aging and Human Development, Duke University, 1978).

9. Duke OARS *Multidimensional Functional Assessment*.

10. G.G. Fillenbaum, "An Examination of the Vulnerability Hypothesis," *Journal of Aging and Human Development* 8 (1977-78): 155-160.

11. E.G. Youmans and M. Yarrow, "Aging and Social Adaptation: A Longitudinal Study of Healthy Old Men," in *Human Aging II: An Eleven Year Follow-up Biomedical and Behavioral Study*, DHEW pub. no. (HSM) 71-9037, eds. S. Granick and R. D. Patterson (Washington, D.C.: U.S. Department of Health, Education and Welfare, 1971).

Older Americans Resources and Services (OARS) Instrument

Source: Duke University Center for the Study of Aging and Human Development, Duke University Medical Center, Durham, North Carolina, © 1975.

OARS MULTIDIMENSIONAL FUNCTIONAL ASSESSMENT QUESTIONNAIRE   CARD 1

Subject # _____
                                                                    1-4

Subject Number _*Mr. Edward Johns*_   Card # __01__
                                                              5-6
Subject's Address _____
                   Street & Number   City   State   Mo Day Yr

Date of Interview ___*9 - 5 - 79*_____
                                                             7-8 9-10 11-12
Time Interview Began ___*9:30 a.m.*___

Interviewer's Name ___*Alan Myers*___
                                                             _____
Relationship of Informant to Subject _*no informant*_   13-14

Place of Interview [BE SPECIFIC.]   15

*OARS - GET Clinic*
                                                             16
Subject's Residence
[SPECIFY HOME OR TYPE OF INSTITUTION.]

_____
                                                             17-18

OLDER AMERICANS RESOURCES AND SERVICES PROGRAM
OF THE
DUKE UNIVERSITY CENTER FOR THE STUDY OF AGING AND HUMAN DEVELOPMENT
DURHAM, NORTH CAROLINA 27710

April, 1975

CARD 1

PRELIMINARY QUESTIONNAIRE
[ASK QUESTIONS 1-10 AND RECORD ALL ANSWERS. (ASK QUESTION 4a.
ONLY IF SUBJECT HAS NO TELEPHONE.) CHECK CORRECT (+) OR
INCORRECT (-) FOR EACH AND RECORD TOTAL NUMBER OF ERRORS BASED
ON TEN QUESTIONS.]

1 +	0 -		
✓		1.	What is the date today? Sept- 5 1979 Month Day Year
✓		2.	What day of the week is it? Wed.
✓		3.	What is the name of this place? Pickens Build.
✓		4.	What is your telephone number? 963-9876
			a. [ASK ONLY IF SUBJECT DOES NOT HAVE A PHONE.] What is your street address?
✓		5.	How old are you? 65
✓		6.	When were you born? June 9, 1914 Month Day Year
✓		7.	Who is the president of the U.S. now? Carter
✓		8.	Who was the president just before him? Ford
✓		9.	What was your mother's maiden name? Thomas
✓		10.	Subtract 3 from 20 and keep subtracting 3 from each new number you get, all the way down.

[CORRECT ANSWER IS: 17, 14, 11, 8, 5, 2]

O Total number of errors.

19
20
21
22

23
24
25

26
27
28
29

30-31

1. Telephone number [IF SUBJECT IS RELIABLE TRANSFER FROM   CARD 1
    PRELIMINARY QUESTIONNAIRE; OTHERWISE, OBTAIN FROM INFORMANT
    OR LOOK ON TELEPHONE.] ____963-9876____

2. Sex of Subject
    1 Male
    2 Female
                                                                    ____32____

3. Race of Subject
    1 White (Caucasian)
    2 Black (Negro)
    3 Oriental
    4 Spanish American (Spanish surname)
    5 American Indian
    6 Other
    - Not answered
                                                                    ____33____

4. [GET FROM PRELIMINARY QUESTIONNAIRE IF SUBJECT IS RELIABLE;
    FROM INFORMANT IF NOT.]   Mo   Day   Yr
    a. When were you born? __June__   __9__   __1914__   _____
                            (Month)   (Day)   (Year) 34-35 36-37 38-39

    b. How old are you? ____65____
                                                                    ____40-42____

5. How far did you go (have you gone) in school?
    1 0-4 years
    2 5-8 years
    3 High school incomplete
    4 High school completed
    5 Post high school, business or trade school   - come back
    6 1-3 years college   to this
    7 4 years college completed
    8 Post graduate college
    - Not answered
                                                                    ____43____

SOCIAL RESOURCES

Now I'd like to ask you some questions about your family and friends.

6. Are you single, married, widowed, divorced or separated?
    1 Single
    2 Married
    3 Widowed   " Wife died 10 years ago "
    4 Divorced   pt. sad
    5 Separated
    - Not answered
                                                                    ____44____

7. Who lives with you?

CARD 1

[CHECK "YES" OR "NO" FOR EACH OF THE FOLLOWING.]

	1 YES	0 NO	
	✓		No one
45		✓	Husband or wife
46		✓	Children
47		✓	Grandchildren
48		✓	Parents
49		✓	Grandparents
50		✓	Brothers and sisters
51		✓	Other relatives [Does not include in-laws covered in the above categories.]
52		✓	Friends
53		✓	Non-related paid* helper [*Includes free room]
54		✓	Others [SPECIFY.] _____
55			

8. How many people do you know well enough to visit with in their homes?
3 Five or more
② Three to four
1 One to two
0 None
- Not answered

who are important to him?

56

9. About how many times did you talk to someone--friends, relatives, or others on the telephone in the past week (either you called them or they called you)? [IF SUBJECT HAS NO PHONE, QUESTION STILL APPLIES.]
③ Once a day or more
2 2-6 times
1 Once
0 Not at all
- Not answered

"Son visits daughter calls since stroke"

57

10. How many times during the past week did you spend some time with someone who does not live with you, that is you went to see them or they came to visit you, or you went out to do things together?
3 Once a day or more
② 2-6 times
1 Once
0 Not at all
- Not answered

" my son "
(I want to see what social contacts were before stroke)

58

11. Do you have someone you can trust and confide in?
    ② Yes
    0 No   *"my brother"*
    - Not answered

                                                  59

12. Do you find yourself feeling lonely quite often, sometimes, or almost never?
    0 Quite often
    ① Sometimes
    2 Almost never
    - Not answered

                                                  60

13. Do you see your relatives and friends as often as you want to or are you somewhat unhappy about how little you see them?
    ① As often as wants to
    2 Somewhat unhappy about how little *pt seems uncertain*
    - Not answered

                                                  61

14. Is there someone who would give you any help at all if you were sick or disabled, for example your husband/wife, a member of your family, or a friend?
    ① Yes
    0 No one willing and able to help
    - Not answered

                                                  62

    [IF "YES" ASK a. AND b.]

    a. Is there someone who would take care of you as long as needed, or only for a short time; or only someone who would help you now and then (for example, taking you to the doctor, or fixing lunch occasionally, etc.)?
        .1 Someone who would take care of Subject indefinitely (as long as needed)
        2 Someone who would take care of Subject for a short time (a few weeks to six months)
        ③ Someone who would help the Subject now and then (taking him to the doctor or fixing lunch, etc.)
        - Not answered

                                                  63

    b. Who is this person?

        Name _____

        Relationship *brother and sister*

                                                  64

ECONOMIC RESOURCES

Now I'd like to ask you some questions about your work situation.

CARD 1

15. Are you presently:

[CHECK "YES" OR "NO" FOR EACH OF THE FOLLOWING.]

	1 YES	0 NO	
65		✓	Employed full-time
66	✓		Employed part-time *"on sick leave"*
67	✓		Retired
68		✓	Retired on disability
69		✓	Not employed and seeking work
70		✓	Not employed and not seeking work
71		✓	Full-time student
72		✓	Part-time student

16. What kind of work have you done most of your life?

[CIRCLE THE MOST APPROPRIATE.]

1 Never employed
2 Housewife
3 Other [STATE THE SPECIFIC OCCUPATION IN DETAIL.] _____

73

(occupation) _____ *Salesman* _____

74 - Not answered

works in office supply now — seems embarrassed about job

17. Does your husband/wife work or did he/she ever work? [QUESTION APPLIES ONLY TO SPOUSE TO WHOM MARRIED THE LONGEST.]
(1) Yes
2 No
3 Never married
- Not answered

75

[IF "YES" ASK a.]

a. What kind of work did or does he/she do?

[STATE THE SPECIFIC OCCUPATION IN DETAIL.] _____

76

_____ *Secretary* _____

CARD 2

18. Where does your income (money) come from (yours and your husband's/
wife's)?

[CHECK "YES" OR "NO" FOR EACH OF THE FOLLOWING AND IF "YES" ENTER
THE AMOUNT AND CIRCLE "Weekly", "Monthly", OR "Yearly".]

S# _____
1-4 _____

Card# 02
5-6 _____

1 YES	0 NO	IF YES HOW MUCH			CODE 1 Yes 0 No
	✓		Weekly Monthly Yearly	Earnings from employment (wages, salaries or income from your business) *on sick leave now*	7
	✓		Weekly Monthly Yearly	Income from rental, interest from investments, etc. [Include trusts, annuities, & payments from insurance policies & savings.]	8
✓		$280.	Weekly (Monthly) Yearly	Social Security (Include Social Security disability payments but not SSI.)	9
	✓		Weekly Monthly Yearly	V.A. benefits such as G.I. Bill, and disability payments	10
	✓		Weekly Monthly Yearly	Disability payments not covered by Social Security, SSI, or VA. Both government & private, & including Workmen's Compensation	11
	✓		Weekly Monthly Yearly	Unemployment Compensation	12
✓		95.	Weekly (Monthly) Yearly	Retirement pension from job	13
	✓		Weekly Monthly Yearly	Alimony or child support	14
	✓		Weekly Monthly Yearly	Scholarships, stipends (Include only the amount beyond tuition.)	15
	✓		Weekly Monthly Yearly	Regular assistance from family members (including regular contributions from employed children)	16
	✓		Weekly Monthly Yearly	SSI payments (yellow government check)	17
	✓		Weekly Monthly Yearly	Regular financial aid from private organizations and churches	18
	✓		Weekly Monthly Yearly	Welfare payments or Aid for Dependent Children	19
			Weekly Monthly Yearly	Other	20

[IF COMPLETE INCOME AMOUNTS ARE OBTAINED IN QUESTION 18 SKIP TO
QUESTION 19, BUT IF ANY AMOUNTS ARE MISSING ASK a.]

CARD 2

a. How much income do you (and your husband/wife) have a year?

IF ALL AMOUNTS
OBTAINED ON 18,
TOTAL AND CODE
IN 18a.

[SHOW ANNUAL INCOME LADDER AND CIRCLE THE LETTER WHICH
IDENTIFIES EITHER YEARLY OR MONTHLY INCOME CATEGORY.]

CODE		YEARLY	MONTHLY
01	A.	0 - $499	(0 - $41)
02	B.	$500 - $999	($42 - $83)
03	C.	$1,000 - $1,999	($84 - $166)
04	D.	$2,000 - $2,999	($167 - $249)
05	E.	$3,000 - $3,999	($250 - $333)
06	F.	$4,000 - $4,999	($334 - $416)
07	G.	$5,000 - $6,999	($417 - $583)
08	H.	$7,000 - $9,999	($584 - $833)
09	I.	$10,000 - $14,999	($834 - $1249)
10	J.	$15,000 - $19,999	($1250 - $1666)
11	K.	$20,000 - $29,999	($1667 - $2499)
12	L.	$30,000 - $39,999	($2500 - $3333)
13	M.	$40,000 or more	($3334 or more)

21-22

23-24

19. How many people altogether live on this income (that is it
provides at least half of their income)? _____ / _____

20. Do you own your own home?

25

┌─ 1 Yes
└─ 0 No ─────────────────────→ [IF "NO" ASK c. AND d.]
   - Not answered

[IF "YES" ASK a. AND b.]

a.
26
↳ a. How much is it worth?
      1 Up to $10,000
      2 $10,000 - $24,000
      3 $25,000 - $50,000
      4 More than $50,000
      - Not answered

b.
27
b. Do you own it outright
   or are you still
   paying a mortgage?
      1 Own outright
      2 Still paying
      - Not answered

b(1)
28

[IF 2 ASK (1).]

c.
29

(1) How much is the
    monthly payment?
      1 0-$59
      2 $60-$99
      3 $100-$149
      4 $150-$199
      5 $200-$249
      6 $250-$349
      7 $350 up
      8 Not answered

c(1)
30

d.
31

c. Do you (and your husband/wife)
   pay the total rent for your
   house (apartment) or do you
   contribute to the cost, or
   does someone else own it or
   pay the rent?
      1 Subject pays total rent
      2 Subject contributes to
         the cost
      3 Someone else owns it or
         pays the rent (Subject
         doesn't contribute)
      - Not answered
   [IF 1 OR 2 ASK (1.).]
   (1.) How much rent do you pay?
      1 0-$59 per month
      2 $60-$99 per month
      3 $100-$149
      4 $150-$199
      5 $200-$249
      6 $250-$349
      7 $350 up
      - Not answered

d. Do you live in public housing
   or receive a rent subsidy?
      1 No, neither
      2 Yes, live in public housing
      3 Yes, receives a rent subsidy
      - Not answered

CARD 2

21. Are your assets and financial resources sufficient to meet
    emergencies?
    1 Yes
    ⓪ No
    - Not answered   *pt sod*

    _____
    32

22. Are your expenses so heavy that you cannot meet the payments,
    or can you barely meet the payments, or are your payments no
    problem to you?
    1 Subject cannot meet payments
    ② Subject can barely meet payments
    3 Payments are no problem
    - Not answered

    _____
    33

23. Is your financial situation such that you feel you need
    financial assistance or help beyond what you are already
    getting?
    ① Yes
    0 No
    - Not answered

    _____
    34

24. Do you pay for your own food or do you get any regular help
    at all with costs of food or meals?
    ① Subject pays for food himself
    2 Subject gets help
    - Not answered

    _____
    35

    [IF 2 ASK a.]

    a. From where?
        [CHECK "YES" OR "NO" FOR EACH OF THE FOLLOWING.]

1	0		
YES	NO		
		Family or friends	36
		Food stamps	37
		Prepared food (meals) from an agency or organization program [SPECIFY NUMBER OF MEALS PER WEEK.] _____	38

    39-40

CARD 2

25. Do you feel that you need food stamps?
  1 Yes
  (0) No " *I don't want to apply* "
  - Not answered

41

26. Are you covered by any kinds of health or medical insurance?
  (1) Yes
  0 No
  - Not answered

42

[IF "YES" ASK a.]

a. What kind?

[CHECK "YES" OR "NO" FOR EACH OF THE FOLLOWING.]

1 YES	0 NO	
	✓	Medicaid
		Medicare Plan A only (hospitalization only)
✓		Medicare Plan A and B (hospitalization and doctor's bills)
✓	✗	Other insurance: hospitalization only (Blue Cross or other)
	✓	Other insurance: hospitalization and doctor's bills (Blue Cross and Blue Shield, major medical or other)

43
44
45
46
47

27. Please tell me how well you think you (and your family) are
now doing financially as compared to other people your age--
better, about the same, or worse?
[PROBE AS NECESSARY.]
  2 Better
  1 About the same
  0 Worse " *I don't know,*
  (-) Not answered   *I don't know* "

48

28. How well does the amount of money you have take care of your
needs--very well, fairly well, or poorly?
  2 Very well
  1 Fairly well   " *I don't know* "
  0 Poorly
  (-) Not answered   *stressful subject*

49

29. Do you usually have enough to buy those little "extras";
that is, those small luxuries?
  2 Yes
  0 No   *I didn't ask because*
  - Not answered   *of answers to 27 & 28*

50

CARD 2

30. Do you feel that you will have enough for your needs in the future?
   2 Yes
   0 No
   - Not answered

I didn't ask — stressful see z ↑ ↓ 28

51

MENTAL HEALTH

Next, I'd like to ask you some questions about how you feel about life.

31. How often would you say you worry about things--very often, fairly often, or hardly ever?
   0 Very often
   1 Fairly often
   2 Hardly ever
   - Not answered

52

32. In general, do you find life exciting, pretty routine, or dull?
   2 Exciting
   1 Pretty routine
   0 Dull
   - Not answered

53

33. Taking everything into consideration how would you describe your satisfaction with life in general at the present time-- good, fair, or poor?
   2 Good
   1 Fair
   0 Poor
   - Not answered

54

CARD 2

CODE
1 Yes
0 No

34. Please answer the following questions "Yes" or "No" as they apply to you now. There are no right or wrong answers, only what best applies to you. Occasionally a question may not seem to apply to you, but please answer either "Yes" or "No", whichever is more nearly correct for you.

[CIRCLE "YES" OR "NO" FOR EACH.]

(1) Do you wake up fresh and rested most mornings?...............yes NO

55

(2) Is your daily life full of things that keep you interested?..yes NO

56

(3) Have you, at times, very much wanted to leave home?.........YES no

57

(4) Does it seem that no one understands you?...................YES no

58

(5) Have you had periods of days, weeks, or months when you couldn't take care of things because you couldn't "get going"?..YES no

59

(6) Is your sleep fitful and disturbed?..........................YES no

60

(7) Are you happy most of the time?......*pt. uncertain*....yes NO

61

(8) Are you being plotted against?..........*pt. laugh*....YES no

62

(9) Do you certainly feel useless at times?...................YES no

63

(10) During the past few years, have you been well most of the time?..yes NO

64

(11) Do you feel weak all over much of the time?...............YES no

65

(12) Are you troubled by headaches?............................YES no

66

(13) Have you had difficulty in keeping your balance in walking?..YES no

67

(14) Are you troubled by your heart pounding and by a shortness of breath?..YES no

68

(15) Even when you are with people, do you feel lonely much of the time?..YES no

69

Sum of Responses in Capital letters ___7___

Sum of Responses in Capital Letters

70-71

CARD 2

35. How would you rate your mental or emotional health at the
present time--excellent, good, fair, or poor?
   3 Excellent
   2 Good   *pt uncertain*
   1 Fair
   0 Poor
   - Not answered   72

36. Is your mental or emotional health now better, about the
same, or worse than it was five years ago?
   3 Better
   2 About the same
   0 Worse
   - Not answered   73

PHYSICAL HEALTH   CARD 3

Let's talk about your health now.   S# ___
                                                 1-4

37. About how many times have you seen a doctor during the past
six months other than as an inpatient in a hospital?   Card# 03
[EXCLUDE PSYCHIATRISTS.]   5-6

    __4__ Times   7-9

38. During the past six months how many days were you so sick
that you were unable to carry on your usual activities--such
as going to work or working around the house?
   0 None
   1 A week or less
   2 More than a week but less than one month
   3 1-3 months
   4 4-6 months
   - Not answered   10

39. How many days in the past six months were you in a hospital
for physical health problems?

    _15_ Days   11-13

40. How many days in the past six months were you in a nursing
home, or rehabilitation center for physical health problems?

    _0_ Days   14-16

41. Do you feel that you need medical care or treatment beyond
what you are receiving at this time?
   1 Yes
   0 No
   - Not answered   17

        "Dr Smith is taking care
of me. . . . he's fine
. . . he referred me few."

CARD 3

42. I have a list of common medicines that people take. Would you please tell me if you've taken any of the following in the past month.

[CHECK "YES" OR "NO" FOR EACH MEDICINE.]

COL.

	1 YES	0 NO	
18____		✓	Arthritis medication
19____		✓	Prescription pain killer (other than above)
20____		✓	High blood pressure medicine
21____		✓	Pills to make you lose water or salt (water pills)
22____		✓	Digitalis pills for the heart
23____		✓	Nitroglycerin tablets for chest pain
24____		✓	Blood thinner medicine (anticoagulants)
25____		✓	Drugs to improve circulation
26____		✓	Insulin injections for diabetes
27____		✓	Pills for diabetes
28____		✓	Prescription ulcer medicine
29____		✓	Seizure medications (like Dilantin)
30____		✓	Thyroid pills
31____		✓	Cortisone pills or injections
32____		✓	Antibiotics
33____	✓		Tranquilizers or nerve medicine
34____		✓	Prescription sleeping pills (once a week or more)
35____		✓	Hormones, male or female (including birth control pills)

CODE # OF
"others"
THAT CANNOT
BE ENTERED
IN ABOVE
CATEGORIES.

36-37

43. What other prescription drugs have you taken in the past month?

[RECORD THE "others". THEN ENTER THEM IN APPROPRIATE CATEGORIES ABOVE IF POSSIBLE.]

[SPECIFY.] *lithium*

meprobamate

CARD 3

44. Do you have any of the following illnesses at the present time?

[CHECK "YES" OR "NO" FOR EACH OF THE FOLLOWING. IF "YES", ASK:
"How much does it interfere with your activities, not at all,
a little (some), or a great deal?" AND CHECK THE APPROPRIATE BOX.]

```
CODE
0,1,2,3 ;
OR 4 FOR
YES BUT
NOT HOW
MUCH.
```

[IF "YES", ASK:] How much does it interfere with your activities?

YES (0)	NO (1)	NOT AT ALL (1)	A LITTLE (2)	A GREAT DEAL (3)		COL.
✓			✓		Arthritis or rheumatism	___38
	✓				Glaucoma	___39
	✓				Asthma	___40
	✓				Emphysema or chronic bronchitis	___41
	✓				Tuberculosis	___42
	✓				High blood pressure	___43
✓		✓			Heart trouble	___44
	✓				Circulation trouble in arms or legs	___45
	✓				Diabetes	___46
	✓				Ulcers (of the digestive system)	___47
	✓				Other stomach or intestinal disorders or gall bladder problems	___48
	✓				Liver disease	___49
	✓				Kidney disease	___50
	✓				Other urinary tract disorders (including prostate trouble)	___51
	✓				Cancer or Leukemia	___52
	✓				Anemia	___53
✓			✓		Effects of stroke	___54
	✓				Parkinson's Disease	___55
	✓				Epilepsy	___56
	✓				Cerebral Palsy	___57
	✓				Multiple Sclerosis	___58
	✓				Muscular Dystrophy	___59
	✓				Effects of Polio	___60
	✓				Thyroid or other glandular disorders	___61
	✓				Skin disorders such as pressure sores, leg ulcers or severe burns	___62
	✓				Speech impediment or impairment	___63

45. Do you have any physical disabilities such as total or partial
    paralysis, missing or non-functional limbs, or broken bones?
    - 0 No
    - 1 Total paralysis
    - 2 Partial paralysis
    - 3 Missing or non-functional limbs
    - 4 Broken bones
    - - Not answered

64 ____

46. How is your eyesight (with glasses or contacts), excellent,
    good, fair, poor, or are you totally blind?
    - 1 Excellent
    - 2 Good
    - 3 Fair
    - 4 Poor
    - 5 Totally blind
    - - Not answered

65 ____

47. How is your hearing, excellent, good, fair, poor, or are you
    totally deaf?
    - 1 Excellent
    - 2 Good
    - 3 Fair
    - 4 Poor
    - 5 Totally deaf
    - - Not answered

66 ____

48. Do you have any other physical problems or illnesses at the
    present time that seriously affect your health?
    - 1 Yes
    - 0 No
    - - Not answered

67 ____

[IF "YES" SPECIFY.] _____

_____

SUPPORTIVE DEVICES AND PROSTHESES
49. Do you use any of the following aids all or most of the time?

[CHECK "YES" OR "NO" FOR EACH AID.]

CARD 3

YES	NO		
1	0		
	✓	Cane (including tripod-tip cane)	68
✓		Walker *"sometimes, I don't have it with me today"*	69
	✓	Wheelchair	70
	✓	Leg brace	71
	✓	Back brace	72
	✓	Artificial limb	73
	✓	Hearing aid	74
	✓	Colostomy equipment	75
	✓	Catheter	76
	✓	Kidney dialysis machine	77
		Other [SPECIFY.] _____	78

CARD 4
S# ____
1-4
Card# __04__
5-6

50. Do you need any aids (supportive or prosthetic devices) that you currently do not have?
    1   Yes
    ⓪   No
    -   Not answered

7 ____

[IF "YES", ASK a.]

a. What aids do you need? [SPECIFY.]

_____

_____

_____   8-9

51. Do you have a problem with your health because of drinking or has your physician advised you to cut down on drinking?
    1   Yes
    ⓪   No   *"I've never liked to drink"*
    -   Not answered   10 ____

CARD 4

52. Do you regularly participate in any vigorous sports activity
    such as hiking, jogging, tennis, biking, or swimming?
    1   Yes   *I didn't ask*
    0   No
    -   Not answered

11 ———

---

53. How would you rate your overall health at the present time--
    excellent, good, fair, or poor?
    3   Excellent
    2   Good
    1   Fair
    (0) Poor
    -   Not answered

12 ———

54. Is your health now better, about the same, or worse than it
    was five years ago?
    3   Better
    2   About the same
    (0) Worse
    -   Not answered

13 ———

55. How much do your health troubles stand in the way of your
    doing the things you want to do--not at all, a little (some)
    or a great deal?
    3   Not at all
    2   A little (some)
    (0) A great deal   *this answer disagrees*
    -   Not answered   *with one given earlier Q 44*

14 ———

ACTIVITIES OF DAILY LIVING

Now I'd like to ask you about some of the activities of daily
living, things that we all need to do as a part of our daily
lives. I would like to know if you can do these activities
without any help at all, or if you need some help to do them,
or if you can't do them at all.

[BE SURE TO READ ALL ANSWER CHOICES IF APPLICABLE IN QUESTIONS
56. THROUGH 69. TO RESPONDENT.]

Instrumental ADL

56. Can you use the telephone...
    (2) without help, including looking up numbers and dialing
    1   with some help (can answer phone or dial operator
        in an emergency, but need a special phone or help
        in getting the number or dialing),
    0   or are you completely unable to use the telephone?
    -   Not answered

15 ———

57. Can you get to places out of walking distance...   CARD 4
    2 without help (can travel alone on buses, taxis, or drive
       your own car),
    1 with some help (need someone to help you or go with you
       when traveling) or
    0 are you unable to travel unless emergency arrangements are
       made for a specialized vehicle like an ambulance?
    - Not answered   ___
                                                                      16

58. Can you go shopping for groceries or clothes [ASSUMING S HAS
    TRANSPORTATION]...
    2 without help (taking care of all shopping needs yourself,
       assuming you had transportation),
    1 with some help (need someone to go with you on all
       shopping trips),
    0 or are you completely unable to do any shopping?
    - Not answered   ___
                                                                      17

59. Can you prepare your own meals...
    2 without help (plan and cook full meals yourself),
    1 with some help (can prepare some things but unable
       to cook full meals yourself),
    0 or are you completely unable to prepare any meals?
    - Not answered   ___
                                                                      18

60. Can you do your housework...
    2 without help (can scrub floors, etc.),
    1 with some help (can do light housework but need help
       with heavy work),
    0 or are you completely unable to do any housework?
    - Not answered   ___
                                                                      19

61. Can you take your own medicine...
    2 without help (in the right doses at the right time),
    1 with some help (able to take medicine if someone
       prepares it for you and/or reminds you to take it),
    0 or are you completely unable to take your medicines?
    - Not answered   ___
                                                                      20

62. Can you handle your own money...
    2 without help (write checks, pay bills, etc.),
    1 with some help (manage day-to-day buying but need help
       with managing your checkbook and paying your bills),
    0 or are you completely unable to handle money?
    - Not answered   ___
                                                                      21

Physical ADL

63. Can you eat...
    2) without help (able to feed yourself completely),
    1 with some help (need help with cutting, etc.),
    0 or are you completely unable to feed yourself?
    - Not answered

    _22_

64. Can you dress and undress yourself...
    2 without help (able to pick out clothes, dress and
    undress yourself),
    1 with some help,
    0 or are you completely unable to dress and undress
    yourself?
    - Not answered

    _23_

65. Can you take care of your own appearance, for example
    combing your hair and (for men) shaving...
    2) without help,
    1 with some help,
    0 or are you completely unable to maintain your
    appearance yourself?
    - Not answered

    _24_

66. Can you walk...
    2 without help (except from a cane),
    1 with some help from a person or with the use of a
    walker, or crutches, etc.,
    0 or are you completely unable to walk?
    - Not answered

    _25_

67. Can you get in and out of bed...
    2 without any help or aids,
    1 with some help (either from a person or with the
    aid of some device),
    0 or are you totally dependent on someone else to
    lift you?
    - Not answered

    _26_

68. Can you take a bath or shower...   *d worder ??.*
    2 without help,
    1 with some help (need help getting in and out of
    the tub, or need special attachments on the tub),
    0 or are you completely unable to bathe yourself?
    - Not answered

    _27_

69. Do you ever have trouble getting to the bathroom on time?
    2) No
    0 Yes
    1 Have a catheter or colostomy
    - Not answered

    _28_

[IF "YES" ASK a.]

CARD 4

a. How often do you wet or soil yourself (either day or night)?
   1 Once or twice a week
   0 Three times a week or more
   - Not answered   ___29___

70. Is there someone who helps you with such things as shopping,
    housework, bathing, dressing, and getting around?
    1 Yes
    0 No
    - Not answered   ___30___

[IF "YES" ASK a. AND b.]

a. Who is your major helper?

   ✗ Name ___Will Johns___ Relationship ___son___   ___31___
b. Who else helps you?

   Name _____ Relationship _____   ___32___

✗ _son is only visiting for short time_

I stopped Q here because it seemed frail
& I wanted to start clinical
UTILIZATION OF SERVICES _eval. in remaining time_

71. Now I want to ask you some questions about the kinds of help you
    are or have been getting or the kinds of help that you feel you
    need. We want to know not only about the help you have been
    getting from agencies or organizations but also what help you
    have been getting from your family and friends.

    TRANSPORTATION
    (1) Who provides your transportation when you go shopping,
        visit friends, go to the doctor, etc.?

        [CHECK "YES" OR "NO" FOR EACH.]

1 YES	0 NO		
		Yourself	___33___
		Your family or friends	___34___
		Use public transportation (bus, taxi, subway, etc.)	___35___
		Public agency [SPECIFY.] _____	___36___
		Other [SPECIFY.] _____	___37___

a. On the average how many round trips do you make a week?
    0 None
    1 Less than one a week
    2 One to three a week
    3 4 or more
    - Not answered

_____
38

b. Do you feel you need transportation more often than it
    is available to you now for appointments, visiting,
    social events, etc.?
    1 Yes
    0 No
    - Not answered

_____
39

SOCIAL/RECREATIONAL SERVICES
(2) In the past six months (since _____ [SPECIFY MONTH.]) have
     you participated in any planned and organized social or
     recreational programs or in any group activities or classes
     such as arts and crafts classes? [EXCLUDE EMPLOYMENT-RELATED
     CLASSES.]
     1 Yes
     0 No
     - Not answered

_____
40

[IF "NO" SKIP TO c.; IF "YES" ASK a., b., AND c.]

a. About how many times a week did you participate in these
    activities?
    1 Once a week or less
    2 2-3 times a week
    3 4 times a week or more
    - Not answered

_____
41

b. Do you still participate in such activities or groups?
    1 Yes
    0 No
    - Not answered

_____
42

c. Do you feel you need to participate in any planned and
    organized social or recreational programs or in any
    group activities or classes?
    1 Yes
    0 No
    - Not answered

_____
43

EMPLOYMENT SERVICES
(3) Has anyone helped you look for or find a job or counseled you
     in regard to getting employment in the past six months (since
     _____ [MONTH])?
     1 Yes
     0 No
     - Not answered

_____
44

[IF "NO" SKIP TO b.; IF "YES" ASK a. AND b.]

a. Who helped you?
    1 Family members or friends
    2 Someone from an agency
    3 Both
    - Not answered

———
45

b. Do you feel you need someone to help you find a job?
    1 Yes
    0 No
    - Not answered

———
46

SHELTERED EMPLOYMENT
(4) During the past six months have you worked in a place like
a sheltered workshop which employs people with disabilities
or special problems?
    1 Yes
    0 No
    - Not answered

———
47

[IF "NO" SKIP TO b.; IF "YES" ASK a. AND b.]

a. Do you still work there?
    1 Yes
    0 No
    - Not answered

———
48

b. Do you feel you need to work in a sheltered workshop?
    1 Yes
    0 No
    - Not answered

———
49

EDUCATIONAL SERVICES, EMPLOYMENT RELATED
(5) In the past six months have you had any occupational
training or on the job training to further prepare you
for a job or career?
    1 Yes
    0 No
    - Not answered

———
50

[IF "NO" SKIP TO c.; IF "YES" ASK a., b., AND c.]

a. Was this full or part-time training?
    1 Full-time
    2 Part-time
    - Not answered

———
51

b. Are you still in classes or training?
    1 Yes
    0 No
    - Not answered

———
52

CARD 4

c. Do you feel you need education or on the job training to prepare you for a job?
   1 Yes
   0 No
   - Not answered

53

REMEDIAL TRAINING

(6) In the past six months have you had any remedial training or instruction in learning basic personal skills, for example speech therapy, reality orientation, or training for the blind or physically or mentally handicapped? [EXCLUDE PHYSICAL THERAPY.]
   1 Yes
   0 No
   - Not answered

54

[IF "NO" SKIP TO c.; IF "YES" ASK a., b., AND c.]

a. On the average about how many training sessions a week did you have over the past six months?
   1 Less than one a week
   2 One a week
   3 Two or more a week
   - Not answered

55

b. Are you currently receiving this type of training or instruction?
   1 Yes
   0 No
   - Not answered

56

c. Do you think you need remedial training or instruction in basic personal skills?
   1 Yes
   0 No
   - Not answered

57

MENTAL HEALTH SERVICES

(7) Have you had any treatment or counseling for personal or family problems or for nervous, or emotional problems in the past six months, that is, since _____ [SPECIFY MONTH.]?
   1 Yes
   0 No
   - Not answered

58

[IF "NO" SKIP TO d.; IF "YES" ASK a., b., c., AND d.]

a. Were you hospitalized for nervous, or emotional problems at any time during this period? (Last six months)
   1 Yes
   0 No
   - Not answered

59

b. During the past six months how many sessions have you CARD 4
    had with a doctor, psychiatrist or counselor for these
    problems (other than those when you were an inpatient
    in the hospital)?
    0 None, had treatment only as an inpatient
    1 Less than 4 sessions (only occasionally
       or for evaluation)
    2 4-12 sessions
    3 13 or more sessions
    - Not answered
                                                              ‾‾60‾‾

c. Are you still receiving this help?
    1 Yes
    0 No
    - Not answered
                                                              ‾‾61‾‾

d. Do you feel that you need treatment or counseling for
    personal or family problems or for nervous or emotional
    problems?
    1 Yes
    0 No
    - Not answered
                                                              ‾‾62‾‾

PSYCHOTROPIC DRUGS
(8) Have you taken any prescription medicine for your nerves
    in the past six months, like medicine to calm you down or
    to help depression?
    1 Yes
    0 No
    - Not answered
                                                              ‾‾63‾‾

[IF "NO" SKIP TO b.; IF "YES" ASK a. AND b.]

a. Are you still taking it?
    1 Yes
    0 No
    - Not answered
                                                              ‾‾64‾‾

b. Do you feel you need this kind of medicine?
    1 Yes
    0 No
    - Not answered
                                                              ‾‾65‾‾

PERSONAL CARE SERVICES
(9) In the past six months has someone helped you with your
    personal care, for example helping you to bathe or dress,
    feeding you, or helping you with toilet care?
    1 Yes
    0 No
    - Not answered
                                                              ‾‾66‾‾

[IF "NO" SKIP TO d.; IF "YES" ASK a., b., c., AND d.]

CARD 4

a. Who helped you in this way?
   1 Unpaid family members or friends
   2 Someone hired to help you in this way
     or someone from an agency
   3 Both
   - Not answered

_____
67

b. On the average, how much time per day has this
person helped you to bathe, dress, eat, go to the
toilet, etc.?
   1 Less than ½ hour per day
   2 ½ to 1½ hours per day
   3 More than 1½ hours per day
   - Not answered

_____
68

c. Are you still being helped in this way?
   1 Yes
   0 No
   - Not answered

_____
69

d. Do you feel you need help with bathing, dressing,
eating, or going to the toilet, etc.?
   1 Yes
   0 No
   - Not answered

_____
70

NURSING CARE
(10) During the past six months have you had any nursing care,
in other words did a nurse or someone else give you treatments or medications prescribed by a doctor? [EXCLUDE
NURSING CARE WHILE IN THE HOSPITAL.]
   1 Yes
   0 No
   - Not answered

_____
71

[IF "NO" SKIP TO e.; IF "YES" ASK a., b., c., d., AND e.]

a. Who helped you in this way?
   1 Unpaid family members or friends
   2 Someone hired to help you in this way
     or someone from an agency
   3 Both
   - Not answered

_____
72

b. On the average, how many hours a day did you receive
this help?
   0 Only occasionally, not every day
   1 Gave oral medicine only
   2 Less than ½ hour per day
   3 ½ to 1 hour per day
   4 More than 1 hour per day
   - Not answered

_____
73

CARD 5

S# _____
                                                                        1-4
c. For how long did you have this help within the
    past six months?   Card# ___05___
        1 Less than one month   5-6
        2 1-3 months
        3 More than 3 months
        - Not answered
                                                                      _____
                                                                        7
d. Are you still receiving nursing care?
        1 Yes
        0 No
        - Not answered
                                                                      _____
                                                                        8
e. Do you feel you need nursing care?
        1 Yes
        0 No
        - Not answered
                                                                      _____
                                                                        9
PHYSICAL THERAPY
(13) During the past six months have you received physical
     therapy?
        1 Yes
        0 No
        - Not answered
                                                                      _____
                                                                        10
[IF "NO" SKIP TO d.; IF "YES" ASK a., b., c., AND d.]

a. Who gave you physical therapy or helped you with it?
        1 Unpaid family members or friends
        2 Someone hired to provide this or someone
           from an agency
        3 Both
        - Not answered
                                                                      _____
                                                                        11
b. On the average how many times a week did someone
    help you with your physical therapy activities?
        1 Less than once a week
        2 Once a week
        3 2 or more times a week
        - Not answered
                                                                      _____
                                                                        12
c. Are you still receiving physical therapy?
        1 Yes
        0 No
        - Not answered
                                                                      _____
                                                                        13
d. Do you think you need physical therapy?
        1 Yes
        0 No
        - Not answered
                                                                      _____
                                                                        14

CARD 5

CONTINUOUS SUPERVISION
(14) During the past six months was there any period when
someone had to be with you all the time to look after
you?
   1 Yes
   0 No
   - Not answered

15

[IF "NO" SKIP TO c.; IF "YES" ASK a., b., AND c.]

a. Who looked after you?
    1 Unpaid family members or friends
    2 Someone hired to look after you or
       someone from an agency
    3 Both
    - Not answered

16

b. Do you still have to have someone with you all
    the time to look after you?
    1 Yes
    0 No
    - Not answered

17

c. Do you feel you need to have someone with you
    all the time to look after you?
    1 Yes
    0 No
    - Not answered

18

CHECKING SERVICES
(15) [IF S IS STILL RECEIVING CONTINUOUS SUPERVISION, ASK ONLY c.]

[PERSONS WHO NEED CHECKING WHO ARE LIVING IN INSTITUTIONS
OR WITH FAMILY MEMBERS MAY BE PRESUMED TO BE RECEIVING IT.]

During the past six months have you had someone regularly
(at least five times a week) check on you by phone or in
person to make sure you were all right?
   1 Yes
   0 No
   - Not answered

19

[IF "NO" SKIP TO c.; IF "YES" ASK a., b., AND c.]

a. Who checked on you?
    1 Unpaid family members or friends
    2 Someone from an agency, a volunteer,
       or someone hired to help you
    3 Both
    - Not answered

20

b. Is someone still checking on you at least five
times a week?
1 Yes
0 No
- Not answered

c. Do you feel you need to have someone check on you
regularly (at least five times a week) by phone or
in person to make sure you are all right? [CIRCLE
"NO", IF S FELT HE NEEDED CONTINUOUS SUPERVISION,
(14c.)].
1 Yes
0 No
- Not answered

RELOCATION AND PLACEMENT SERVICES
(16) In the past six months have you had any help in finding a
new place to live, or in making arrangements to move in?
[THIS INCLUDES PLACEMENT IN INSTITUTIONS.]
1 Yes
0 No
- Not answered

[IF "NO" SKIP TO b.; IF "YES" ASK a. AND b.]

a. Who helped you with this?
1 Unpaid family members or friends
2 Other, such as someone from an agency
3 Both
- Not answered

b. Do you feel you need help in finding a (another)
place to live?
1 Yes
0 No
- Not answered

HOMEMAKER-HOUSEHOLD SERVICES
(17) During the past six months did someone have to help you
regularly with routine household chores such as cleaning,
washing clothes, etc.? That is did your wife/husband or
someone else have to do them because you were unable to?
1 Yes
0 No
- Not answered

[IF "NO" SKIP TO d.; IF "YES" ASK a., b., c., AND d.]

CARD 5

a. Who helped with household chores?
   1 Unpaid family members or friends
   2 Other, such as a paid helper or agency person
   3 Both
   - Not answered

27

b. For about how many hours a week did you have to
   have help with household chores?
   1 Less than 4 hours a week
   2 4-8 hours a week (a half-day to a day)
   3 9 or more hours a week (more than one day a week)
   - Not answered

28

c. Are you still getting this kind of help?
   1 Yes
   0 No
   - Not answered

29

d. Do you feel you need help with routine housework?
   1 Yes
   0 No
   - Not answered

30

MEAL PREPARATION
(18) During the past six months did someone regularly have to
prepare meals for you? That is did your wife/husband or
someone else regularly cook because you were unable to,
or did you have to go out for meals?
   1 Yes
   0 No
   - Not answered

31

[IF "NO" SKIP TO c.; IF "YES" ASK a., b., AND c.]

a. Who prepared meals for you?
   1 Unpaid family members or friends
   2 Other, such as a paid helper or agency person
   3 Both
   - Not answered

32

b. Is someone still having to prepare meals for you?
   1 Yes
   0 No
   - Not answered

33

c. Do you feel that you need to have someone regularly
prepare meals for you because you can't do it yourself?
   1 Yes
   0 No
   - Not answered

34

ADMINISTRATIVE, LEGAL, AND PROTECTIVE SERVICES
(19) During the past six months has anyone helped you with any legal matters or with managing your personal business affairs or handling your money, for example paying your bills for you?
   1 Yes
   0 No
   - Not answered

_____
35

[IF "NO" SKIP TO c.; IF "YES" ASK a., b., AND c.]

a. Who helped you?
   1 Family members or friends
   2 A lawyer, the Legal Aid Society, other agency personnel, or someone hired to help you?
   3 Both
   - Not answered

_____
36

b. Are you still getting help with legal matters or with managing your personal business affairs?
   1 Yes
   0 No
   - Not answered

_____
37

c. Do you think you need help with these matters?
   1 Yes
   0 No
   - Not answered

_____
38

SYSTEMATIC MULTIDIMENSIONAL EVALUATION
(20) In the past six months has anyone like a doctor or social worker thoroughly reviewed and evaluated your overall condition including your health, your mental health, and your social and financial situation?
   1 Yes
   0 No
   - Not answered

_____
39

a. Do you think you need to have someone review and evaluate your overall condition in this way?
   1 Yes
   0 No
   - Not answered

_____
40

COORDINATION, INFORMATION AND REFERRAL SERVICES
(24) During the past six months did someone see to it that you got the kinds of help you needed? In other words did someone give you information about the kind of help that is available or put you in touch with those who could help you?
   1 Yes
   0 No
   - Not answered

_____
41

CARD 5

[IF "NO" SKIP TO c.; IF "YES" ASK a., b., AND c.]

a. Who was this person?
    1 A family member or a friend
    2 Someone from an agency
    3 Both
    - Not answered

42

b. Is there still someone who sees to it that you get
    the kinds of help you need? In other words is there
    someone who gives you information about the kind of
    help that is available or puts you in touch with
    those who can help you?
    1 Yes
    0 No
    - Not answered

43

c. Do you feel you need to have someone organize or
    coordinate the kinds of help you need and make
    arrangements for you to get them?
    1 Yes
    0 No
    - Not answered

44

45

72. ⌈QUESTION 71 WAS ASKED OF:⌉
     1 Subject
     2 Informant
     ⌊3 Both   ⌋

CONCLUDING STATEMENT TO THE SUBJECT

[MAKE A BRIEF CONCLUDING STATEMENT TO THE SUBJECT INDICATING THE
CONCLUSION OF THE INTERVIEW AND EXPRESSING YOUR APPRECIATION
FOR HIS COOPERATION.]

QUESTIONS TO BE ASKED OF AN INFORMANT
BASED ON HIS KNOWLEDGE OF THE SUBJECT

No informant today

[IF THE SUBJECT IS UNRELIABLE THESE QUESTIONS MUST BE ASKED OF AN   CARD 5
INFORMANT.]
[IF THE SUBJECT IS RELIABLE, THE QUESTIONS MUST BE ASKED IF AN
INFORMANT IS AVAILABLE.]

SOCIAL RESOURCES

73. How well does _____ (Subject) get along with his/her family
    and friends--very well, fairly well, or poorly (has considerable
    trouble or conflict with them)?
    1 Very well
    2 Fairly well (has some conflict or trouble with them)
    3 Poorly (has considerable trouble or conflict with them)
    - Not answered
                                                                    ____
                                                                     46

74. Is there someone who would help _____ (Subject) at all if
    he/she were sick or disabled, for example his/her husband or
    wife, a member of the family or a friend?
    1 Yes
    0 No
    - Not answered
                                                                    ____
                                                                     47

    [IF "YES" ASK a. AND b.]

    a. [CIRCLE THE MOST APPROPRIATE.]
        Is there someone who would take care of him/her as long as
        needed, or only for a short time, or only someone who would
        help now and then (for example, taking him/her to the
        doctor, fixing lunch, etc.)?
        1 Someone who would take care of Subject indefinitely
           (as long as needed)
        2 Someone who would take care of Subject a short time
           (a few weeks to six months)
        3 Someone who would help him now and then (taking him
           to the doctor or fixing lunch, etc.)
        - Not answered
                                                                    ____
                                                                     48

    b. Who is this person?

        Name _____

        Relationship _____
                                                                    ____
                                                                     49

ECONOMIC RESOURCES

75. In your opinion are _____'s (Subject's) needs for the following basic necessities being well met, barely met, or are they not being met?

[CHECK THE APPROPRIATE BOX FOR EACH NEED.]

2 WELL MET	1 BARELY MET	0 NOT MET	
			Food
			Housing
			Clothing
			Medical care
			Small luxuries

50

51

52

53

54

MENTAL HEALTH

76. Does _____ (Subject) show good, common sense in making judgments and decisions?
    1 Yes
    0 No
    - Not answered

55

77. Is _____ (Subject) able to handle (cope with) major problems which occur in his/her life?
    1 Yes
    0 No
    - Not answered

56

78. Do you feel that _____ (Subject) finds life exciting and enjoyable?
    1 Yes
    0 No
    - Not answered

57

79. How would you rate _____'s (Subject's) mental or emotional health or ability to think at the present time compared to the average person living independently--excellent, good, fair, or poor?
    3 Excellent
    2 Good
    1 Fair
    0 Poor
    - Not answered

58

80. Is _____ (Subject's) mental or emotional health or ability to think-- better, about the same, or worse than it was five years ago?
    3 Better
    2 About the same
    0 Worse
    - Not answered

59

PHYSICAL HEALTH

CARD 5

81. How would you rate _____ (Subject's) health at the present time--excellent, good, fair, or poor?
    3 Excellent
    2 Good
    1 Fair
    0 Poor
    - Not answered

_____
60

82. How much do _____ (Subject's) health troubles stand in the way of his/her doing the things he/she wants to do--not at all, a little (some), or a great deal?
    3 Not at all
    2 A little (some)
    0 A great deal
    - Not answered

_____
61

[THE REMAINING QUESTIONS ARE TO BE ANSWERED BY THE INTERVIEWER IMMEDIATELY AFTER LEAVING THE INTERVIEW SITE.]

83. Length of interview _____*30*_____
                                   Minutes

_____
62-64

84. Factual information obtained from:
    1 Subject
    2 Relative
    3 Other [SPECIFY.] _____

_____
65

85. Factual questions (obtained from Subject and/or informant) are:
    1 Completely reliable
    2 Reliable on most items
    3 Reliable on only a few items
    4 Completely unreliable

_____
66

86. Subjective questions (those in boxes, obtained from Subject only) are:
    1 Completely reliable
    2 Reliable on most items
    3 Reliable on only a few items
    4 Completely unreliable
    5 Not obtained

_____
67

    [IF 5 ANSWER a.]

    a. Why didn't the Subject answer the Subjective questions? [BE SPECIFIC.]

    _____

    _____

    _____

_____
68-69

SOCIAL RESOURCES

CARD 5

87. Which of the following best describes the availability of help for the Subject if he(she) were sick or disabled?

[CIRCLE THE MOST APPROPRIATE.]

1 At least one person could and would take care of the Subject indefinitely (as long as needed).
2 At least one person could and would take care of the Subject for a short time (a few weeks to 6 months).
3 Help would only be available now and then for such things as taking him(her) to the doctor, fixing lunch, etc.
4 No help at all (except possible emergency help) would be available.

70

88. Which of the following best describes the Subject's social relationships?

[CIRCLE THE MOST APPROPRIATE.]

1 Very satisfactory, extensive
2 Fairly satisfactory, adequate
3 Unsatisfactory, of poor quality, few

71

ECONOMIC RESOURCES

89. In your opinion which of the following best describes the Subject's income?

1 Ample
2 Satisfactory
3 Somewhat inadequate
4 Totally inadequate
5 No income at all

72

90. In your opinion does the Subject have any financial reserves?

1 Yes, has reserves
0 No, has (little or) no reserves

73

91. In your opinion which of the following statements best describes the extent to which the Subject's needs are being met?

1 Food, housing, clothing, and medical needs are met; Subject can afford small luxuries.
2 Food, housing, clothing, and medical needs are met; Subject cannot afford small luxuries.
3 Either food, or housing, or clothing, or medical needs are unmet; Subject cannot afford small luxuries.
4 Two or more basic needs (housing, food, clothing, medical care) are unmet; Subject cannot afford small luxuries.

74

MENTAL HEALTH   CARD 5

92. Is it your impression that the Subject shows good, common
     sense in making judgments and decisions?
        1 Yes
        0 No
        - Not answered   *I'm not sure at this point —
                                in eval — see clenical eval.*   ___
                                                                      75

93. Is it your impression that the Subject is able to handle
     (cope with) major problems which occur in his/her life?
        1 Yes
        0 No
           Not answered   ___
                                                                      76

94. Is it your impression that the Subject finds life exciting
     and enjoyable?
        1 Yes
        0 No
           Not answered   ___
                                                                      77

                                                                    CARD 6

                                                             S# ___
                                                                 1-4

95. During the interview did the Subject's behavior strike you Card# 06
     as: 5-6

     [CHECK "YES" OR "NO" FOR EACH OF THE FOLLOWING.]

| 1 | 0 | |
YES	NO	
✓		Mentally alert and stimulating
✓		Pleasant and cooperative
✓		Depressed and/or tearful
	✓	Withdrawn or lethargic
	✓	Fearful, anxious, or extremely tense
	✓	Full of unrealistic physical complaints
	✓	Suspicious (more than reasonable)
	✓	Bizarre or inappropriate in thought or action
	✓	Excessively talkative or overly jovial, or elated

(alignment with numbers 7, 8, 9, 10, 11, 12, 13, 14, 15)

PHYSICAL HEALTH
96. Is the Subject either extremely overweight, or malnourished
     and emaciated?
        0 No, neither
        1 Yes, extremely overweight
        2 Yes, malnourished or emaciated
        - Not answered   ___
                                                                      16

CARD 6   SOCIAL RESOURCES RATING SCALE

<u>17</u>

97. [RATE THE CURRENT SOCIAL RESOURCES OF THE PERSON BEING
    EVALUATED ALONG THE SIX-POINT SCALE PRESENTED BELOW.
    CIRCLE THE <u>ONE</u> NUMBER WHICH BEST DESCRIBES THE PERSON'S
    PRESENT CIRCUMSTANCES. SOCIAL RESOURCES QUESTIONS ARE
    NUMBERS 6-14, 73, 74, 87, AND 88.]

1. <u>Excellent social resources.</u>
   Social relationships are very satisfying and extensive;
   at least one person would take care of him(her)
   indefinitely.

2. <u>Good social resources.</u>
   Social relationships are fairly satisfying and
   adequate and at least one person would take care
   of him(her) indefinitely.
   OR
   Social relationships are very satisfying and extensive;
   and only short term help is available.

3. <u>Mildly socially impaired.</u>
   Social relationships are unsatisfactory, of poor quality,
   few; but at least one person would take care of him(her)
   indefinitely.
   OR
   Social relationships are fairly satisfactory, adequate;
   and only short term help is available.

4. <u>Moderately socially impaired.</u>
   Social relationships are unsatisfactory, of poor quality,
   few; and only short term care is available.
   OR
   Social relationships are at least adequate or satisfactory;
   but help would only be available now and then.

5. <u>Severely socially impaired.</u>
   Social relationships are unsatisfactory, of poor quality,
   few; and help would only be available now and then.
   OR
   Social relationships are at least satisfactory or adequate;
   but help is not even available now and then.

6. <u>Totally socially impaired.</u>
   Social relationships are unsatisfactory, of poor quality,
   few; and help is not even available now and then.

ECONOMIC RESOURCES RATING SCALE   CARD 6

98. [RATE THE CURRENT ECONOMIC RESOURCES OF THE PERSON BEING EVALUATED
     ALONG THE SIX-POINT SCALE PRESENTED BELOW. CIRCLE THE ONE NUMBER
     WHICH BEST DESCRIBES THE PERSON'S PRESENT CIRCUMSTANCES. ECONOMIC
     QUESTIONS ARE NUMBERS 15-30, 75, AND 89-91.]

     1. Economic Resources are excellent.   ___
         Income is ample; Subject has reserves.   18

     2. Economic Resources are satisfactory.
         Income is ample; Subject has no reserves
         or
         Income is adequate; Subject has reserves.

     3. Economic Resources are mildly impaired.
         Income is adequate; Subject has no reserves
         or
         Income is somewhat inadequate; Subject has reserves.

     4. Economic Resources are moderately impaired.
         Income is somewhat inadequate; Subject has no reserves.

     5. Economic Resources are severely impaired.
         Income is totally inadequate; Subject may or may not
         have reserves.

     6. Economic Resources are completely impaired.
         Subject is destitute, completely without income or reserves.

     [INCOME IS CONSIDERED TO BE ADEQUATE IF ALL THE SUBJECT'S
     NEEDS ARE BEING MET.]

CARD 6

19

MENTAL HEALTH RATING SCALE

99. [RATE THE CURRENT MENTAL FUNCTIONING OF THE PERSON BEING
EVALUATED ALONG THE SIX-POINT SCALE PRESENTED BELOW.
CIRCLE THE ONE NUMBER WHICH BEST DESCRIBES THE PERSON'S
PRESENT FUNCTIONING. MENTAL HEALTH QUESTIONS ARE THE
PRELIMINARY QUESTIONNAIRE, AND NUMBERS 31-36, 76-80,
AND 92-95.]

1. Outstanding mental health.
   Intellectually alert and clearly enjoying life.
   Manages routine and major problems in his life
   with ease and is free from any psychiatric
   symptoms.

2. Good mental health.
   Handles both routine and major problems in his life
   satisfactorily and is intellectually intact and free
   of psychiatric symptoms.

3. Mildly mentally impaired.
   Has mild psychiatric symptoms and/or mild intellectual
   impairment. Continues to handle routine, though not
   major, problems in his life satisfactorily.

4. Moderately mentally impaired.
   Has definite psychiatric symptoms, and/or moderate
   intellectual impairment. Able to make routine,
   common-sense decisions, but unable to handle major
   problems in his life.

5. Severely mentally impaired.
   Has severe psychiatric symptoms and/or severe
   intellectual impairment, which interfere with routine
   judgments and decision making in every day life.

6. Completely mentally impaired.
   Grossly psychotic or completely impaired intellectually.
   Requires either intermittent or constant supervision
   because of clearly abnormal or potentially harmful
   behavior.

Maybe
(4)
see denied
eval.

CARD 6

PHYSICAL HEALTH RATING SCALE

100. [RATE THE CURRENT PHYSICAL FUNCTIONING OF THE PERSON BEING
EVALUATED ALONG THE SIX-POINT SCALE PRESENTED BELOW. CIRCLE
THE ONE NUMBER WHICH BEST DESCRIBES THE PERSON'S PRESENT
FUNCTIONING. PHYSICAL HEALTH QUESTIONS ARE NUMBERS 37-55,
81, 82 AND 96.]

20

1. In excellent physical health.
   Engages in vigorous physical activity, either regularly or
   at least from time to time.

2. In good physical health.
   No significant illnesses or disabilities. Only routine
   medical care such as annual check ups required.

3. Mildly physically impaired.
   Has only minor illnesses and/or disabilities which might
   benefit from medical treatment or corrective measures.

4. Moderately physically impaired.
   Has one or more diseases or disabilities which are either
   painful or which require substantial medical treatment.

5. Severely physically impaired.
   Has one or more illnesses or disabilities which are either
   severely painful or life threatening, or which require
   extensive medical treatment.

6. Totally physically impaired.
   Confined to bed and requiring full time medical assistance
   or nursing care to maintain vital bodily functions.

PERFORMANCE RATING SCALE FOR
ACTIVITIES OF DAILY LIVING

CARD 6

21

101. [RATE THE CURRENT PERFORMANCE OF THE PERSON BEING EVALUATED
ON THE SIX-POINT SCALE PRESENTED BELOW. CIRCLE THE ONE
NUMBER WHICH BEST DESCRIBES THE PERSON'S PRESENT PERFORMANCE.
ACTIVITIES OF DAILY LIVING QUESTIONS ARE NUMBERS 56-69.]

1. Excellent ADL capacity.
   Can perform all of the Activities of Daily Living
   without assistance and with ease.

2. Good ADL capacity.
   Can perform all of the Activities of Daily Living
   without assistance.

3. Mildly impaired ADL capacity.
   Can perform all but one to three of the Activities
   of Daily Living. Some help is required with one to
   three, but not necessarily every day. Can get through
   any single day without help. Is able to prepare his/her
   own meals.

4. Moderately impaired ADL capacity.
   Regularly requires assistance with at least four
   Activities of Daily Living but is able to get
   through any single day without help. Or regularly
   requires help with meal preparation.

5. Severely impaired ADL capacity.
   Needs help each day but not necessarily throughout
   the day or night with many of the Activities of
   Daily Living.

6. Completely impaired ADL capacity.
   Needs help throughout the day and/or night to carry
   out the Activities of Daily Living.

....

Summary of Ratings

Social Resources	3 — ?
Economic Resources	3
Mental Health	3 — ?
Physical Health	3
Activities of Daily Living	3
Cumulative Impairment Score (Sum of the five ratings)	5

22-23

Summary of Psychoactive Drugs for Geriatric Patients

Alan D. Whanger

The drug lists in Table B-1 are not exhaustive but rather reflect clinical usage and experience. The drugs are listed in general descending order of frequency of the author's use of them in older patients. The dose range is in broad terms only, and cannot completely reflect the wide physiologic range of need and tolerance in the elderly. The doses are in milligrams per day unless noted otherwise. They reflect the total daily dose and not the actual frequency or individual dosages. The best general dose rule is to "start low and go slow." Only the more common side effects are noted.

Table B-1 Psychoactive Drugs Prescribed for Older Patients

Generic Name	Trade Name	Dose Range	Side Effects
Major Tranquilizers			
1. Haloperidol	Haldol	0.2–10	Hypotension,
2. Thiothixene	Navane	0.3–10	drowsiness,
3. Perphenazine	Trilafon	2–12	extrapyramidal symptoms,
4. Thioridazine	Mellaril	10–300	EKG changes,
5. Trifluoperazine	Stelazine	1–10	tardive
6. Fluphenazine	Prolixin Decanoate (IM)	6.25–25 every 3/wks.	dyskinesia, anticholinergic
	Prolixin Enanthate (IM)	6.25–25 every 2/wks.	effects, rigidity; can
7. Chlorprothixene	Taractan	25–200	potentiate other
8. Fluphenazine	Prolixin (oral)	1–5	drugs
9. Prochlorperazine	Compazine	5–20	
10. Chlorpromazine	Thorazine	10–300	
11. Molindone	Moban	10–50	

Table B-1 continued

Generic Name	Trade Name	Dose Range	Side Effects
Minor Tranquilizers			
1. Lorazepam	Ativan	0.5–6	Drowsiness,
2. Oxazepam	Serax	10–60	ataxia,
3. Alprazolam	Xanax	0.25–1.5	confusion,
4. Diazepam	Valium	2–20	habituation; can
5. Chlordiazepoxide	Librium	5–30	potentiate other
6. Meprobamate	Equanil, Miltown	200–1,200	drugs
Sedative Antihistamines			
1. Diphenhydramine	Benadryl	12.5–50	Drowsiness,
2. Hydroxyzine	Atarax, Vistaril	20–100	dizziness,
3. Promethazine	Phenergan	12.5–50	anticholinergic effects
Antidepressants— Tricyclic and Others			
1. Doxepin	Sinequan, Adapin	30–150	Drowsiness,
2. Imipramine	Tofranil	30–150	hypotension,
3. Trazodone	Desyrel	50–300	blurred vision,
4. Amoxapine	Asendin	25–150	dry mouth,
5. Maprotiline	Ludiomil	25–75	constipation,
6. Nortriptyline	Pamelor, Aventyl	30–150	anticholinergic effects,
7. Desipramine	Norpramin, Pertofrane	25–100	hypertension,
8. Amitriptyline	Elavil	30–150	confusion
Antidepressants— MAO Inhibitors			
1. Phenelzine	Nardil	15–60	Hypotension,
2. Tranylcypromine	Parnate	10–30	hypertensive crises, interactions
Stimulants			
1. Methylphenidate	Ritalin	5–15	Agitation,
2. Dextroamphetamine	Dexedrine	2.5–10	CV stimulation, habituation
Antimanic Drugs			
1. Lithium carbonate	Lithonate, Eskalith	150–900	Tremor, ataxia, confusion

Table B-1 continued

Generic Name	Trade Name	Dose Range	Side Effects
Hypnotics			
1. Chloral hydrate	Noctec	0.5–1.5 g.	Gastritis,
2. Temazepam	Restoril	15–30	dizziness,
3. Flurazepam	Dalmane	15–30	hangover,
			habituation
Vasodilators			
1. Cyclandelate	Cyclospasmol	400–800	Flushing,
2. Isoxsuprine	Vasodilan	30–60	weakness
Antiparkinson Agents			
1. Diphenhydramine	Benadryl	12.5–50	Anticholinergic effects,
2. Trihexyphenidyl	Artane	1–6	confusion,
3. Benztropine	Cogentin	0.5–2	urinary retention,
4. Amantadine	Symmetrel	100–300	depression
Miscellaneous Drugs			
1. Ergot Alkaloids, hydrogenated	Hydergine	1–3	Mild agitation, nausea

Index